WHO SHALL LEAD THEM?

Who Shall Lead Them?

The Future of Ministry in America

Larry A. Witham

OXFORD
UNIVERSITY PRESS

2005

OXFORD
UNIVERSITY PRESS

Oxford University Press, Inc., publishes works that
further Oxford University's objective of excellence
in research, scholarship, and education.

Oxford   New York
Auckland   Cape Town   Dar es Salaam   Hong Kong   Karachi
Kuala Lumpur   Madrid   Melbourne   Mexico City   Nairobi
New Delhi   Shanghai   Taipei   Toronto

With offices in
Argentina   Austria   Brazil   Chile   Czech Republic   France   Greece
Guatemala   Hungary   Italy   Japan   Poland   Portugal   Singapore
South Korea   Switzerland   Thailand   Turkey   Ukraine   Vietnam

Published by Oxford University Press, Inc.
198 Madison Avenue, New York, New York 10016
www.oup.com

Library of Congress Cataloging-in-Publication Data
Witham, Larry, 1952–
Who shall lead them? : the future of ministry in America / Larry A. Witham.
p. cm.   Includes bibliographical references and index.
ISBN-10: 0-19-516697-3
ISBN-13: 978-0-19-516697-2
1. Pastoral theology—United States.
2. Christianity—Forecasting.
I. Title.
BV4011.3.W58 2005
262'.1'0973—dc22   2005006364

9 8 7 6 5 4 3 2 1
Printed in the United States of America
on acid-free paper

For Jackson W. Carroll and a generation of
"clergy watchers," and for my family.

Acknowledgments

A BOOK ABOUT THE AMERICAN CLERGY could easily be written as a vocational guide or a dry-as-dust look at a labor force. My attempt to do something different owes its inspiration to a lifetime of encounters with ministers, in my hometown, in a graduate theological school, and for twenty years on a newspaper beat.

I am particularly indebted to clergy I have met most recently, either on research for this book or during a nine-year stint of covering weekly sermons for *The Washington Times*. In 2001, I also had the pleasure of working on a five-part series, "Pulpits in Peril," with writer Julia Duin, photographer Maya Alleruzzo, and editor Ken McIntyre. The series was a great warm-up for this more in-depth work. For all my interest in this topic, I have not written a particularly pious book. Yet as a summation of ministry today it hopes to inform, sober, and inspire. My reliance on so much sociological data probably makes it more the Book of Numbers than the Acts of the Apostles, but I have tried to keep the narrative lively enough, and acknowledge that some readers will feel that their church or tradition was not duly covered.

Studies of the clergy are legion. Sociologists produced 485 of them between 1930 and 1970, showing that "the ministry is one of the favourite themes of modern socio-religious studies." Seven hundred modern studies have reportedly been done on just the psychology of ministers. Add to this thousands of articles on the theology and practice of ordained ministry, and then major surveys conducted in 1914, 1934, 1954, 1967, and 2000, and a veritable mountain of research materializes. But as one seminary president said, the topic remains elusive: "Christian ministry is inherently a mystery, not easily studied, measured, or quantified by social science instruments."[1] I hope this modest work adds something fresh, if only an accessible overview on a vast topic. Thanks are due to a host of people who read and commented on parts of the manuscript: Jackson Carroll, Randel Everett, James Guth, Lawrence Mamiya, John Odean, Vicki Phelps, Russell Shaw, Peter Theusen, James Wall, and Barbara Brown Zikmund. The long list of sociologists I am indebted to shows up in the notes section, and this is particularly true for the Pulpit and Pew research project out of Duke Divinity School. Its ecumenical reach and variety of findings have made it a rough benchmark of ministerial life at the start of the twenty-first century. Cynthia Read, my editor at Oxford University Press, has again been a wise and felicitous guide. As usual, my wife has provided the friendship and support that a Psalms writer might envy. In all such writing projects, however, it's wise to remember what the Preacher in Ecclesiastes said about human vanity: "Of making many books there is no end, and much study is a weariness of the flesh."

Contents

Introduction

Interesting Times

CLERGY AND LAWYERS shared equal prominence in English lore, particularly as rivals to kings. Faced with the intransigence of Thomas à Becket, Henry II supposedly asked, "Will no one rid me of this turbulent priest?" In Shakespeare's tale of King Henry VI, the conspirators declared, "The first thing we do, let's kill all the lawyers."[1]

The age of kings is over, but the fates of clergy and lawyers are still being worked out. Lawyers have prospered in the United States. Since 1970 their number has nearly tripled to more than three for every thousand Americans. Over the same decades, the share of clergy has practically stayed flat, hovering just above one minister for every thousand Americans.[2] English monarchs notwithstanding, it seems that clergy today are losing the proverbial battle with Henry II. For some, the comparison between the pulpit and the bench is enough to declare that Christian ministry in America is in decline.

At the start of the twenty-first century, both clergy watchers and ministers themselves sense that something is slipping in this great American vocation. In the comparison with lawyers, the decline could simply hinge on this: A nation once described as having "the soul of a church" now has the soul of a courtroom. The signals are mixed, of course. Ministers still hold the esteem of society. "Most Americans trust the clergy, at least more than they trust leaders of government and industry," said sociologist Robert Wuthnow, and that would go for lawyers as well.[3]

Yet while praised in general, ordained ministry is not receiving many of society's rewards. A study on the mean salaries in modern professions found, "The clergy's place within the professional middle class is becoming increasingly tenuous. Mean clergy income has remained relatively flat

1

over the past 20 years, while others with graduate degrees, especially those in medicine and law, have seen their salaries rise."[4]

As American society goes about its business, the minister has been eclipsed on many fronts. With the expansion of government, "salvation through welfare" may have overshadowed offerings through churches. When psychiatrists and psychologists appeared with their clinical vantage on the soul, ministers "were the heaviest losers." Film and television treat ministers as "the establishment's human face," said one media report, but another added that they are otherwise treated with "indifference" as players in modern society. There was a time when preaching and theological debate were popular forms of public entertainment. Yet in many ways, television and other media have forever stolen the clergy's thunder.[5]

When assessing their own current status, ministers themselves can be either optimists or pessimists. Listening to the latter produces the outlines of a "crisis" in ministry—even an unprecedented crisis. One Catholic clergyman and vicar limns the past two decades as "the priesthood's dark night." Evangelical pollster George Barna calls ministry "one of the most frustrated occupational groups in the country." And Methodist minister and sociologist Jackson W. Carroll, a leading "clergy watcher" of this era, laments a "troubled profession."[6]

Yet something about Christian ministry itself makes it far different from any job, profession, or social class: "We are viewed as representatives of God," said one minister.[7] Belief in God in the United States is still widespread, and in some sectors religious practice remains robust indeed. What is more, Christian belief, with the Crucifixion and Resurrection, allows the assumption that it is often darkest before the dawn. In some communities and lives, ministers still loom larger than any other figure in society. The pastor remains central to the rites of human passage—birth, marriage, and death. Ministers pray at civic events and inaugurations of the president of the United States.

The nation's Christian clergy, during four centuries on the American scene, have never lacked a challenge. It would be easy enough to declare the full-time, ordained, and official ministry in "crisis." But there is an alternative besides simply rejecting the gloom and proclaiming all is sweetness and light. Another approach is to consider the ancient Chinese curse: "May you live in interesting times." The goal of this book is to consider those two scenarios. Is American ministry in crisis, or simply in the thick of very interesting times?

Siding with the optimists, there are several reasons to step back from the precipice. Most of them have to do with considering the complexity of a "clergy crisis," especially when the question is put: crisis compared to what? Was there ever a golden age for the Christian ministry? Historians speak of bright spots, great revivals, and remarkable individuals—but not halcyon eras.

Without doubt dark spots appear everywhere, from a decline in mainline Protestant membership, sexual abuse and cover-up in the Catholic priesthood, and the entrapment of evangelical, Pentecostal, or black clergy by what Quaker writer Richard J. Foster lists simply as "money, sex, and power." The ultimate comparison might be Jesus' first disciples, said Assemblies of God minister Russell P. Spittler. "Even Jesus in his band of twelve had one rascal, who fell on financial matters," he said, referring to Judas Iscariot. "I, not entirely insincerely, figure as long as we're not above one in twelve who has that kind of problem we are in the statistical parameters of the ministry of Jesus."[8]

When ministry is declared a failure or success, what plumb line should that comparison be against? Clergy today do live in the shadows of a kind of golden age, namely the 1950s, probably the peak period of economic, educational, and religious growth in American history. Many of the nation's best and brightest entered ministry, and local pastors had civic standing. Church construction and attendance hit dizzying heights. *Newsweek* declared a "resurgent Protestantism" in 1955, and in 1960 a Massachusetts pastor still testified, "People keep joining the church without my lifting a finger."[9] Perhaps the clergy crisis is more a question of comparing then and now and coming up short.

Or it could be a matter of comparing one profession to another, which is important for young people who ask, "Will I be a doctor, lawyer, businessman, priest, or preacher?" Lutheran pastor and church historian Martin Marty suggests that no profession will come out looking rosy under too much analysis of its image or probing of its inner life. "Have stockbrokers today high morale? Or auto makers? Savings and Loan executives?" he asks. "Will physicians and lawyers find happiness?"[10]

The expectations put on clergy in the United States are colored by a culture of evangelical immediacy and business-world pragmatism—ministers must bring results. For conservative believers this result is pietistic transformation—the proverbial revival. For more liberal or communitarian believers, clergy are expected to erect "the kingdom of God," a world of better health, education, peace, and justice.

Barna traces every pastor's frustration to the "inability to live up to expectations placed upon them." As one minister said, "Pastors can rarely say, 'Look at the difference I helped make in this person's life. . . . ' The fruit of effective ministry may not be visible for many years." In Montana one recent year, "Pastor Steve" emerged from a particularly tough season, marred by a teen suicide in a church family. "Sometimes you see fruit, sometimes you don't," he said. Or let an ordinary churchgoer speak: "Even a pastor who walks on water is not going to satisfy everyone."[11]

Expectations placed on individual clergy are only part of the story, for the entire profession has been tossed about by the stormy changes in American society. In the century of America's founding, the European elite spoke of the "three professions of Divinity, Law, and Physic." In early America, "ministry was a learned calling, and until the 1740s only a few 'hot-gospelers,' Quakers, and other eccentrics questioned that."[12]

While the learned calling still exists, American ministry has far more testimonies of walking a knife's edge. The Massachusetts Bay Puritans worried about leaving "an illiterate ministry to the Churches, when our present ministers shall lie in the Dust." The unexceptional Anglican priests of the Virginia colony were known to "babble in a pulpit, roar in a tavern." When the first Great Awakening hit the Carolinas, residents "complained of being eaten up by itinerant preachers." And Thomas Jefferson looked askance at ministers for making people "give up morals for mysteries."[13]

Visiting the young American democracy in the early 1800s, Alexis de Toqueville marveled at the freewheeling and politicized clergy, for "you meet with a politician where you expected to find a priest." And another French chronicler was equally surprised that the ordinary farmer "conceives no other idea of a clergyman than that of a hired man." If he does not do his work well, the farmer "will dismiss him, and do without his sermons, and let his church be shut up for years."[14]

This was the start of the Jacksonian era. Rapid democratization, frontier growth, and the Second Great Awakening (1780–1830) dramatically increased the ranks of ministers. But the era also produced the first Society for the Relief of Aged and Destitute Clergymen. The large clergy ranks, now with more mix in quality, prompted one churchman in the decade before the Civil War to report "an impression, somewhat general, that an intellectual clergyman is deficient in piety, and that an eminently pious minister is deficient in intellect."[15]

After the Civil War, when the independent black church flourished, African Methodist Episcopal minister Henry McNeal had to preach ten times a week and said he was "accused of recklessly licensing preachers by the cargo" so great was the need. The white churches of the late 1800s produced nationally known "princes of the pulpit." But by 1920, seminary recruits were coming from the nation's humbler families and "more than half of the American clergy had neither a college nor a seminary degree." From the laboratories of the new social sciences in 1935 came the remark that the ministerial profession was a "victim of a mild vocational psychosis." And ministers themselves likened it to "entering the army, where one never knows where he will land or live or what specific work he will be called upon to perform."[16]

Even in the booming 1950s, Protestant leaders worried about a "perplexed profession," the "minister's dilemma," and "recruitment of clergy willing to serve in local parishes." As the number of Catholic priests in the United States was reaching a high point, the Second Vatican Council nevertheless declared in 1965 a "regrettable shortage of priests" and "so few clerics to evangelize." By 1963 a "crisis of identity" was declared in mainline Protestant circles. Subsequent race riots, assassinations, Vietnam drafts, resurgent secularism, and sexual liberation quite naturally left "the clergyman with considerable ambiguity and lack of clarity as to his role in society."[17]

Yet people continue to go into the ministry and remain there. "For all its problems," historian Marty said, "professional ministry endures, revives, finds new niches, attracts talent, enjoys support." Even amid the gloomy prognosis of the tumultuous 1960s, those who found the clergy most at risk added that, nevertheless, there was "no other group in our society that has a greater potential and, indeed, a graver responsibility, for generating great concerns for human destiny."[18]

American ministry is as diverse as the people who enter its calling and as varied as the traditions that have arisen over the past two millennia. For a start, the clergy divide up by titles, a spectrum that runs from the high-church sacramental "priest" to the low-church egalitarian "pastor." English Reformers rebuked the British monarch's "clergy" and Rome's priests by using the title "minister." While "parson" (*the* person) has fallen by the wayside, "preacher" stays in currency. In the South, every kind of minister is simply "the preacher."[19]

Disagreements go deeper still, of course. The church split between Roman Catholic and Eastern Orthodox in 1054. And the sixteenth-century clash of the Reformation and Counter Reformation created the basic contours of most ministry in the western world today, including its seminary systems. On American shores, colonial divines were prone to calling each other "dead" or "unconverted." What Abraham Lincoln said about civil war applies to every other biblical, moral, and social disagreement: "Both read the same Bible and pray to the same God, and each invokes His aid against the other."

The tensions can extend to the relations between clergy and laity, the other major group of workers in the church since time immemorial. In the current era of clergy shortages, lay innovation has become common in both Protestant and Catholic circles, producing what some call a proliferation of quasi-clergy roles. Indeed, the number of theologically trained Catholic lay leaders today is about to surpass the number of priests in America. The growth in new lay roles has prompted some to speak of a "new clericalism"—that is, laity with ministry titles short of ordination.[20] Drawing lines between ordained and lay ministry is a perennial challenge to the churches, one likely to continue in the future.

With all these demarcations crisscrossing the Christian ministry, how does one begin to look at ministry in America, especially in hopes of talking about "ministry as a whole?" This book makes that attempt by focusing on ordained ministry, giving emphasis to its largest sector: parish ministry. The ordained minister will be considered in the traditional sense: a person trained, appointed, or elected to a full-time spiritual occupation. "The Church has never been without persons holding specific authority and responsibility," agreed one hundred theologians, hailing from all traditions. "The very existence of the Twelve and other apostles shows that, from the beginning, there were differentiated roles in the community."[21]

Ordained clergy have traditionally engaged in "general" ministry in a local church or in "specialized" ministries such as counseling, teaching, or administration. Of all ordained clergy in America, about 60 percent work in general ministry, while the rest are specialized or retired. For this study, general ministry has pride of place and is seen as the front line on so many issues. Loren Mead, an Episcopal priest who pioneered consulting work with congregations, has stated the case even more unequivocally: "A pastor who gets caught up in anything else—from pastoral counseling to social action to theological study—and neglects the task of preaching and leadership for worship is in the wrong business."[22]

Beyond this, the unity of all the clergy forces in America is a reality not to be overlooked. They circulate from one task to another, sometimes across denominations, but always seem to be roughly in the same boat. In this sense it is very realistic to speak of "clergy as a whole" in the American setting. First of all, it is a nation that extols religious liberty and thus encourages a kind of live and let live attitude regarding people who feel called by God to minister. In the long tradition of denominationalism in America, "no denomination claims that all other churches are false churches," and this too allows clergy to feel they share a common vocation.[23]

Their common tasks unite them, as do their common enemies. The vocational challenges are great, and that alone tends to forge a healthy camaraderie. They all face the same indifferent public, which tells Gallup polls that four in ten are in church on a given weekend, when it may be just half that. One Missouri pastor felt he was always "fighting against the world." But that would ease when he met fellow combatants at the ministerial association: "You see that you're all in the same work." And in the same boat. The actor Robert Duvall, who plays a Pentecostal preacher in *The Apostle*, put it nicely when he sees a Catholic bishop blessing fishing vessels in Louisiana: "You do it your way, I do it mine. But we get it done, don't we?"[24]

The story that follows will look at ministry in its separate parts, yet in the spirit of considering ministry as a whole. The parts of ministry are being played out among mainline and evangelical Protestants, women, Roman Catholic priests, minority clergy, the massive Southern Baptist clergy corps, and the growing spirit-filled entrepreneurs. (Regrettably, the Eastern Orthodox clergy, the Mormon priesthood, and Jewish rabbis are beyond the scope of the narrative). By looking at various precincts of ministry, the more universal issues for clergy also emerge. All ministers, for example, face questions of recruiting a next generation, the friction between a "calling" and a "profession," and their stances on women's ordination. They wrestle with the prophetic voice, political involvement, use of the Bible, handling the "worship wars" over music and style, and the lifestyle of "health and wealth" clergy.

The closing chapters look at other general aspects of ministry. In organized religion, ministers get their pay, try new methodologies, and confront the church growth movement. They are also party to the widening "fault lines" over sexual and behavioral controversies in the church, and become larger than life in the images of literature, news media, and popular culture. By the end of this story, we will have met ministers who combine four kinds of approaches in their work. Theologically, some clergy take an exclusive approach to ministry, preaching "the only way," while others prefer an open approach to ministry, offering "a good way." Temperamentally, some clergy want to generate vision and growth, while others offer a quieter stability and individual care.

Whatever that combination, and whether clergy are in crisis or merely living in "interesting times," they have survived while kings have disappeared, and they have survived because of ministerial integrity. English lore also points to how this clergy requirement is unlikely to vanish. Ministers must try to live what they preach, as a character in Shakespeare's *Hamlet* eagerly reminded: "Do not, as some ungracious pastors do, Show me the steep and thorny way to heaven, While, like a puffed and reckless libertine, Himself the primrose path of dalliance treads." Chaucer rhymes it in his *Canterbury Tales*: "The true example that a priest should give, is one of cleanness, how the sheep should live."[25]

Chaucer notwithstanding, this book will take those demands on clergy rather lightly, hewing instead to a descriptive look at ministerial variety, a daunting enough task to do well. Today "there is less discernment of what the life of a priest or minister is really like," said one study of clergy in literature. "But perhaps there never was a time when those outside this or any profession really penetrated its nature."[26] Heeding such limitations, our story begins with the call to ministry itself, its modern experience in America, and its historical roots.

1

Call to Ministry

BETWEEN PARACHUTE JUMPS with the Army Rangers and setting off explosives, Nathaniel Brewster used to experience a gentle tug on his soul. Melissa Keeble, who went to Romania on a Christian youth mission, also felt the "tugging" on her heart—and on her arms, as Romanian women who had lived under a secular dictatorship turned to her for spiritual advice.

Each in their own way, Brewster and Keeble had felt "the call" to ministry. It drew the West Point graduate and member of the 82nd Airborne into the Catholic priesthood. "Mostly, it was just recognizing how much God loved me," he said. "I'm a demolition engineer turned Catholic priest." The call drew Keeble to an evangelical seminary, where she met her husband, who like herself was in training for ordination as a Presbyterian minister. "We both felt a kind of tugging," said Keeble, whose home church is in Danville, California. "This is what I've been led to do. It terrifies me in a lot of ways, and it excites me."[1]

Christianity has always enjoyed a backdrop of dramatic stories about being called by God, with St. Paul's vision on the road to Damascus or St. Augustine's hearing a voice in his garden being just two examples of how dramatically it could happen. Across history, the experience of the call has often been "disturbing, frightening, and awesome," writes one contemporary minister. The average experience is far less demonstrative, but no less decisive. While ministers are careful not to exaggerate, they still liken the call to the experience of Isaiah saying to God, "Here am I! Send me," or Jesus summoning fishermen at the Sea of Galilee.[2]

Many Christian traditions, eager to encourage the call, have downplayed the drama to emphasize that it can come both by a tugging on the heart and on the arm—a call by God and by people. "It is emphatically not

9

to be expected that the voice of the Lord calling should come to the future priest's ear in some extraordinary way," the Second Vatican Council of the Catholic Church insisted. Signs in "everyday life" would do. The modern papacy speaks of a twofold "voice of God"—"one interior, that of grace [and] the other one external, human, sensible, social, juridical, concrete." For ordination in the Episcopal Church, the *Book of Common Prayer* speaks of a twofold sense, a belief that "God *and* the church" are beckoning.[3]

The subtlety and complexity of the call should not underestimate the role of a profound episode in a person's life, however. That is what Robert Wicks, an expert in pastoral psychology, has heard hundreds of times when he asks Catholic and Protestant ministers what caused their decision. "The person will often say they had an experience," and usually with an immediacy, said Wicks. "Rarely is it something slow." When the call does come as a slow process, it is typically backed by a family history or social environment: family respect for the priesthood, cultural reverence for the preacher, or the impression made by a relative in ordained ministry.[4]

A country pastor in South Dakota made all the difference for John O. Lundin. Reared on a farm, Lundin's childhood memories opened the way for his own ordination to Lutheran ministry. "The pastor used to come over to hunt and I remember this tall man," Lundin recalled. "It was fun. They tell me I said, 'Someday I want to be like him.'" Such positive environmental factors are still at work today, according to surveys. When asked, a third of the Protestants and Catholics in U.S. seminaries report having been influenced by a "close clergy relative." For most, the call has been enhanced by contact with "congregational clergy." And it seems only logical that nearly half of younger priests in the United States attended parochial schools, in which priests still have an esteemed role.[5]

However the call to ministry begins, its outcome is a distinct population of clergy in the United States. Their precise number has always been elusive. But between census data and reports from denominations, a fairly solid picture may be drawn—over time, at present, and by denominations and regions.

In the past century, remarkably, the call to ministry in America has produced a fairly consistent proportion of ministers. Between 1910 and 2000, for example, the census has regularly found just a fraction more than one "occupational" minister for every one thousand citizens.[6]

Estimating the total number of clergy today, however, requires a reconciling of disparate numbers. For a start, the 2000 census found 388,925 Americans with a "clergy" occupation (in the past five years). Denominational reports come in lower with 351,989 clergy "serving parishes" in about the same year. At the least, these two figures on "active" clergy roughly match the estimated 300,000 to 350,000 congregations in the United States. Yet these numbers do not account for *all* clergy, because many ordained ministers are retired or do not lead local churches. When the *total* number of clergy is considered—595,935 according to denominations—the call in America may be seen in its more complex reality: While 60 percent of *all* clergy lead local churches, there is another 40 percent who are teachers, missionaries, counselors, administrators, freelancers, or retired.[7]

Ministry in America has always had a denominational landscape as well, and clergy are still best known by those affiliations. Using the *total* number of clergy, mainline Protestants (22 percent) make up the largest bloc, followed by Pentecostals (21 percent), Southern Baptists (15 percent), and then Roman Catholics (11 percent). Clergy in the historic black denominations amount to 8 percent of all clergy, while many more black pastors are Pentecostal. Nearly all the rest of the American clergy (23 percent) minister in independent evangelical, Adventist, Latter-day Saints (Mormon), sectarian, or "orthodox" Protestant churches.[8]

Ministers can be found everywhere, and in fairly resilient proportions. The largest segment (40 percent) works in the South, while 25 percent serve churches in the Midwest. The rest divide (17 percent each) between the West and the Northeast. Regional proportions have remained stable in recent decades, with the Sunbelt showing the most growth and the industrial Northeast the most loss. Today, most clergy (52 percent) work in towns and rural settings. A quarter serve in cities with population of ten thousand or more, and the rest carry out ministry in the suburbs.[9]

As every minister knows, the ability to do ministry will be influenced by local cultures as well. The interest in what Christian ministers have to say will differ sharply between urban San Francisco and suburban Atlanta, for example, and even between different states. Accordingly, Nevada has a scarcity of "occupational" clergy (1 to 1,644 citizens) while South Dakota and Arkansas have an abundance (1 to 460 citizens). As a national average, America has 1 "occupational" minister for every 723 citizens, a state of affairs approximated in Wisconsin, Louisiana, and Michigan.[10]

Given the landscape of modern ministry, the call will give people such as Brewster and Keeble unique challenges. At age twenty-nine, Brewster entered the priesthood in the Diocese of Wichita, Kansas. He acknowledges that his vow of celibacy is indeed "a point of no return." But he feels an example has led the way for him: "There is no truer man than Jesus Christ, and the priest is called to act in his person."

If Brewster, in his singleness, hopes to reflect the ministry of God, Keeble will try to do that as part of a clergy couple, a type of marriage seen more often now. At age twenty-five, she was about to finish her studies at

Fuller Theological Seminary. Once ordained, she and her husband would face choices over whose ministry job to follow. Most important is "the couple following the call of God," Keeble said. "Now, does that mean we're each going to have to make sacrifices? Of course it does."

The stories of the call abound, each one unique but every one having something universal as well. Some testimonies lean to the unconventional, while others could not be any more traditional than a pious son following his father's vocation.

Years after they were ordained, evangelical minister Robert K. Johnston and Benedictine brother Gregory Elmer compared notes on the quirky way they felt the call as young men. As ministers, they both had become experts on film and faith. Back in 1964, they both had left a movie theater changed after watching the film *Becket*. Thomas à Becket gave up his freedom, wealth, and privileges to become a tonsured monk, and then archbishop of Canterbury. "Teach me now how to serve you with all my heart, and find my true honor in observing your divine will," Becket prayed. That was enough to spark the imaginations of both Johnston and Elmer.[11]

Bruce Chilton, who entered the Episcopal priesthood, felt his call on a youthful trek across Europe. It was 1967 when he arrived at the seaside town of Dubrovnik in the former Yugoslavia, on a blistering hot day. "I ducked into the dark confines of a medieval church," he recalled, and paced up to the altar, where a frieze depicted Christ on the cross. "I had a momentary but searing impression of agony," he said, "but paradoxically, deep inside myself, I also felt the answering reverberations of something beyond pain, beyond despair." He left the cool sanctuary for an even cooler bottle of beer, but the encounter had sown a seed that "germinated." Chilton said, the "experience eventually led me to seek ordination."[12]

Many ministers, it seems, had other plans in life, and it took some persuading to detour them down the ministerial path. That is the story of a great Southern Baptist figure, George W. Truett (d. 1944), who went on to become one of the "great preachers of his day" at First Baptist Church of Dallas. "His church voted to ordain him to be a minister before he ever experienced the call himself," said K. Randel Everett, whose own family experienced a similarly dramatic shift in priorities. When Randel's father, a college-trained agriculturist in Arkansas, caught tuberculosis, "He said, 'God you help me get well and I'm going to be obedient.'" Health regained, his father moved the family to a seminary town in Texas and began training for Southern Baptist ministry. Randel was among three sons who followed in their father's footsteps."[13]

Episcopal Bishop Jane Holmes Dixon, who was ordained in 1981, is certain that the church called her but is reluctant to second-guess the divine. "Where is God in all of this process? I'm very clear that I don't fully know the mind of God," she said. "That's idolatry. That puts human beings, the preacher, in equal position to God." She recalls when she was fifteen, a Mississippi schoolgirl at a "fundamentalist" Presbyterian church, a young man said, "You know, you ought to be a preacher. You spend so much time in church." When the call became serious in the 1970s, the Episcopal church played a major role: "I feel comfortable in saying that the church has called me to ministry."[14]

When Lloyd John Ogilvie of Wisconsin felt the call he had no idea where it would lead. During his studies at Lake Forest College north of Chicago, he was guided by older students in Bible study. "I went back to my room, got on my knees, and made my commitment to as much as I knew of Christ at that moment," he said. "And that was the beginning." A communications major, Ogilvie said, "Now I had something I wanted to communicate." The "profound experience of being loved" moved Ogilvie to change his major to history and philosophy and aim for seminary, finally studying with divines at the University of Edinburgh: "The passion to preach the gospel became very real." Starting in a small church in 1956, Ogilvie went on to First Presbyterian Church of Hollywood—and then to be chaplain of the U.S. Senate.[15]

At the time when Ogilvie preached in Hollywood, John Odean arrived in Los Angeles to advance his acting career. Inspired by the Jesus people movement in 1972 in his native Spokane, Washington, Odean met the "Jesus freaks" again in the beach towns of Southern California. He believes God even called him at age three, if memory serves. "And I said, 'He did it.' God made it my heart's desire." In the fast-growing Vineyard Church, Odean found himself with a Sunday teaching spot. "I taught everything I knew from Genesis to Revelation, and I was done in fifteen minutes," he said. "It was panic, but I got through that and taught for three months. And that's how I got my feet wet." Now, a next generation comes to him about ministry: "I have these kids here who come to me and say, 'Mentor me. Help me do what you did.'"[16]

A people person of skill and sincerity, Odean knows the Bible inside and out. Yet he hasn't set foot in a seminary. That modern choice—to enter seminary graduate school or learn in the field—is as old as ministry and still part of the call. Siding with the Puritan reforms of his time, the English poet John Milton was convinced that it is "the inward calling of God that makes a minister." But he also believed that the minister must undergo "painful study." His opposite might have been the great Methodist itinerant preacher Peter Cartwright, who dismissed fancy schooling. When the true Methodist preacher "felt that God had called him to preach," Cartwright said, "instead of hunting up a college or Biblical institute, [he] hunted up a hardy pony or a horse, and some traveling apparatus."[17]

Ministers in the black church still debate the emphases of a Milton or a Cartwright, reliving a natural disagreement that has always impassioned the great African-American churchmen, especially as their people emerged from slavery and eyed new opportunities. Around the year 2000, Benjamin Robinson, a native of Oakland, California, reared in the black Pentecostal tradition, was completing his master's of divinity at Fuller Theological Seminary. While definitely for education and credentials, Robinson declared, "Without that call and the anointing for ministry, seminary doesn't do you a lick of good." The Atlanta-based Interdenominational Theological Center stands for an educated clergy and reigns as the largest consortium of black seminaries in America. There, theology professor Jacquelyn Grant would never deny the inner experience, but she emphatically sides with Milton on the necessary pain of learning. "Some folks are stuck on the call," she said. "And whatever they knew at the point of the call, they think that's all they need to learn."[18]

Beyond the apprenticeship, and even the seminary, some clergy hunger to learn more. In the words of one historian, pastors like this perennially leave the pulpit: "Their taste for ideas and their aptitudes for study singled them out for the intellectual life."[19] Of the aforementioned people, Johnston and Chilton became seminary professors, and while Everett has almost never missed a Sunday preaching, late in life he became a seminary president. Of the clergy who leave the full-time pulpit, some become enamored of the "scientific" study of their vocation, and that is the story of the young Methodist pastor Jackson W. Carroll, who today is called a "veteran clergy watcher."

Reared as a Methodist in South Carolina, Carroll was coached in public speaking by a Presbyterian cleric and made his "decision to answer the call" at a Methodist youth conference. There was "no supernatural voice," he said, but a "strong sense" of what God wanted. He graduated from Duke Divinity School in 1956 and returned to South Carolina, only the start of his call being "tested many times." He was a pastor in Rock Hill when it became the first town in South Carolina to experience a civil rights sit-in—which he and fellow clergy supported.

Carroll was invited to be Methodist campus minister at Duke, and there he caught the academic bug. At Princeton, he also studied under the sociologist Samuel Blizzard, who pioneered studies of modern ministry. Carroll followed in his footsteps, producing some of the early social science on trends in seminaries and female clergy. He was about to retire from teaching when the Lilly Endowment asked him to direct Pulpit and Pew, a four-year study of ministry, beginning in 1999. It was no small project, part of the "twists and turns" of ministry, said Carroll, who felt it had "continuity with the call I answered years ago."[20]

The sociological study of ministry, which reached another stage in projects such as Pulpit and Pew, is rarely in the business of reducing the call of God to cold, hard statistics. Yet even ministers, persuaded of the mystery of the call, can be curious about the empirical shape of their vocation. With ample warning to never see the call as simply a "profession"—a word that can smack of pay raises and secular ambition—there is no denying that as a work force in America, the ministerial trade is subject to social forces and trends.

One of the strongest, confirmed by Pulpit and Pew and already hinted at for a decade, is that in both the Protestant and Catholic ministries, Americans are feeling the call later in life. Older men and women are entering ministry, while the path someone like an Everett or Carroll took—being ordained by their mid-twenties—has become exceptionally rare.

At Lutheran Theological Seminary in Gettysburg, Jack Hernstrom knows the data and the debate on second- and third-career clergy pretty well. He entered ministerial studies in his early fifties. While he can picture his future in ordained ministry, Hernstrom said, "There are congregations that won't hire an older pastor," and once that post is obtained, it is harder to move onto a second church posting. Yet Hernstrom won't accept the notion that God only calls youthful initiates. "My first reaction is that the apostles were all 'second career,' including Paul," he said. "My only regret is that I didn't heed God's call when I was young."[21]

The trend toward late-career clergy has been tracked for all to see, with Pulpit and Pew being only the latest and most systematic reading. It found that America's newer ministers—those in ministry for less than ten years—have an average ordination age of thirty-seven. By comparison, ministers with more than thirty years of service were ordained at age twenty-five. In two decades, the age of entering ministry has shifted upward by about twelve years. Denominationally, the highest rates of second-career callings show up among black clergy (83.7 percent) and conservative Protestants (66.1 percent). Mainline Protestantism reports about 41 percent and Roman Catholics are in that lower range as well. The older the minister, however, the shorter the ministry.[22]

Whatever their ages, all of the clergy were active in their churches in their teens. Yet the first-career pastors felt the divine tugging as early as age seventeen. They were ordained about a decade later. Because they had been *more* active as teenagers than their older confreres, Pulpit and Pew wondered, "Could it be that youth ministries are no longer as significant a channel of recruitment to ordained ministry as they once were?" Second-career ministers were more likely to have become active in a local church later in life. They heard the call in their mid-twenties, getting ordained in the mid-thirties.[23]

According to Pulpit and Pew, those who receive the call at a young age are more likely to earn a master's of divinity degree (65 percent as opposed to 39 percent for older people called to serve). Yet the older clergy report advantages that seem to come with age. The second-career pastor is less likely to doubt the call once it comes—about seven in ten

(68.3 percent) have never doubted their path. Only half of first-career ministers can claim such certainty. Four in ten of the first-career clergy, in fact, have doubted the ministry "once in a while." A quarter of second-career pastors have had "once in a while" misgivings.[24]

As a whole, however, the Pulpit and Pew survey found that American clergy are an older group in America. Half of all active clergy are at least fifty years old, and a fifth are sixty-one or older. Catholic clergy are the most senior of the various traditions. In all, clergy are "typically older and more experienced" than the general population of workers. And those under thirty are rare, amounting to no more than 5 or 10 percent of all clergy. Partly due to aging, just 60 percent of all clergy today are active in parishes; a good part of the remaining 40 percent are retired.[25]

The dynamics of the call are also shaped by sex, race, and ethnicity in America. In the past three decades, according to the 2000 census, the number of women in ministry has shot up to 14 percent of all clergy. (This trend is examined further in Chapter 3). More generally, the census shows this: The rates of clergy recruitment are far higher among women and minorities than among men in general. Between 1990 and 2000, the number of men in ministry grew by 15 percent, keeping up with the rate of population growth (13 percent). Meanwhile, the number of female, black, and Hispanic clergy each climbed by 50 percent, and the number of Asian ministers by 40 percent.[26] The white male minister is keeping up, but hardly with the zeal of racial and ethnic minorities.

For Americans feeling the call today, it is hard to avoid a little bit of calculation about the social and economic standing of the minister. In recent decades, studies show, it has been losing status as a promising career. From a crass labor-market perspective, ministry has lost the perks (whether social status, good pay, or opportunity) that once attracted enterprising young men. Using other labor jargon, ministry may have become "feminized," joining such typically underpaid female occupations as secretary, teacher, social worker, or librarian.[27] When Odean took up ministry, his mother stitched a wall hanging that said: "Working for the Lord doesn't pay much, but the retirement plan is out of this world." Still, making a living is reportedly getting harder for ministers, and newcomers certainly mix some of that estimation with their desire to heed the call.

Once ordination has opened the door to ministry, Americans with the call face another disconcerting factor: the challenge of distributing clergy among available jobs in the nation's churches. There are enough ordained individuals to fill every church pulpit in America, and a little more. But the complexity of matching ministers with church needs has produced an "oversupply" in some church sectors and undersupply in others; there are denominations, for example, where 20 to 30 percent of the churches— typically small, unattractive, or struggling—have no resident pastor. The total number of Americans studying in theological seminaries is at a high-water mark. But compared to past generations of seminarians, fewer today want to lead a local church, a fact that will leave many small churches empty of pastors.[28]

While the Protestant churches tend to see the roller-coaster effect of oversupply and undersupply, the Catholic Church generally sees its clergy spread too thin across a system of geographic parishes. The two scenarios have shaped clergy finances as a whole. The median income of all Protestant clergy today is $40,000, meaning that half earn less. On that downward slope, many pastors report a "fear of falling"—falling below a middle-class standard of living. "Compounding his predicament is guilt," said one report. "Why must he be preoccupied with career moves and money when he has responded not to a career, but to a call?" While the earnings of Protestant clergy vary widely, salaries for Catholic priests in U.S. dioceses are lower and far more regulated, with the median financial package for a U.S. priest (salary and housing) being $25,000 a year (not including health-care, education, and retirement benefits).[29]

The full-time career minister is still the rule, but the exception endures. Many clergy hold another job. They have been called "tentmakers" after St. Paul's day job, or "moonlighters" who work after hours for extra income or secular experience. The Catholic "worker priest" was once famed for trying to do both. Now, nearly two in ten Catholic priests (18 percent) are part-time ministers, often because of age or other duties. Among Protestant churches, 27 percent of the clergy are part-time. A church typically needs two hundred members to afford a full-time minister, and many obviously fall short.[30] The remarkable variation in sizes of churches, in fact, bedevils modern ministry as much as anything.

In America today, just 10 percent of clergy serve "large" churches with 350 members or more, and the result is that one tenth of all clergy preach to one half of all churchgoers. The lopsided corollary is just as remarkable. Half of all clergy do the preaching to just 11 percent of churchgoers. These churchgoers belong to congregations with fewer than one hundred members. The groundswell into large churches, meanwhile, has put the spotlight on a corps of clergy who shoulder a bigger leadership task. A few thousand of them, both Protestant and Catholic, lead "megachurches" with at least two thousand members. But even more clergy simply have sizeable church followings and in these cases some experts foresee "a national shortage of ministers who can serve effectively as the senior pastor of a very large congregation."[31]

Such worries might be balanced out by the educational advances in the clergy calling compared to past eras. Catholic priests invariably earn a master's degree in divinity, and now more than six in ten Protestants also have a master's or more advanced degree, while many of the rest have attended Bible college or institutes. Clergy report that the love of learning, in fact, is one of the great motivating factors after the call has been heard.

What all clergy enjoy most is sharing that knowledge as teachers and worship leaders. And despite the constant challenges—the greatest reported by today's clergy as being the conveyance of the gospel to society—seven in ten of the active clergy are nevertheless content with their lifestyle.[32]

Ministry, with all its contemporary flux, has always relied on its two-thousand-year history for perspective and strength. More than most professions, perhaps, ministry comes under the gaze of antiquity, whether it be Jesus calling the fishermen or New Testament stories of the early church. The reaching back in history, as ambiguous as it can be at times, adds power to the Christian sense of calling, shows how ministry has adapted to so many epochs and cultures, and for many holds out some hope of a more united Christian ministry in the future.

Few would contest the claim of one New Testament scholar: "A clear picture of early ministry is simply beyond our reach."[33] Yet the attempts to grasp its essentials have never ceased. While the New Testament term minister means no more than to "serve" (*diakonia* in Greek), the first identified leaders of the church were called "elders," which in the Greek came out as *presbyteroi*. Elders showed up in Jerusalem in the A.D. 50s and later in the outlying churches founded by Paul's missionary work. From early on, said biblical scholar Raymond Brown, "one may strongly suspect" that elders were installed by the laying on of hands, signifying the presence of the Holy Spirit.[34]

Catholics and Protestants still identify clergy as presbyters or elders. But in the ancient church the ministry roles hardly ended there, thanks especially to Paul, whose letters contain the earliest known references to organized ministry. Yet for better or worse, Paul's assertions change over time. He begins with "those over you in the Lord" and "elders" but later speaks of "varieties of ministry," which include "teachers, then workers of miracles, then healers, helpers, administrators, speakers in various tongues." He winnows that down further to "apostles, some prophets, some evangelists, some pastors and teachers."[35]

The narrowing down of ministry continued as the church became more structured. The process, in turn, highlighted two seemingly polar opposite forms of ministry: the independent charismatic leader on the one hand, and the more institutional role of bishop on the other. As Paul's letters suggest, charismatic miracle workers lost ground as the church matured, and as later historians pointed out, bishops became the controlling figures of belief and ordination of others. As "primitive enthusiasm waned, or became corrupted," said biblical scholar John Knox, "the Spirit was thought of as conferred through ordination."[36] Despite this subordination of the charismatic role, it has never been excised from ministry, and the contrast of hierarchical and Pentecostal ministry in America today illustrates the enduring polarity.

Some have seen evidence of the first bishop in Paul's letters, but everyone agrees that before long elders were called "overseers," or *episcopos* in Greek. The overseers seemed to have begun as groups, and were probably viewed as something like a "president," an office known in Roman civic life. By the time of the early church fathers, however, the bishop clearly became something more. Ignatius of Antioch (d. before A.D. 117) likened the bishop to Christ. Clement of Rome struck a different chord, seeing bishops as managerial but no less central to organized ministry.

Either way, governance by a single bishop prevailed by the end of the third century, operating on a "doctrine that a certain priestly power inhered in the office of the bishop," said Knox.[37] The role would become a contentious issue in the history of Christian ministry, especially as the bishop of Rome became the papacy. Disagreement over an even earlier role in the ancient church, the office of deacon, has been mild by comparison to church wrangling over the role of bishops.

Though derived from the Greek term for "minister," the title of deacon came to mean "servant." Acts recounts how the twelve apostles did not want to "give up preaching the word of God to serve tables." They laid hands on seven "men of good repute, full of the Spirit and of wisdom" to do the church's practical and charitable work, presumably the very first *deacons*. The seven have also been interpreted as the first Gentile leaders. In any event, they freed up the apostles to devote themselves to "prayer and to the ministry of the word." Having faded across church history, deacons were revived by Protestants, who found them in the Bible. The Second Vatican Council restored their ordained status, a "different degree" of ordination from priest or bishop but part of the "divinely instituted ecclesiastical ministry." Today, married men play this role widely in Catholicism, but the debate still rages on allowing female deacons, since it confers a kind of "ordination."[38]

By the time Christianity became the established church of the Roman Empire in 325 under Emperor Constantine (d. 337), ministry had gone through three stages, beginning with the "charismatic" phase.[39] The second period, with elders, presidents, and chief pastors, reflected the secular society. Finally, the bishop and presbyter became the "clergy," or *kleros*. They shared the baptismal role, but only the bishop confirmed new members and ordained priests. Under Constantine, clergy were like civic officials: trained, promoted, and moved between parishes. Yet the charismatic and otherworldly element never faded. Monastic and desert ascetics split from the priestly orders. Calls for return to the "primitive church" ministry have been perennial.

During the sixteenth-century Reformation, Martin Luther declared the "priesthood of believers." Still, Luther had restrictions as well. He allowed ordination only for ministers called to a pulpit, an idea that "became the common property of the Reformers [but] was not always observed." The teachings of St. Paul would forever stamp ministry with the Old Testament concept of "priesthood," allowing even radical reformers to take the idea to universal and egalitarian extremes.[40]

When ministry arrived from Europe on American shores, it had both the priestly and egalitarian features. There were Pietists, Quakers, and Baptists to level the ministerial role and Puritans, Anglicans, Catholics, and Lutherans to retain its formal structures. What never arrived, however, were bishops from overseas, and only after the American Revolution and adoption of the U.S. Constitution did Americans raise up their own.

Before the Revolution, five generations of clergy, serving mostly in New England, formed an exclusive circle trained in England or at Harvard and Yale colleges. The religious individualism spawned by First Great Awakening of the 1740s, however, broke the clergy monopoly and then the War of Independence and frontier expansion stoked egalitarian impulses in all aspects of life. In the age of Jeffersonian and Jacksonian democracy, a time of populism, sectarian splits, and millennial fervor, the revivalist impulse called the Second Great Awakening nearly obliterated distinctions between lay and ordained ministers. Modern-day Europeans certainly notice the difference even today. "Faith is more entrepreneurial here," said one Anglican cleric, having worked in England and the United States. "It has depended on lay initiative with the Baptist farmer preachers and the Methodist circuit riders. A kind of frontier religion."[41]

Between 1800 and 1860, a period characterized by an "evangelical consensus," the Protestant ministry in America took on its enduring characteristics. The nation's churches adopted an "evangelical conception of the social order" and rapidly recruited and trained revivalist ministers, according to historian Donald Scott.[42] They built a "benevolent empire" of seminaries, Bible and tract societies, missions, colleges, hospitals, reform groups, and charities. But more than anything, religious revivals became a way for leaders to try to impose social improvement on the masses, and for the masses to organize their own dissenting movements. In the South, the 1801 revival at Cane Ridge, Kentucky, was organized by clergy but in the end launched a new era of "lay exhorters" and Methodist circuit riders, large numbers of whom eschewed the siren call of "respectability, centralization, and education."[43]

In the North, the revival experience around New England—where America's first Protestant seminary was opened in 1808—reflected the national trends of the period. The number of clergy there tripled by the 1840s and the levels of ministerial education diverged widely, according to Scott. Yet for everyone, ministry took on a national, not just local, horizon. Ordinary men, often called by God at revivals, became "full-time clerical functionaries" of the new national projects. The pastor's experience "was no longer a single, lifetime pastorate, but a career involving four or more different positions." The minister became an "agent of organized evangelicalism."[44]

The explosive development also brought its reaction. Churches were now being jostled by the fierce two-party political system, a new sectionalism, and the fight over abolition of slavery, and many withdrew to be safe havens of religious devotion. New clergy handbooks urged ministers to shy from political combat and entanglements, being "the spiritual friend of all but the social friend of none." Compared to the days of Puritan clergy who graduated from Harvard or Yale, the new minister was viewed not as better than ordinary Christians, but as trying harder to achieve Christian character in their "almost exclusively devotional and confessional" role. As Scott said, ministry had been transformed from an "office" to a profession. After the 1840s, "the relationship between a pastor and his people had become essentially a client relationship."[45]

While even today the clergy in America are both appointed to congregations or "hired" by congregational committees, there is no longer the sense of religious "office" as in colonial times. American ministers, it seems, must meet their constituents halfway, if not entirely, in the "client relationship." As this common feature pervaded American ministry, the disestablishment of clergy became a global norm as well. State churches lost centuries of monopoly, and societies became more secular around the world. Naturally, the leaders of the Christian traditions began to seek a common identity for ministry to strengthen its future.

The bellwether of such efforts were the World Council of Churches consultations, held over several decades, which produced a final consensus document in 1982 called *Baptism, Eucharist and Ministry*, or *BEM*. The one hundred theologians from all traditions who adopted *BEM* offered the ancient "threefold pattern" of bishop, elder, and deacon as the basis for a common ministry today. Despite *BEM*'s appeal to ancient roots, it urged every tradition to be humble about making claims from the past: "to avoid attributing their particular forms of the ordained ministry directly to the will and institution of Jesus Christ."[46]

By the nature of compromise, *BEM* ended up a middling document, floating somewhere in the Protestant center. Catholic authorities, feeling the priest had lost some rank, insisted on a "sacramental ordination in the apostolic succession." The Eastern Orthodox had similar worries: They said *BEM* lacked "a sufficiently clear distinction between the ministry of the people of God and the ordained ministry." Evangelicals felt that priestly roles had too much recognition, overriding the Pauline "diversity" of the early church: "Why should the contemporary church be narrower in its understanding of ministry than the New Testament?"[47]

While projects such as *BEM* may have given American clergy a sense of common roots, and even a future horizon for working more closely together, Christian ministry in the United States still is known mainly by its factions. The largest, of course, has been Protestantism. It had formed the "evangelical consensus" at the start of the nineteenth century. The unity was irreparably shattered early in the next century, however, when Protestants divided between modernist and orthodox impulses, creating today what are the more liberal "mainline Protestants" and the more conservative "evangelicals." That division among clergy remains. It becomes a starting point for this survey of contemporary American ministry.

2

The Protestant Divide

Two kinds of protestant clergy walk the land, but describing their different paths has not been easy. Historians have called it the "two-party" system in Protestantism, a split between private salvation and social progress as goals for ministry. Sociologists have a different jargon. They speak of the "church" and "sect" in Protestantism, the former a part of the establishment, the latter a purified outsider. For average Americans, the difference is probably most evident in the messages they hear on Sundays, either the preaching of immediate conversion or of gradual nurture.

In speaking of modern ministry, the Protestant divide falls roughly between the more orthodox clergy of the "evangelical" churches, and the more modernist ministers of "mainline Protestantism." Evangelical pastors are more likely to present the gospel as a moment of decision, a choice against "the world" and for conversion. "You've got to bring them to that point of making that choice," said Chuck Smith, senior minister of Calvary Chapel, a large evangelical congregation in Southern California. The Bible does that everywhere, he said. "Either you do or you don't. Jesus said you're either for me or against me."[1]

Delivering sermons on the same Bible, the mainline Protestant pastor is less likely to see the Christian life so simply as the evangelical. Faith is a complex matter in a "world" that can be as much friend as foe. As one mainline minister wrote during a controversy over prayers with non-Christians, "Though we believe God has been revealed through and incarnated in Jesus, we who follow Jesus don't have a corner on the truth." This was a clergy editorial in the *Christian Century*, a journal for mainline constituents, which concluded: "At best we can witness to the truth as we know it and have experienced it."[2]

The two paths of the Protestant clergy are hardly as bifurcated as the "two-party" system and church versus sect suggest. But in all their meandering, these pathways remain a good map for understanding clergy today.

On any given Sunday in America, the evangelical decision and the mainline nurture are predictable fare. Almost as certain, moreover, the mainline will acknowledge a denominational heritage, whereas evangelicals will speak of dramatic turning points in the early church, as detailed by the New Testament. "Mainline Protestant congregations don't aim for that dramatic encounter on Sunday," said Maria E. Erling, a Lutheran seminary professor who was a New England pastor. "They expect a more textured message that connects them to a living tradition." Ronald Byars, who preached in Presbyterian churches for decades, did not aim for dramatic conversions. "Just the ordinary biblical preaching, week in and week out, is a way of reforming the way people view the world."[3]

Protestant clergy today are in open conversation about their different approaches, hewing to the classic arguments from their traditions, but also recognizing the new debate over which approach is more successful. The simpler and more urgent message, it seems, generates church growth, while a more "textured" gospel may get lost in a society bombarded with information. While mainline clergy may take a lesson from that, they still cherish the mystery and ambiguity of a complex universe. "The gospel should be made simple, not simplistic or simple–minded," said David M. Greenhaw, president of Eden Theological Seminary, a mainline school. "By being too complex, people can't grasp its meaning for their lives."[4]

At the time of this reflection, Greenhaw was part of the Faith Communities Today (FACT) study of congregations and pastoral leadership. One sobering finding was this: Churches with very educated pastors and members with diverse opinions—a recipe for complexity—are "far more likely" to experience conflict. These sanctuaries of diversity will have "more and different kinds of conflict" than churches with less divergence in opinion.[5] Evangelical ministry, meanwhile, tends to produce greater uniformity. While Greenhaw sees lessons in making the gospel simpler, most mainline clergy believe it cannot be reduced to black and white, a world without shades of gray. And in this way, the mainline clergy strongly reflect the American mainstream.

In a nation that is historically Protestant, and has only lost that tacit designation since the 1960s, clergy have always debated which kind of ministry occupies the Protestant mainstream in America. Protestant ministers spend more time preparing sermons, administering a congregation, and visiting the sick than laying claim to that "mainline" status. Yet since the term gained currency in the 1950s to speak of the historic and modernist denominations, the rivalry has not gone away: Who occupies the center lane of American culture, the modernists or the evangelicals?

Whatever the answer, being "mainline" is still about engaging culture, using seminaries, and attracting the nation's young talent into ministry. It is also about clergy as professionals. These remain topics for Protestant ministry today, a half century after the prosperous 1950s raised up and cheered the Protestant establishment, only for it to be shaken by the liberal 1960s.

That Protestant establishment, known today by denominations called the "seven sisters" (listed below), was helping to build American culture since the early twentieth century. That Protestant vitality crested in the 1920s, cut short by the Depression and war, and then in the 1950s the mainline experienced a final "brief shining moment" amid the boom of postwar prosperity. With denominational loyalty still strong in the 1950s, these mainline denominations erected magnificent office buildings in Manhattan and opened tens of thousands of new churches nationwide. Mainline leaders appeared on the covers of *Time* and *Newsweek,* and when *Life* featured "Twelve Great American Preachers" in 1953, all the Protestants were mainliners (except Billy Graham, an evangelical).[6]

When society changed after the 1960s, the mainline had far more institutional overhang than did evangelicals. Much of the mainliners' energy was drained by the typical burdens of a mass bureaucracy: maintaining buildings, departments, legislative conventions, employee benefits, and seminary systems. After 1970 the seven sisters lost two to three million members, and "sagging confidence" characterized mainline Protestant ministry.[7] Today it is commonly said that the "mainline has been sidelined," by an age when denominations don't seem to matter and evangelicals report membership growth and a new role in American politics.

In recent decades, mainline church activity did not really recede, but it seemed so as its cultural voice was overshadowed by a new evangelical prominence. Evangelical clergy took control of television and radio, and the Religious Right made political headlines. The leadership of the Catholic Church also stormed the front pages, debating the U.S. economy, nuclear war, and abortion, and riding the coattails of a media-age pontiff, John Paul II. By comparison, said sociologist Robert Wuthnow, there was a "relative absence of nationally visible mainline clergy." Indeed, a Lutheran theologian declared it "the Catholic moment" in 1987, and an activist manifesto of the 1990s was titled "Evangelicals and Catholics Together." By 2000, the mainline National Council of Churches pursued ties to evangelicals and Catholics, where the action seemed to be happening.[8]

Still, at the dawn of the twenty-first century, mainline Protestantism's 126,283 clergy make up the single largest bloc of ministers, or 22 percent of *all* American clergy. They care for 22.5 million churchgoers in 80,000 congregations. Compared to evangelical ministers, however, a larger share of mainline clergy are retired or doing non-parish work.[9] The mainline denominations are also known by their moderate or liberal leanings, a judgment based on the theological and social positions of governing bodies and clergy. Among the seven sisters the moderates are the United Methodist Church (the largest of the seven), the Evangelical Lutheran Church in America (ELCA), the American Baptist Churches, and the Disciples of Christ. Their more liberal kin are the Presbyterian Church (USA), the Episcopal Church, and the United Church of Christ.[10]

Beyond their differences, the denominations share a common spirit, according to recent surveys. While committed Christians, mainline members have "largely learned to live in a pluralistic world that requires respect for other faiths," according to Wuthnow. Nearly all view the Bible as "the inspired word of God." But more than six in ten said it contains "historical or scientific errors," and just 28 percent take the Bible "literally, word for word." Nearly all believe that God was "fully revealed to humans in Jesus Christ." But fewer (79 percent) assert that Christianity is "the best way to understand God." They are "open to the idea that truth can be found in other religions," Wuthnow said.[11]

As would be expected, half of mainline worshipers say they take the doctrinal middle road. The rest divide between being religious conservatives (22 percent) and religious liberals (26 percent). Mainline churches are places where "people with quite different theological views can come together for worship and service," Wuthnow said. While some still credit the mainline as being a bridge that "holds the center" of Protestantism, its internal clashes have also become legendary. As denominational conventions often show, the mainline is now a cauldron of "conflicts over social issues," which include abortion, war, poverty, church-state issues, and homosexuality.[12]

The conflict shows how porous the mainline is to both modernist and orthodox impulses. Nothing illustrates this better than the new phenomenon of liberal and conservative "special purpose groups" that cross denominational boundaries. On the conservative front, these have been called "evangelical renewal movements," which have "turned their attention to local clergy and congregations, giving less attention to denominational machinery," said sociologist Roger Finke. The result, for example, can be detected in the Midwest region of the United Methodist Church, scene of high "exposure to evangelical associations, especially [for] younger clergy." There, four in ten of the United Methodist mainline clergy sound like evangelicals: They said it is "completely true" that "only those who believe in Jesus Christ can go to heaven."[13]

The remaining six in ten of these Midwest clergy, however, reflect the more modernist outlook of the mainline when it comes to declaring that only believers "can go to heaven": 24 percent said it is "probably true" and 32 percent said it is "probably not true."[14] The Midwest is a more conservative domain of mainline Protestantism, however, and probably the greatest overall contrast is between regions of the country as a whole.

When mainline denominations debate doctrinal and social issues, for example, ministers in urban and western settings are predictably more liberal, while clergy in rural settings and the South lean conservative.

In all, however, it is impossible to put the entire mainline in a box. "At the local level, mainline congregations are as varied as American society itself," said Wuthnow. Congregations reflect their regions, constituents, and needs, and often seek a balance. Take the case of Resurrection United Methodist Church in Leawood, Kansas—a megachurch that, with 5,000 worshipers, is the second largest in the denomination. Its preaching is hardly exclusivist. Its pastor, Adam Hamilton, said the congregation succeeds on "our feeling that truth is not found on either extreme—we learn from both our liberal and conservative friends."[15]

Theology and ideology aside, a "day in the life" of a Protestant minister is not too different for mainline and evangelical clergy. The median work-week for a Protestant minister today is forty-six hours (compared to fifty-three hours for a Catholic priest). While the clergy work ethic can have extremes, from the casual part-timer to the manic workaholic, half of Protestant clergy fall in the middle range: forty-two to sixty-three dedicated ministerial hours a week.[16]

Preparing for the sermon and worship consumes the largest single bloc of time, or about a third of the hours each week. That is followed by pastoral care, a fifth of the minister's hourly labors, according to Pulpit and Pew. Then come administration and meetings (15 percent); teaching and training (13 percent); denominational and community meetings (6 percent). On average, the clergy spend about an hour a day in prayer, and about four hours a week reading independent of sermon preparation.[17]

The workaholic benchmark for mainline Protestant ministers was the 1950s, according to surveys back then by the sociologist Samuel Blizzard. He found that ministers worked an average of sixty-nine hours each week. A repeat study in the 1990s found the ministerial week had shrunk to forty-eight hours. Clergy worked hard, for sure. But the changing hours say something not only about modern efficiency but also about a more tenuous role of the pastor in modern culture and the changing ways of denominational life.

Much of the drop-off in time, according to the recent study, resulted in a decline in "visiting members and potential members, and in attending church and denominational meetings." All of this was not necessarily the modern minister's choice alone, of course. He may not be summoned to city hall or to a member's parlor as much as before. However, there was a time when "the pastor was a shepherd, and that means taking care of a flock," said a Lutheran minister who led his first church in 1958. "It means finding the one lost sheep. But now, the last thing the flock wants is for you to show up at their door."[18]

Whatever the causes, "Protestant clergy are now spending less time with church members, potential members, and religious and civic leaders than they did in the past," said the post-Blizzard study. While time spent in administration also dropped, the time spent counseling and planning church events increased. As to "personal piety," or time in prayer or devotional reading, "Catholics and [Protestant] sectarian clergy towered over the Protestant mainline."[19]

While most congregations in America are small, this is a particularly strong characteristic of the mainline denominations. And those demographics have set up obstacles to recruiting clergy for the future. Mainline churchgoers, for example, are more likely than other Americans to live in small towns. The small church, in turn, typically has half the members required, usually estimated at 200, to pay a full-time minister. For the ELCA, having 10 percent of churches pastorless is a healthy nudge for rotation and change. But today, 20 percent of ELCA churches are looking for the next minister. Similarly, 30 percent of Presbyterian Church (USA) churches lack a resident pastor. These hardship postings tend to be in rural or economically depressed regions. Filling pulpits around prosperous urban centers like the San Francisco Bay Area and Washington, D.C., is easy. "People fall all over themselves to work here," said one Washington-area minister.[20]

For both the city and the countryside in the 1950s, the story was different. Everywhere, mainline churches had stable memberships, and they could be counted on to send money to headquarters and students to seminary. "None of those things can be taken for granted any more," said Michael L. Cooper-White, a pastor who became president of the ELCA's Lutheran Theological Seminary in Gettysburg, Pennsylvania. "Congregations here today may not exist twenty years from now," the Minnesotan said at the turn of the new century. "The church is no longer the center of communities, even in small towns. So its future depends on continual evangelism and reaching out."[21]

The roughly 11,000 congregations of the ELCA are served by 9,379 clergy (with nearly that many more retired or in other work). Pastors are now being urged to be mission-minded workers and "transformational" leaders, seeing American society as an exotic mission field and the church as ripe for innovations. And one hopes clergy will show young people the joys of ministry. "Too many of my clergy colleagues don't speak enthusiastically about their ministries," Cooper-White said. It is part self-effacement and part career burnout. "We're really encouraging our clergy to talk with people, particularly younger people, about the rewards."[22]

The clergy rolls of the United Methodist Church make up nearly 40 percent of all mainline ministers serving local churches. While the sheer number is plentiful enough, the challenge is matching them to a new spectrum of tasks, from reviving small congregations to imbuing young people with Methodist loyalty. "The question is not whether we have enough pastors, but whether we have the right pastors to do what needs to be done," said Robert Kohler, head of clergy personnel.[23]

In the long run, part of being the "right pastor" will include being a young minister—with ample years to serve and a willingness to start out in a small congregation. Yet the number of young ministers in the mainline has dropped dramatically. The number of United Methodist ministers who are thirty-five years old or younger is just 6.7 percent. While that gives the Methodists a better rate than the ELCA (with 6.1 percent) and just behind the leading Presbyterian Church (USA) (with its 7 percent of clergy in this young category), the trend does not bode well across the seven historic denominations. The others range from 3.7 to 5.8 percent of clergy being that young.[24]

If the mainline has become sidelined, what might ministry learn from that experience? There are several theories of decline in mainline Protestantism: demographic, sociological, and historical. None of them has proven a silver bullet in finding solutions, but all of them point to feasible causes.

At the most practical level, the Protestant mainline may have grown and then shrunk by the sheer force of American birthrates. By this argument, the mainline church "revival" of the 1950s was a fertility spike and the decline a "return to normalcy." In another view, the educational and career goals of mainline churchgoers have caused them to marry later and have fewer children, giving a growth advantage to evangelicals and Catholics. What is more, the "worldly" success of mainliners may have given them a more tolerant and less evangelistic outlook. More than a third of mainline churchgoers have college degrees (compared to a quarter of all Americans), and twice as many are professionals, managers, and business owners (49 percent) than the general population. The mainline is also aging, with an average membership age of fifty-two to the national average of forty-six. Fewer than a third are under age forty.[25]

Another kind of sociological explanation may dig deeper into the minds of American Christians. It is the secularization theory, articulated particularly well by sociologist Peter Berger, a mainline Lutheran. He said that supernatural beliefs simply became harder to hold as Americans became more educated and worldly. The "sacred canopy" of belief, which had always made religious teachings "plausible," withered away under modernity and under its pluralism. For the mainline, this meant that organized Christianity had lost relevance, and many Americans simply stopped joining or attending churches. Berger reversed his "secularization" position later as religion, especially among evangelicals and Pentecostals, began to grow.[26]

But the "sacred canopy" problem did not go away entirely, and may have shifted to a more local setting: the dinner table of mainline parents—who failed to inculcate their children, the baby-boomer generation, with the particulars of their faith. For one thing, said Wuthnow, mainliners allowed their children "to explore spiritual alternatives." More broadly, according to another study, secularization, tolerant trends in society, and education produced a growing number of "lay liberals" in the church who were not assertively orthodox in rearing their children. According to the "lay liberal" theory, the mainline shrinkage after the 1960s was not a return to normal birthrates, or even dissatisfaction with top mainline leadership; it was the loss of baby boomers who might have filled mainline Protestant pews.[27]

One of the most prominent explanations of decline, however, has been set in the context of a religious marketplace. Faiths that were stricter, yet offered greater spiritual rewards, seemed to draw more customers. Hence evangelical and sectarian groups grow, while liberal ones dissipate. Dean Kelley, a United Methodist minister, made this case in *Why Conservative Churches Are Growing* (1972), which illustrated the point on an "exclusivist-ecumenical gradient." An exclusive faith, with its higher demands, high walls against the world, and clear eternal rewards, was more effective at keeping membership. Ecumenical churches, which lowered walls, were not distinct enough to keep their zeal. Kelley's argument was expanded by others into the economic parlance of "rational choice"; Americans choose the best product for the price, resulting in "winners" and "losers" in the church marketplace.[28]

Whatever the merits of the marketplace theory, there also seemed to be an historic inevitability about the direction of mainline Protestantism at the end of the twentieth century. In the words of historian Peter Thuesen, a "logic of mainline churchliness" was established in the heyday of evangelical Protestantism of the early nineteenth century and has simply played itself out in the present.[29] The "logic" of antebellum Protestantism was for Protestant ministry to engage secular society as a reformist and progressive force. This was done by the formation of denominations, agencies, and bureaucracies. At the end of the 1800s, however, the "evangelical consensus" in America was shattered by the new forces of modernity—urbanization, sectionalism, natural science, industrialization, and immigration.

As the split widened in the early 1900s, giving rise to fundamentalist Protestants who opposed the modernist trends, the mainline "logic" continued on the path of Protestant institution building. This was the era of the Social Gospel for the mainline, whose leaders and programs criticized capitalism's excesses, on the one hand, but extolled moral uplift and modern scientific efficiency on the other. The old logic of pre-Civil War evangelism now became the "liberal institutional logic" of progressive social causes, ecumenical cooperation, and new kinds of national agencies, said Thuesen. "Social Gospelers were clearly enamored of corporate, bureaucratic models for realizing God's kingdom," he said.[30]

Nothing represented the new mainline spirit better than the Federal Council of Churches, organized by thirty-three Protestant denominations. Its leaders "partook deeply of the bureaucratic ethos of big business and the scientific ethos of the university," and by the 1920s the fundamentalist-modernist split had become irreversible. In his famous 1922 sermon, "Shall the Fundamentalists Win?" modernist Baptist minister Harry Emerson Fosdick epitomized the battle, decrying the effort "to drive out of the evangelical churches men and women of liberal opinions." And he pleaded "the cause of magnanimity and liberality and tolerance of spirit."[31]

When the fundamentalists finally left these denominations, they ceded all their resources to the modernists: "The spoils of victory included everything from church buildings and denominational offices to pension funds and seminary scholarships." Mainline Protestantism was shaken, but moved on to apparent prominence in American culture, despite the 1930s "religious depression" that followed the economic shocks of the Great Depression. Seeking to improve ministry, the mainline launched the 1934 study on *The Education of Ministers in America* and afterward formed the American Association of Theological Schools, the first agency to accredit seminary degrees for ministers.[32] And in 1952, the mainline National Council of Churches further parted ways with the "evangelicals" by sponsoring the publication of a modern-language Bible, the *Revised Standard Version*.

Two versions of Protestant ministry were now in place, though society might have been slow to recognize the early accomplishments of the fundamentalists, said historian Joel Carpenter. "Fundamentalism provided a believable faith and a strong, lively religious community for hundreds of thousands in the 1930s and 1940s," he said. The "come-outers" who left the old denominations may have ceded the historic spoils, but they propagated a whole new world of publications, Bible institutes, and radio programs. That unnoticed success, Carpenter said, marked the beginning of the "disestablishment" of mainline Protestantism.[33]

After the pitched battles between fundamentalists and modernists in the 1920s, however, the spirit of evangelical ministry underwent its own transformation, driven by internal struggles among the orthodox themselves. What united them, on one hand, was the soul-winning evangelical zeal of the late 1800s, seen in the likes of salesman turned evangelist Dwight L. Moody, who preached a "sinking ship" world before Christ returned. "Moody was never ordained, yet few who heard him ever doubted the validity of his 'call.' " The fundamentalist view of the ministry was much the same, eschewing the credentialism of the mainline for entrepreneurship and biblical authority alone. Indeed, Billy Graham, an early fundamentalist, projected that classic demeanor. A Bible college graduate with no divinity degree, he was "an unassuming, unadorned man of God, standing with Bible in hand, expounding on the gospel of salvation."[34]

But finally, fundamentalism had to decide its ultimate attitude toward "the world," a question of temperament in ministry, and toward national organizations. By the 1940s, separatism no longer suited many conservative Protestants. They split away to produce today's evangelical mainstream, characterized by the National Association of Evangelicals (1943) and the new Graham, who by abandoning fundamentalism became no less than "the nation's preacher" in the 1950s. The fundamentalists kept their "oppositional spirit," urging the continued "coming out" of worldly churches, while at a new evangelical institution, Fuller Theological Seminary, the president denounced "come-outism."[35]

Though distinguishing itself with the "evangelical" term, the new movement still resisted national organization, preferring no structure or authority other than local churches and pastors. The National Association of Evangelicals, which viewed the NCC as an "ominous superchurch," struggled for four decades to gain its own membership: "While evangelicals sense the value of some level of structure, the dynamic nature of their movement would only tolerate a limited amount of centralization." The 1960s took its toll on both the conservative and liberal Protestants, but a harbinger of who survived best might have been seen in the 1976 *Newsweek* headline, "Year of the Evangelical."[36]

Already by mid-century, the term evangelical had been expanded beyond the fundamentalist Baptist, Presbyterian, and Congregationalist origins of the movement. It came to include Pentecostals and holiness churches—such as the Assemblies of God and Wesleyan Methodists—called a "third force" even by the mainline Protestants.[37] In the late 1960s, meanwhile, the Southern Baptists outpaced the Methodists as the largest denomination in America, and it was certainly more evangelical than it was mainline Protestant. In the twenty-first century, in fact, the Southern Baptist Convention declared itself "the evangelical behemoth."[38]

As a whole, however, evangelicals differ from mainline Protestant denominationalism by their fierce independence. They all want to protect from polluting or compromising their "distinctives"—which are many, from views on baptism, the Holy Spirit, and salvation to ordination and the return of Christ. Yet on the exclusive claim of Christian salvation—only believers would go to heaven—they varied not at all.

Given the broad coverage of a term like "evangelical," its conservative Protestant ministers make up a remarkable 74 percent of "active" clergy serving local churches today. In an overall comparison with mainline

Protestant ministers, one feature stands out: Evangelical clergy are more plentiful because more are "active" as pulpit ministers. The number drops, however, when compared to the total number of mainline ministers, including those who are retired or do other work. In this case, the evangelicals are just 59 percent of *all* Protestant clergy. This points to two trends: (1) mainline clergy hold many church jobs besides local pastor and perhaps retire earlier; and (2) the fluid nature of evangelicalism provides few ordained posts *besides* pastor. In such an entrepreneurial setting, many evangelicals found their own ministries. Many serve as pastor for life.[39]

While "evangelical" clergy may be the vast majority in modern-day Protestantism, a different picture emerges when only the modernist-fundamentalist split is considered. Two traditions that did not participate directly in the split—the Southern Baptist Convention and the Pentecostal movement—now make up most of America's evangelical clergy. And that means that the heirs of the proverbial "come-outers" of the early 1900s— fundamentalist clergy in the Presbyterian, Baptist, Congregational, Church of Christ and later Lutheran, Methodist, and Wesleyan traditions—today amount to just 22 percent of all ministers serving U.S. congregations. Contrasted with today's Protestant mainline clergy, these "evangelicals" may have more preachers in Sunday pulpits (77,000 versus 61,000 mainline), but the mainline has more total clergy (126,000 versus 103,000 evangelical).[40]

The head counts of clergy will always be less relevant than the challenge of matching ministers with the various needs of Protestantism, both mainline and evangelical. Yet this numerical picture of the mainline—fewer clergy in pulpits, more doing other work, and perhaps more retired— invariably springs from the more structured history of mainline denominations. They have required seminary education, used appointive systems, limited tenures, sought to make ministry a profession—and weighed in on a range of social controversies, especially in the 1960s.

Mainline churches today generally require that pastors earn a master's of divinity degree. In the actual field the reality is more complex. The study of Methodist ministers in the Midwest (see above) found that half had no theological degree. That is comparable to Southern Baptist pastors, half of whom do not earn a master's of divinity. Where the degree is found in the American church landscape, however, it is more than likely held by a mainline (or Roman Catholic) cleric and by clergy who lead any kind of large church. A 2001 survey found that 61 percent of American ministers had a master's degree, 27 percent had studied at a Bible college, and the rest lacked formal training.[41]

The choice between highly trained or a less trained clergy was given to American Protestantism in the age of Jacksonian democracy, when, as historian Nathan Hatch said, "Ordinary folk came to distrust leaders of genius and talents and to defend the right of common people to shape their own faith and submit to leaders of their own choosing." Nevertheless, evangelicals had become great seminary builders as well, claiming in the 1990s slightly more institutions (sixty-three) than the mainline denominations (fifty-seven) and higher enrollments (thirty thousand compared to seventeen thousand). Again, evangelical numbers are bolstered by Southern Baptists participation, with the largest seminary system in the world.[42]

Yet by emphasizing theological graduate school, and moving toward the mainstream of culture, the evangelicals have begun to experience the same kind of "crisis" as the mainline. By spending time earning degrees, candidates for ministry missed out on the local apprenticeships that have been classic to building ministry staff by fundamentalists, evangelicals, and now the megachurches, some of which will not hire seminary graduates. On this front, however, the diversity of the mainline Protestant congregations is helping out: Many of them, being more conservative and going outside the denominational "supply" system, are looking for their next ministers at the evangelical seminaries.[43]

Mainline Protestants like to work within their system, for cooperation and "connection" are the essence of their modern traditions. Yet some congregations have gone outside their denominational system to look for clergy, taking note of the great ideological differences between mainline and evangelical seminary training. It is a story told by researchers who spent three years looking at each kind of school. Their final report, *Being There* (1997), presented the anonymous institutions as Mainline Seminary and Evangelical Seminary. At Mainline, a "brick chapel rests on the crest of a hill." Evangelical did "not look very ecclesiastical at all." Mainline organized around "ethnic and gender diversity." Students learned that "the world and the church are missing not order and discipline but inclusiveness and justice." They were "challenged to confront their own deep prejudices and intolerance." Mainline gave particular attention to "two forms of injustice: racism and sexism," putting the onus "most heavily on white males."[44]

Evangelical Seminary, guided by Reformation belief, or a "mild generic Calvinism," "warned [students] away from persons, ideas, and institutions that seem to have given in to humanism and the emotional excesses of revivalistic religion." Study at Evangelical Seminary is a cognitive search for "tools" for Bible-centered Christian living. "Virtually all the students . . . have had a heavy dose of evangelical youth culture." Seminary life is about "a relationship, a deeply personal and emotional one, between the individual student and God." And yet the key issue is the *"right doctrine about God,"* said one professor. "If we preach wrong, your faith is futile, and the end is the grave." The difference in emphasis seemed to be this: "Mainline's dominant message is on behavior and attitudes more than assent to doctrinal affirmations." The student's "struggle" is paramount. One professor at Mainline Seminary said her goal was "to prepare students never to be comfortable in the church."[45]

One concern voiced by both Protestant and evangelical leaders who believe in graduate school seminary is the lowering of standards—and thus a decline in quality of students who will become the next generation of clergy. Auburn Seminary president Barbara Wheeler, who participated in the *Being There* study, points to law, medicine, and the Jewish rabbinate to strike a comparison. Today, law students pick a career at age twenty-six and doctors twenty-four. Divinity students come in at thirty-five. The rabbinic students, however, still are relatively young when they make a commitment, according to a national survey of the nation's entering class of seminarians in 1998.

Conducted by Auburn Seminary staff, the survey found a new kind of generational challenge for Christian seminaries.[46] While younger students are typically from well-educated families and have good college grades, they are less interested in being parish ministers. The number of older students, meanwhile, has risen dramatically. They are typically from average backgrounds with modest academic success but are most eager to be a local minister. They have been called by experiences in a local church, whereas in the past the young seminarian matriculated through a church college and was ordained by age twenty-five.

"There is a problem overall," Wheeler concluded. Generally with the older students, "their religious commitments, though intense, are not long established," she said. The older students are eager for ordination (65 percent). Four in ten say congregational ministry is their first choice. "Younger students often lack interest in ministry, especially congregational ministry," the survey found. Just half on an ordination track want to lead a local church. And only a third of all the younger master's degree seminarians relished a pulpit. Many prefer teaching, social work, a chaplaincy, or administration.

Modern culture is clearly not helping to focus the dreams of talented young people on being ministers, especially when better ways to make money beckon on all sides. Still, the success with rabbinic students stood out: 56 percent of them wanted to lead a synagogue. "The marginal status of organized religion is very likely the basic cause of the difficulty of attracting leaders for religious organizations," Wheeler said. "People of ability, especially the young, seek social roles that position them to make a substantial difference."

The rabbinate seems to have kept this "high status" and the marks of "quality": Younger students with better grades are eager to train for a lifetime ministry. "Though their course of study is longer and their debt load higher, rabbinical students, as a group, have most of the characteristics of 'quality,' " Wheeler said. "Compared with Christian students, they are religiously well trained and enculturated." And the status goes "hand-in-hand with strong salaries." Indeed, starting salaries of rabbis are double those of other clergy.

Yet even the rabbinate is challenged. Rabbi pay has "reached impressive levels," with $100,000 not an unusual wage-and-housing package for newer rabbis, according to Jack Wertheimer, provost of Jewish Theological Seminary. Still, synagogues face "a crisis of personnel," he said. Talented students are less interested today in leading congregations. Jewish studies at university compete with seminary tracks and "the title of professor inevitably [has] outranked that of rabbi." Reform, Conservative, and Reconstructionist synagogues have become more "anti-clerical," Wertheimer said. Many churches place "grossly unrealistic expectations" on their ministers, and the same goes for synagogues and rabbis. So Jewish seminarians look elsewhere, often for jobs in the many secular Jewish organizations. "Rabbis and prospective rabbis still fare considerably better than their Christian counterparts," Wertheimer said, citing the Auburn study.[47]

That study recommended that churches and seminaries do more to recruit and support young candidates: "Some persons who might make good religious leaders are lost to the profession simply because they made early decisions to take other paths." It also said that theological schools should raise the admissions bar: They presently accepted 87 percent of all applicants. With the bar set too low, "religious communities cannot assume that a professional degree from an accredited theological school guarantees genuine promise for ministry."

The term *professional* has been part of the mainline since the "evangelical consensus" was formed: Seminaries trained clergy with credentials, and ministers put their names on the rolls for hire. Yet it was also the period when, according to historian Samuel Haber, the "egalitarian onslaught" of Jacksonian democracy before and after 1830 dismantled all the nascent professions, in protest of the experts and elites who seemed to be monopolizing medicine, law, and even ministry. The American professions—of which the numbers greatly multiplied—regrouped themselves in the late 1800s and early 1900s. Some clergy were irked by the way a major 1933 study, *The Professions*, excluded ministry. But in time they got their revenge. By the 1950s, the minister was becoming less a master of theological disciplines and more a "professional manager and therapist."[48]

When H. Richard Niebuhr wrote his benchmark study on Protestant ministry in the fifties, he described it as the "perplexed profession." He nevertheless saw an "emerging new conception" of the minister as both spiritual and managerial. He called this role "pastoral director." While once a strong prayer and sermon by the pastor might suffice each week, the complex modern church required more. Niebuhr said the minister would of course carry out the traditional functions: "preaching, leading the worshiping community, administering the sacraments, caring for souls, presiding over the church." But more than that, "His first function is that of building or 'edifying' the church; he is concerned in everything that he does to bring into being a people of God who as a Church will serve the purpose of the Church in the local community and the world."[49]

That vision, which was both about leadership and institution building, was appealing enough. Yet in the same decade, another student of mainline ministry, the sociologist Samuel W. Blizzard, announced the "minister's dilemma." While clergy entered ministry with one set of priorities—preaching first, followed in importance by being pastor, priest, teacher, organizer, and last of all administrator—the church demanded an opposite "use of time." Most time was spent on administration and pastoral services. "Men who are recruited for the ministry usually have an image of the preacher, priest, teacher and pastor as a servant of God," Blizzard wrote in the *Christian Century* in 1956. "But they actually spend most of their time doing those things they feel are least important. Denominational goals and programs and local parish needs determine the use of their time."[50]

The American middle class naturally began to view the local sanctuary as a place for user-friendly services, not just a Sunday exhortation. "The clergy need to be engaged in activity that is useful in the eyes of the laity if they are to be maintained in their positions," one minister said in 1963. "The praise of God for his goodness and power does not legitimate a clergyman in the United States." Other pressures descended on mainline clergy as well. They were caught in the crossfire of the new social criticism, which took aim at middle-class conformity, white-collar success, and the "organization man." Liberal clergy began to decry the "suburban captivity of the churches," a slogan heard in 1961. Indeed, some clergy had tired of "churchianity"—for "some young clergymen are 'pro-Christ' and 'anti-church.'" The time seemed ripe for another Jacksonian-like revolt, but now among the clergy themselves. "All in all it was fairly easy to be an ordained minister until the 1960s."[51]

As the Roman Catholic Second Vatican Council of 1962–65 cited "signs of the times" for its own global changes, the polestars for mainline Protestant clergy had been secularization of belief and urbanization. The themes were put forth in two bestsellers: Anglican Bishop John A. T. Robinson's *Honest to God* (1963), which said the idea of God "up there" or "out there" was obsolete, and liberal Baptist Harvey Cox's *The Secular City* (1965), which said Christianity was losing its power as a "commanding system of personal and cosmic values and explanations." While these ideas percolated in seminaries, clergy read headlines about conflicts of race, poverty, and the Vietnam War. A minister could hardly "isolate himself or his decisions from the social milieus," said sociologist Jeffrey Hadden, who conducted a survey of mainline clergy in the 1960s.[52]

His report, *The Gathering Storm in the Churches*, said that religious "doubt" shifted the clergy "away from the next world to a deeper concern about the meaning and implications of the Christian faith for this world." As a result, "The laity have one church and the clergy have another," especially clergy fresh out of seminary, on campuses, and working in urban ministry. They became a "challenge-oriented" generation, confronting the "comfort-oriented" preference of churches. If the "new breed" of clergy viewed the church "as an institution for challenging man to new hopes and new visions of a better world," the laity still favored it as "a source of comfort for them in a troubled world." Many clergy would leave ministry over the ensuing conflict, but many more make up the aged liberal wing of mainline Protestantism today.[53]

The pivotal issues for these clergy had become the blacks' struggle for civil rights, the government-expanding War on Poverty, and opposition to the war in Vietnam. Hadden found that clergy generally sympathized with the civil rights struggle, much more than did their congregations. A smaller number of mainline clergy who became activists on poverty and Vietnam stood out even more from people in the pew. And it had dramatic career implications as well, with more clergy creating free-lance ministries or roles. "Innovative clergy have been systematically separated from the parish pastorate," Hadden reported.[54]

All of this, of course, created a "crisis of identity" for clergy in middle-class churches. While Hadden sympathized with the "new breed," he conceded that many were out of their depth on complex social issues, preferring a prophetic stance to patient consciousness-raising of parishioners: "Facing the jeers and insults of an angry crowd of racial bigots or war hawks may be easier than facing a congregation that feels the Christian gospel is a source of comfort and protection from a troubled world rather than a radical charge to go into the world and make it more human." What was more, "the leadership of a voluntary association can only be so far out of line with the expectations of its constituency before that leadership is questioned."[55]

Despite the tumult and what another commentator called "acute anomie" among mainline Protestant clergy in the 1960s, the quest to improve, deepen, and strengthen the religious call as a "profession" continued. Speaking of the sixties, Haber said "these tumults had few lasting effects" on the status of professions, including the clergy, as had happened so dramatically in the early 1800s. Nevertheless, the feverish decade did renew calls for a movement of ministerial refurbishment. In 1968, for example, a group of mainline pastors incorporated the Academy of Parish Clergy on the model of the medical profession. It continues today as a modest network encouraging excellence, ethics, and continuing education. That same year, theologian James Glasse at Vanderbilt Divinity

School published his book, *Profession: Minister,* which envisioned an American Academy of Pastoral Clergy (never organized) where members took "responsibility for their own self-improvement."[56]

As professionals, Glasse argued, clergy needed one overall status in society, especially as new vocations—from psychiatrists to Rotary Club presidents—overlapped clerical turf. His rubrics for the divine profession were training and expertise, a common ethical code, dedication to human improvement, and the inclusion of several kinds of practitioners. A profession "has the quality of a group photo," he said. "One professional does not have to look just like another, but all are recognizable as belonging in the same picture."[57]

He raised an issue of concern in all churches today: the long-term spiritual development of the overworked minister. In his day, Glasse said ministers were dealt with in segments. First they were the religious "personality type" who heard God's call. Once trained in a denomination, they become an institutional representative, an image of particular ecclesiastical trappings. Finally, clergy do a specific skilled job that becomes their "occupational-type image" and how society will classify them. "We tend to recruit ministers through one kind of image, train them in light of another kind, and then require them to practice in terms of yet another kind," Glasse said. "We do not have an image of the ministry which can picture all the stages of the process," including a fourth stage of long-term renewal, education, and motivation for clergy.[58]

Writing more recently, Gilbert R. Rendle said the reclaiming of professional clergy status means re-establishing a "jurisdiction" in which they have something special to offer. While a century ago that used to be community leadership and general knowledge, now it is narrowed to being a spiritual "interpreter" of modern life. "What may be required is learning a complex professional practice in order to return to a claim of simplicity in one's faith," Rendle said. "Professional ministry is now challenged to reassert itself in an immense new-but-ancient jurisdiction—a place where people are asking questions and facing problems of meaning."[59]

In their own ways, mainline Protestant and evangelical ministry try to give America its modern meaning, a task that can overlap often enough. Such was the case three days after the September terrorist attacks on America, when Billy Graham, the war horse of evangelicalism, took the pulpit of the Washington National Cathedral, a mainline bastion. To a pluralistic nation, Graham did not deliver an evangelical call for decision, but rather offered ways to interpret the horrifying events. The Bible "speaks of evil as a mystery," he said, and offers the cross as assurance of God's ultimate love. It was a message that all Protestant ministry, and indeed Catholic ministry as well, could unite around.[60]

Moments of consensus like this are especially precious when the number of modern social issues that divide ministers are considered. One of the largest divisions has been spurred by the revolution in women's roles in society, a change that has propelled a new wave of female clergy into the pulpit.

3

Women in Ministry

ON A SWELTERING JULY DAY in 1974, three rebel Episcopal bishops, safely retired, ordained eleven women to the priesthood at the Church of the Advocate in Philadelphia. The "irregular" action defied the church's General Convention, which had twice voted against female priests. Yet the Philadelphia events forced the church's hand. At the next convention, in 1976, the policy was approved. The following year, eighty-two Episcopal women, some of whom were already ordained deacons, were made priests.

"We all worried we could be excommunicated—if we lived that long," the Reverend Nancy Wittig recalls about Philadelphia a quarter century later, when women made up about 13 percent of Episcopal priests. "Maybe God would strike us dead."[1]

The dramatic increase of female ordinations in the United States over the past three decades—from a few percent of all American clergy to as many as 14 percent today—has included both highly public events and quiet, gradual changes. There has been advocacy, hyperbole, opposition, and patient dignity. The more radical trajectories are not exactly new, for as early as the 1890s *The Woman's Bible* had already sought "to expose the repressiveness of the Bible's teachings about women." More recently, this same concern has been echoed in new versions of feminist theology. The "Women-Church" outlook advocated for a separate sisterhood based on biological differences from man. The "Re-Imagining" conference followed in 1993, when female clergy gathered to venerate goddess rites, the fertility cycle, and Christian liturgies side by side.[2]

While those episodes stole the headlines, the more gradual and more conventional process of expanding the female ministerial ranks has been the rule. The Lutherans who merged to form the Evangelical Lutheran

41

Church in America (ELCA) are typical of this quiet gradualism. By 2000, when the ELCA celebrated thirty years since they decided to ordain women, the ranks of active clergy had grown to 20 percent female. "I suspect the people who made the original decision never dreamed that we would get to 30 years," said Joanne Chadwick, head of the Commission for Women in the 5.2 million-member denomination.[3]

This gradualism toward more female leadership has been afoot in unexpected places as well. While Pope John Paul II has made clear that the Roman Catholic Church will not ordain women to the priesthood, in the United States female Catholic leadership has been growing quietly. They are the lay ecclesial ministers, theologically trained and increasingly running the administration of and teaching within the nation's Catholic parishes. Indeed, the United States Conference of Catholic Bishops reported in 2004 that women made up nearly half of all administrators in the nation's dioceses, a percentage that "compares favorably" with women in managerial leadership in America's secular workforce.[4]

The last three decades, which have been some of the most active in history regarding women's ordination, illustrate also the inevitable ebbs and tides, and even cycles, that the women's cause in Christian ministry tends to undergo. Overall, for example, the tide has been toward more acceptance of female leadership from the pulpit or at the church executive's desk. Over the past century, the share of U.S. denominations giving women "full clergy rights" rose from 7 percent to around 50 percent.[5]

Yet there has been regress at the same time, as exemplified by views of female leadership in the more conservative Holiness, Pentecostal, and evangelical traditions. After 1853, more than half of all women who were ordained worked in these sectors of American Christianity. That growth was reversed, however, by the fundamentalist clash with modernism in the 1920s, a date that marked the gradual rolling back of women's leadership roles. The independent churches so characteristic of evangelicalism have nevertheless harbored the vast majority of women in church leadership, despite the attention given to ordination struggles in mainline Protestantism. A study in the 1970s, for example, found that the nation's ten largest Protestant groups accounted for just 17 percent of all ordained women. In other words, most female leaders were in small denominations or local, independent, and non-hierarchical Protestant sectors—all of them less visible on the national scene.[6]

The rise of female ordinations in mainline Protestantism, which by its denominational structures have been easier to track, has also produced a cycle effect: a cycle of victory and excitement followed by limits and disappointment. As the "visibility" of women in ministry has increased, churches can "feel that it is no longer necessary to get more women into lay and pastoral leadership positions," said Barbara Brown Zikmund, ordained in the United Church of Christ in 1964. Fewer women than expected have landed top clergy jobs—just 8 percent are senior pastors. While nearly half are sole pastors, they serve mostly small churches. As a result, perhaps, many "pioneer" women have left the ministry. Others detoured into "special ministries." Thirty years after the revolution, complaints about "token levels" of female leadership are heard.[7]

In the more bureaucratic churches, in fact, the room for more ordained women may have evaporated, in a world "increasingly crowded with female colleagues in the lower to mid-level placements as the occupation continues to feminize," said feminist sociologist Paula D. Nesbitt. She said that the ferment over female leadership in U.S. Catholicism may finally be more consequential to "restructuring" church institutions. Perhaps it promises a "radical occupational and organizational change" overshadowing even the mainline, "where women have been ordained, co-opted, job segregated, and to some extent pacified, mollified or frustrated."[8]

The experiences of recent decades have also produced what some call three "waves" of women seeking to do ministry, especially in Protestantism. By their different experiences and goals, they also show the ebb and flow of female opinion amid their common goal of seeking ordination. The opinions range from the more radical to the more conciliatory. "Women should only [enter the ministry] if they intend to work to change the system," said Allison Cheek, a first-wave member of the "Philadelphia eleven" who now teaches liberation theology at the Episcopal Divinity School in Cambridge, Massachusetts. "Otherwise they are undermining women's protest against unjust structures by helping cement them in place."[9]

A still earlier pioneer was Zikmund, who is a bit more philosophical about the ambiguity that remains from three decades of activism. "There was a sense that, 'We're going to go into this church and we're going to change the system,'" she said nearly four decades later. "Some have tried and said it can't be done and gone their own way. Others say there are other important goals besides the top job." Most significant, she believes, is that women have begun "reinventing ministry, refusing the old definitions and expectations." More of them "say they don't want to be head pastor. But is that because they hit a brick wall or because their innate interest was not on the senior pastorate?"[10]

When Zikmund surveyed women serving as ordained ministers in the United States, she found a change in mood about obstacles to their work in the church. Clergywomen in the mid-1990s, experiencing the second wave, were not as concerned about "the sexist nature of the church" as were female clergy in the early 1980s. Back then, a majority of clergywomen (56 percent) felt that changing a sexist church was "quite" or "somewhat" important. A short era later, a third felt that way (35 percent).[11]

Women have testified to greater acceptance in the churches. But experience has brought wisdom as well. When Joy Charlton, the sociologist and minister's daughter, tracked women in Methodist and Lutheran ministry over two decades, she found that many had left the ministry, unhappy with their parish assignments or lack of opportunities. Their decisions to leave often revealed a career "narrative" that mimicked that of male ministers. Women should consider looking at "alternative models" of ministry that suits their nature and needs, Charlton concluded: " 'composing a life' rather than climbing a career ladder."[12]

A third wave of women is now studying for the ministry or just entering the field. The emotion of change is still fresh. "I was almost in tears when I first saw a woman celebrate the Eucharist," said Laurie Brock, an Alabaman studying at General Theological Seminary, an Episcopal school, in 2001. "It gave me a whole different view of God." For Melissa Keeble, a Presbyterian studying at Fuller Theological Seminary in the same period, the challenge of ministry is not "balancing out the number of clergy" between male and female but in finding godly clergy at all. "The worst thing I can imagine is someone going into ordained ministry who is not called by God," she said. "If that means it will always be 10 percent women and 90 percent men, then that's how it should be."[13]

The focus on women's ordination struggles should not suggest that they have lacked centrality, or even leadership, in the church until the present. They "sometimes outnumbered men two to one in many colonial congregations," says one history. Anne Hutchinson famously dissented in Puritan Boston and female Quakers preached in New Amsterdam. Women's voices testified in both Great Awakenings, and in 1853 the first woman was ordained. All along, testimony of the call has been deeply authentic. As missionary doctor Catherine C. Bushnell said around the turn of the twentieth century, it was not about "interests of merely a few ambitious women, [but] the very fundamentals of our faith."[14]

Yet ordained ministry has historically been the domain of men, so the comparison of the two sexes in ministry is invariably a part of its modern understanding. The religious leadership of women in local congregations of the United States today has been best captured by the National Congregations Survey of 1998. By its estimation, women lead 10 percent of all U.S. congregations. Their small churches, however, contain just 6 percent of all churchgoers. They have shorter tenures than male clergy. And they lead 16 percent of churches with no full-time paid staff—meaning the clergywoman herself is part time.[15]

Women are not ordained in Catholic, Eastern Orthodox, or Mormon ministry. Actual congregational leadership in historic black denominations (1 percent) and white conservative churches (5 percent) is not much higher. Women lead 4 percent of Catholic parishes, but these are nuns or lay supervisors in the absence of a priest (the growing number of lay women leading in parishes still are assistants to priests). Women have their strongest showing among mainline Protestant clergy, leading 21 percent of those congregations in America. Yet they are small houses of worship, often "declining in membership and heavily populated by older women."[16]

While both men and women in ministry lead congregations with a predominantly female membership—a widespread fact in American Christianity—female pastors are *more* likely to have this characteristic in their local church, according to the Congregations Survey. Women-led churches are more likely to have less than a third males and fewer two–parent families. The picture shows a "similarity between female ministers and female managers more generally: women tend to occupy authoritative roles in settings in which women, not men, predominate," said one analysis of the Congregations Survey. While some say the "feminization" of ministry has depressed its social rank and income by flooding it with cheaper female labor, the decline seemed underway in the 1950s—without the presence of women. "The occupational decline, as measured by a clergy oversupply, was well established before women began to enter the professional clergy job market in substantial numbers," one study argues.[17]

To the surprise of some, the Congregations Survey found that women are twice as likely to be found in urban congregations than in rural ones. Moreover, the thirteen states of the West have become their haven, home to nearly half of all women-led churches. Next in concentration, twelve Atlantic states from New York to Florida host 29 percent of such congregations. The vast South and compact New England each have 7 to 8 percent of the nation's women-led churches.[18]

Where women serve in ordained leadership their salaries are comparable to those of men with similar positions, years of experience, and education, according to the Pulpit and Pew study of 2002. As suggested by the proverbial "stained-glass ceiling," however, women "do not seem to have equal access to the higher-paying jobs," which generally means larger churches. Whether because of a crowded job market, church policy, social resistance, or naked bias, "female pastors tend to have lower average career attainment than their male counterparts in many Protestant denominations," said another study.[19]

Yet most women have had the advantage of coming to ministry with a second-income spouse, who usually earn far more than even the male clergymen of the nation. "Women who do enter ministry do so because they have on average higher paid working spouses than clergy men." On average they live in households with 20 percent more total income than households of male ministers. "Many married clergywomen live a more secure life than that of their male counterpart." Even though "clergy women may be in a more privileged position overall," they may also be forced to compromise, turning down a call because the husband cannot move from his job.[20]

The social profile of men and women in ministry fairly reflects the population as a whole: For example, they reflect similar rates when it comes to divorces and being single. Yet in local churches conventions prevail. When they have a say in who will be their next minister, the preference is typically for a married man under forty with a homemaker wife and children—an idealistic profile, considering that it encompasses no more than 5 percent of the population. "Many committees do not much want a divorced man—especially not a divorced woman—particularly if that person might be involved in dating," a Pulpit and Pew study reports. Said a member of another search committee, "Half of the ministers whose names we got were females and half of [the females] were divorced."[21]

At the Episcopal Church's General Seminary in New York, half the students were single in 2001. At that time, student placement officer Alon White, a female priest, noted that despite the dilemma of churches seeking a "family man" as pastor, limited budgets bode well for the hiring of single women. "For their money, [churches] get women with a [graduate] degree or commensurate experience, versus a younger man or a harder–to–place man."[22]

The entry of women into ministry has also leavened the debate about leadership styles. In modern-day congregations, according to surveys, a democratic approach is at least reported to be preferred over a more autocratic style of religious leadership. What a local church really wants, however, can be elusive—and usually is proven as ministers and congregations work out their lives together. Either way, however, this is a democratic age: "All pastoral leaders in the 1990s tend to have more of an inclusive, democratic leadership style than a directive, autocratic style." Even bigger-than-life megachurch pastors boast this ameliorative style, at least when asked.[23]

This democratic approach is also called a "relational" style of leadership, and women and men in ministry diverge on how well each is doing under this criterion in a local church. Women by their nature or upbringing may have the advantage here. "There's a relational emphasis among women's lives," Zikmund said. "It's a luxury in a way. You have time for friendships because you are not so goal–oriented." Some goals may suffer. "But I think it strengthens ministry. The Christian faith and religious and spiritual issues are often relational, like your relationship with others and with God, the two great commandments."[24]

One study asked male and female clergy about this and found more women than men (three-fifths to one-fifth) claimed that "women leaders tend to share power more than men leaders." Leadership style may also differ by position, denomination, and stage of proving oneself in ministry. For the past century, three kinds of church structures—institution-centered, congregation-centered, and spirit-centered—have influenced clergy appointments *and* styles of leadership. Theologically, women in spirit-centered churches favor autocratic leadership. So do some women in institution-centered hierarchical churches, such as Episcopal and Lutheran, though this may be more to prove authority than personal preference. Even where democracy is supposed to prevail, "Southern Baptist clergywomen are 20 percent more likely than clergymen in their denomination to see themselves as *very* democratic in leadership style."[25]

What women leaders want in their churches varies widely, and most have no other goal but to serve the Lord, achieve excellence—and be happy. Faced with the challenges of ministry, of course, women are just slightly more likely than men (32 to 28 percent) to have seriously considered leaving the paid profession "sometime during the last year" in the 1990s. For some women, satisfaction or otherwise may have hinged on goals, even agendas, they had in seeking ordination. For women with agendas, two kinds have traditionally stood out. One has been called "institutional feminism," which sought to undermine occupational sexism: it was a head-on competition with men for power. The other is "spiritual feminism," focused more on confronting patriarchal religion by changing theology, symbols, and language. When female clergy are asked about such reformations, more than a third (36 percent) feel their womanhood indeed was "changing the meaning of ordination" (27 percent are mixed and 37 disagreed). They are also more likely than male clergy (72 to 49 percent) to believe "more women should be ordained."[26]

From a historical vantage, both secular and ecclesiastical forces have determined the various fates of women in ministry. After the Civil War, Protestant denominations began to allow lay female leadership and inevitably some kind of ordination, a process that happened earlier and more quickly in congregation-based denominations than in hierarchical ones. When women gained decision-making status in clerical bodies, policies changed. With the modern quest of ecumenism, or Christian unity, women's ordination was singled out, and by the mid-1960s ecumenical talks and the attitudes in many seminaries had torn down remaining theological barriers.[27]

And what of the secular forces? The manifesto of modern feminism, Betty Freidan's *Feminine Mystique*, hit bookstores in 1963, and four years later the National Organization for Women set up its "ecumenical" task force to engage churches. Even before, however, the tides of democracy, liberalism, and equal rights had buffeted Protestantism, prompting votes for women's ordination in the 1950s. After surveying those early dates in

U.S. churches, sociologist Mark Chaves concluded that outside pressure was greater than inside theologies or parish experiences: "Formal rules about women's ordination are, in large part, generated by external pressure on denominations." Economics made theology as well. Industry and world wars pushed women into the workplace, banishing the "cult of domesticity." When churches grew on the wealth of the 1920s and 1950s, women were summoned to fill empty pulpits.[28]

Similarly, the arguments for and against the right of women to preach or lead churches has included both ecclesiastical and social elements. This has been a perennial discussion: hence the key arguments on both sides are fairly pat. In support of women clergy, personal testimony, the need for exhorters, and the simple fact of women's ministry are brought to bear. In regard to the Bible, St. Paul's various bans on women are explained away as part of an ancient social "context" of the writing. In turn, the Bible's endorsement of women's prophetic roles, which even Paul had recognized, are emphasized.[29]

The exclusion of women has its set arguments as well. The view of some black ministers toward female peers may represent some general attitudes. Just more than half of black ministers disapprove of women in the pulpit. One opponent explained that the "responsibility of the pastor is too strenuous," while another fixed on the power of preaching: "She has no voice." Faith-healer Kathryn Kuhlman acknowledged the stress. "This is really a man's job," she said, citing her seventeen-hour days. But "someplace man failed." During the 1920s, Methodist advocate Georgia Harkness listed (and rebutted) six reasons to exclude women, beginning with the words of St. Paul. The others, however, were biological and social: Women departed a natural sphere to do ministry, they were unfit for success, and childbearing cut the work short. They also "interfere with the tenure or salaries of men" and cause the church to "lose in public esteem."[30]

Some male preachers have assured women that motherhood is more influential, for "training in the salvation of her children is mighty and decisive; the influence of the minister over his hundreds is slight." Yet M. Madeline Southard, who organized the American Association of Women Ministers, was not mollified by such praise for the fairer sex. "Men were not disturbed when women washed the world's dirty clothes and scrubbed dirty office floors," she said in 1921. Only when women sought careers did "they became fearful of what would happen to their children and their femininity."[31]

Whether riding on providential or secular energies, the fate of clergy-women orbits around two key doctrines of Christianity—the sacramental priesthood and the authority of biblical texts. This theological concern is eminently practical as it plays out in two sectors of American Christianity, the more liturgical and hierarchical churches and the other more independent, "democratic" Bible ministries.[32]

The Episcopal Church, with its sacramental priesthood, and the Southern Baptist Convention, with its more fundamentalist view of the Bible, are sterling examples of these two kinds of approaches to women in ministry. Their recent conflicted experiences, moreover, illustrate how women's leadership brushes up against sacramental or biblical claims—and how clergy find ways to "agree to disagree" once the disputes are well under way.

Ever since the Anglican Church set foot on American soil in 1607, and its American branch, the Episcopal Church, was formed in 1789, Eucharist worship has been central. As the Catholic-derived tradition argues, Jesus was male with male disciples, the start of an "apostolic succession" that ever since has administered God's grace in the bread and wine, baptism, and the hands-laying of ordination—all male hands until 1977. "Women have the most resistance over celebrating the Eucharist," said Jane Holmes Dixon, who became an Episcopal bishop in 1992. "We believe God is present in that act. People are more willing to accept women in the pulpit, which is not sacramental. Celebration of the Holy Eucharist is, in fact, exactly that."[33]

Once women started handling the Eucharist in 1977, it was a short step to 1989, when the election of a female bishop in the Diocese of Massachusetts brought women into the line of the twelve apostles. For Episcopalians, both were monumental steps, arrived at by a slow progress in history or a leap of heresy—for Episcopalians declared both joy and grief at the developments. Recognizing this division, the House of Bishops passed a resolution the next year known as the "conscience clause," which said bishops and clergy may in good conscience not accept female priests. The measure was never legislated in General Convention, however, making appeals to the conscience clause in later years contentious indeed. When the first female bishop was elected in 1989, the House of Bishops reaffirmed that right of conscience-driven dissent among members of the hierarchy. But perhaps the pivotal year was 1992, when the mother church itself, the Church of England, narrowly voted to ordain its first female priests. Rome recoiled, and if Anglicanism at the time had been a bridge between Catholics and Protestants, "now the bridge is burning."[34]

For two new Episcopal bishops, Jane Holmes Dixon of Washington, D.C., and Jack Iker of Fort Worth, Texas, 1992 was a fateful year. Both were elected to the episcopacy. By general account, she was elected to put a second woman in the American hierarchy, he to represent traditionalists who rejected a female priesthood. "I am a symbol of the inclusiveness of God," Dixon said at her consecration. In contrast, Iker recalls, "When I got elected bishop of Fort Worth, I got known as an 'outspoken opponent' of women to the priesthood. . . . I get labeled as if that's the only thing I'm concerned about."[35]

As required, both Dixon and Iker were confirmed by majority votes from the nation's one hundred Episcopal Church dioceses. But not surprisingly, liberal Washington, D.C., voted against elevating him to the Episcopal hierarchy. If "irregular" ordinations were the dissent of the 1970s, the tables had turned. Upholding a male priesthood was the dissent of the 1990s.

Iker had graduated from General Seminary in 1974, a time when nearly everyone he knew opposed women priests. Over the years of dispute, the doctrinal issues at stake were changing as well. "Nobody asked me if I believe in Christ's resurrection from the dead, but I'm constantly asked if I believe in women's ordination," Iker said. "The Episcopal Church welcomes pluralism and diversity only when it comes from the left or the innovative side; if it's traditional or from the right, there's no tolerance."

A native of Mississippi, Dixon became a public school teacher in Tennessee and then a housewife with three children. In 1964, the family moved to Washington, D.C., where her husband worked as a lawyer. Talk of women's ordination had just begun, and in time Bishop William F. Creighton of Washington became a strong advocate of the proposed change. After the church rejected it in 1973, Creighton took a radical stance and postponed ordination of men until the church reversed its decision. Washington, too, had its own rebellion of four "irregular" ordinations in 1975. The next year, as Dixon recalls, she too felt the spark. Over lunch one day, she mused to Verna Dozier, a black church educator, about her twelve-year-old son becoming a priest. "If you want to be a priest, you be one," Dozier replied. "But you leave that boy alone!" By 1981, Dixon had graduated from seminary and became a candidate for priesthood. "Getting that first position, getting the church that had the confidence and courage to call a woman, was a huge obstacle in those days," she said.

As a deacon since 1982, Dixon had assisted priests until she was called to lead a parish in 1986, a year after another woman became the first female rector of a church in the diocese. "So, you see, from the time the regular ordinations began in 1977, it took until 1985 for a woman to be called as a lead pastor." After six years of parish service, and a top post in the Diocese of Washington, Dixon was elected suffragan, or assistant, bishop in 1992. She pledged to "live as a symbol of hope," presumably for other outsiders.

By 1997, only three Episcopal bishops still opposed women's ordination, and one was Iker. That year at General Convention, the church swept aside all allusions to a conscience clause and mandated in canon law that every diocese allow female priests, following up with a task force to "assist" prelates with "full compliance." Amid cries of coercion, the task force adopted a "slower and gentler process" to simply "gather information."

A small number of ordained women felt the measure—Canon III.8.I— was too harsh. "It felt like the first time we were enshrining coercion into the canon," said Alison Barfoot, a female priest at Christ Church in Overland Park, Kansas, who believed to coerce "is thoroughly un–Anglican." She circulated a petition urging the church not "to indulge in the sin of impatience toward those who clearly differ from us," and 91 of the church's 1,995 female clergy agreed—but to no avail. "Obviously we want all dioceses to ordain women," she said, but the appeal was "to let the Holy Spirit work in people's lives."[36]

Iker saw the canon as a final blow from the velvet fist of feminism. "They aim to have women priests in every diocese no matter what," he said. "I've always been open to the Holy Spirit. But you don't get someone to listen to the Holy Spirit by putting a gun to their head." In this clash over sincere beliefs, both Iker and Dixon had found ways for there to be an agreement to disagree within their church tradition.

For Iker the solution was a kind of overlapping of jurisdictions, what became known as the "flying bishop" arrangement. For example, in Iker's Fort Worth Diocese, he would not ordain or appoint female clergy. But in a friendly arrangement with the Diocese of Dallas next door, a Fort Worth woman could seek ordination under the Dallas bishop, and the Dallas bishop could provide a female priest for any Fort Worth parishes that sought one. This jurisdiction swapping began as a domestic alternative after 1976. But it became international as the Church of England ordained women, more bishops ordained homosexuals, and finally the first openly gay bishop entered the Episcopal apostolic line and was voted into office in New Hampshire in 2003. But the jurisdiction crossing of having "churches within a church" has become strained. The ultimate alternative for traditionalists is to break away under their own apostolic succession, an action they suggest regularly.

In her support of female priests, Bishop Dixon has taken a different view of how to agree to disagree. Once installed in the Washington Diocese, she made "pastoral visits" to five congregations that rejected women priests. The receptions ranged from outright protest to cool acceptance of the inevitable. "It was painful that people didn't want to be at service with me." But each church had two Eucharistic services, she said, so they still had a male-priest option that Sunday. "I would never deny them the only sacrament they could have because I was there," Dixon said. "For me, that is agreeing to disagree."

Looking back, Dixon believes that the Holy Spirit works in an Episcopal Church structure that "lets us have all those different voices" but calls for majority rule. "When final decisions have to be made we vote," she said. "Now you could say, 'That's not of God. That's not how things ought to be done.' But it's worked really well for over four centuries." Though she herself has disagreed with vestries, diocesan rulings, General Convention, and the House of Bishops, she complied: "If you can't live with that, you have to find a different way to be"—by leaving. "Jack Iker has every right to believe his theology is of God, but I expect him to accept the same for me. And then the vote settles it."

The case of the Episcopal Church points to the sacramental boundaries that have been part of the women's ordination debate, but it also illustrates how sacramental systems are closely tied to hierarchical and appointive structures for ministry. If the Anglican tradition is a bridge between Catholics and Protestants, then its child, Methodism, plays that same role between high and low Protestantism.

The end result is that Methodism, though slightly lower in its view of the sacraments, has bishops who appoint clergy. Indeed, when founder John Wesley's advice is heeded, clergy appointments last no more than a year. Of the three styles of church organization—institution-centered, congregation-centered, and spirit-centered—the United Methodist Church reflects the first, where the appointive system bodes well for female clergy being given local church leadership. The church today has nearly 8,000 "clergywomen serving in some capacity," though just 4,460 "are elders in full connection"—meaning fully ordained and appointed ministers. The appointive power of bishops has boosted this number. "The system has been a big help for women in ministry, even though there are still inequities in receiving good appointments," said Marion Jackson, a clergywoman with the Division of Ordained Ministry.[37]

Roman Catholicism, of course, has both a high sacramental idea and an appointive system, building a fairly impregnable wall against such "irregular" ordinations of women as happened in the Episcopal Church (though they have happened as well, with no real impact, in independent Catholic circles). But as even liberal Protestants have noted, women in Catholicism are nevertheless on the verge of changing the practical governance of American churches, what Catholic researchers call the "marked increase in the number of lay ministers, especially lay ministers who are women." As this happens, the number of women in religious orders is dropping faster than the number of priests. Of the thirty thousand lay ecclesial ministers, "the vast majority are women," and they constitute the majority of parish leaders at national diocesan conferences. Heralding such lay enthusiasm, John Paul II has also warned about confusing secular rights and divine design. As a "climate of dissatisfaction" arises in some church sectors, "the distinction between a person's human and civil rights and the rights, duties, ministries and functions which individuals have or enjoy within the church is not clearly understood," he said. "A faulty ecclesiology can easily lead to presenting false demands and raising false hopes."[38]

The Holy See is nevertheless "studying" what it would mean to revive the ancient office of deacon for women. While a female term such as "deaconess" is not used in the New Testament, there is little dispute that women filled such key serving roles in past church history. Scholar Phyllis Zagano said the key question is whether women had a "sacramental" appointment or an informal one. The current Vatican study document "strenuously avoids concluding that women ever received the sacrament of holy orders," she said. "The unstated fear evident in the document is the specter of women priests; if you can ordain a woman a deacon, you can ordain a woman a priest." Whatever the Vatican may finally rule on whether a woman, by nature, can be a vehicle for sacramental grace, it "is not likely to dampen growing worldwide enthusiasm for women deacons."[39]

On the opposite pole from the sacramental and hierarchical churches stand those that focus on biblical authority most of all and that typically call clergy under the "congregational" approach. The two do not always coincide, of course. The liberal United Church of Christ (UCC), while very congregational, is very liberal in approaching the teachings of the Bible. By combing congregational governance with a more liberal theology, the UCC, which is a smaller denomination, has otherwise placed a large percentage of women in its active, non-retired clergy ranks (27 percent).[40]

For discussion about the role of biblical authority in women's ordination, however, the Southern Baptist Convention has no peer in its dramas. As the nation's largest non-Catholic body, it follows a congregational polity—and declares having the Bible as its "only creed." The story of the Southern Baptists, moreover, reflects the stresses and strains in modern evangelicalism, which includes the Pentecostal churches.

"Baptists for the most part have not placed great emphasis on ordination," said Russell Dilday, former president of Southwestern Seminary in Fort Worth, Texas. "You don't find the word in the Bible or a lot about it." While ordination is not spelled out, Paul's view on women in the presence of men may surely be. Writing to the churches at Corinth, Paul said, "Women should keep silence in the churches . . . for it is shameful for a woman to speak in church." And one letter to Timothy declares, "I permit no woman to teach or to have authority over men; she is to keep silent."[41]

With no creed but the Bible, Southern Baptists have been reluctant to inscribe doctrinal statements. During the 1920s, with the rise of modernism and evolution, it was deemed necessary, producing in 1925 the Baptist Faith and Message. When ferment in Bible scholarship and race relations arose in 1963, more creedal amendments were necessary to defend biblical authority. Neither occasion, however, spoke on women.[42]

By the turn of the century, when conservatives and fundamentalist pastors amended the 2000 Baptist Faith and Message, barring women as pastors was front and center. "Southern Baptists, by practice as well as conviction, believe leadership is male," said Tennessee's Adrian Rogers, chairman of the revision committee. Alluding to St. Paul's words, the new clause said: "While both men and women are gifted for service in the church, the office of pastor is limited to men as qualified by Scripture."[43]

At the time, nearly 1,200 women were ordained in the Southern Baptist Convention. But only a few dozen were reported to be senior pastors over men. "Fewer than 1 percent of our churches have ever called a woman to preach," said seminary president and conservative R. Albert Mohler Jr. "The issues are settled by the word of God." With so few actual female pastors, critics of the ban said it was like a cannon killing a gnat—more a battle with the culture and feminism than a daily church issue. Mohler said as much, that the churches "are applying the brakes" to a cultural slouching toward abortion, homosexuality—and away from "traditional roles of women."[44]

Though at first a non-binding document, the Baptist Faith and Message soon became a doctrinal test. All seminary professors and missionaries were required to sign it, and at Southwestern Theological Seminary in Fort Worth, where 26 percent of students were women, some professors refused and left. Women at the seminary held all possible views.[45] "My preference is to teach women," said Judith Kimsey, a master's of divinity student. "Men as leaders in the church is more the biblical pattern. I did not always feel that way. I was raised to be independent, so God had to bring me to a place where I was comfortable with my role." Her fellow student, Catherine Bryan, taught the Old Testament as she earned a doctorate in the subject. And for the fourteen men who took her class on the book of Exodus, her womanhood has "not been an issue."

But for Carla Works, who was studying for a master's in theology, the new credo went too far, even though the biblical issue was really moot. "There is no such thing as a senior pastor in the Bible," she said. "That is a modern distinction we have forced into the text. I'm personally saddened that anyone would put limitations on anyone's call to the ministry."

Dilday, the longtime president ousted from Southwestern Seminary in Fort Worth by a conservative board, supports women leadership. "They say Jesus didn't have women disciples," he said. "Well, he didn't have Gentile ones either." Around the time of the new theological stance, Anne Graham Lotz, daughter of Billy Graham, was conducting evangelical crusades nationwide and "preaching in places around the convention," Dilday noted. "She's a symbol of the future that women are gifted and will be moving into places of responsibility. She had an evangelistic rally here in Fort Worth, and that was downright preaching."

In the recent past, Southern Baptist discipline regarding women was amply demonstrated by one Tennessee church association. These local groups are the only real Southern Baptist authority besides the congregation itself. So this collective body "disfellowshiped" Prescott Memorial Baptist Church when it called Nancy Hastings Sehested as pastor. Lotz preaching to men is hardly the same. But it shows the ambiguous wiggle room between preacher and pastor. To preach to men—in what Lotz calls a "Bible teacher" role—is not to be "over" them. Traveling to Amsterdam to teach world evangelists, Lotz said she had her father's "blessing"—he called her "the best preacher in the family." But she had no ambition to lead. "For myself," she said, "I feel God has forbidden me to be ordained or be a senior pastor."[46]

This is the kind of assessment also taking place in the conservative holiness, Pentecostal, and charismatic churches, which otherwise differ on many points with their strict Calvinist and Baptist brethren (who don't recognize modern "gifts" of the Holy Spirit). The holiness and Pentecostal churches have a rich history of female pioneers and expanders, from the co-founder and leader of the Salvation Army, Catherine Booth, to Aimee Semple McPherson, who started the International Church of the Foursquare Gospel. In Kansas, the Bible student who ignited Pentecostalism itself was Agnes Ozman. "She was not trying to make a point about women's ministry," said historian Grant Wacker. "The sole issue was that she, no less than the men who experienced the Holy Spirit's touch, felt called to proclaim what she knew."[47]

The record on women in these traditions today is mixed. With its sheer size, the predominantly white Assemblies of God in 1999 could boast 5,225 women in ministry (16.2 percent of the total), though just a third of these women are fully ordained. Women make up 8.5 percent of all ordained Assemblies clergy, but as senior pastors they are fewer still: just 3.5 percent. Most women in Assemblies ministry are "certified" or "licensed" as preachers. Yet this is quite progressive compared to another large Pentecostal denomination, the predominantly black Church of God in Christ—which does not ordain women at all.[48]

Over the past century, as the spirit-filled churches became more bureaucratic and reflected more cultural conservatism, their structures became the least likely of all to put women into ministry. Still, much of charismatic Protestantism works outside denominational controls. That is what happened among the black churches, said historian C. Eric Lincoln. Beginning with the migrations of blacks to northern cities during World War I, Lincoln said, "women preachers avoided the structures of the traditional black denominations by founding independent storefront churches." Today, the Congregations Survey has found that "female organizational leadership is more common on the entrepreneurial margins than at the bureaucratic center of the religious world." Nearly a fifth of all black congregations are female-led.[49]

While the concern of conservative churches over secular feminism and the breakdown of the family is always in the background, arguments for exclusive male leadership typically turn to St. Paul in the New Testament. What Paul had forbidden, however, other texts in the Bible allowed. Even Paul's letter to the Corinthians has the "apparent discrepancy" of demanding female silence here but asking a woman to be veiled when she "prays or prophesies" there. In his letter to the Romans, Paul speaks of Phoebe as a deacon. He acknowledged how Mary "worked hard among you" and called Tryphanaena and Tryphosa "workers in the Lord." By Paul's definition of an apostle—one who saw the risen Christ—women were included. Since Jesus once appeared to five hundred people, "it would be rather surprising if there were not women apostles in this sense," said biblical scholar Raymond Brown. Indeed, Paul speaks of Junia, probably a woman, as "outstanding among the apostles."[50]

This search for texts for or against women is well known. New Testament scholar Benjamin Witherington, a Wesleyan, said any agenda can simply "choose between Paul as a chauvinist or feminist." The broader context, he believes, was the tension between the role of women in the new Christian family, their physical families, the society, and anticipation of Christ's return. Hence, Paul probably wanted to avoid conflict with the society—supporting government, subordination of women, and even slavery—while trying to transform women's place in the church and their physical families. "Women's ordination is not discussed or dismissed in the New Testament, but there is nothing in the material that rules out such a possibility," Witherington said. "Women in the [New Testament] era already performed the tasks normally associated with ordained clergy in later eras."[51]

During the development of the early church, moreover, women were attracted by the Gnostic and Montanist heresies, the latter being a Holy Spirit, apocalyptic sect founded by Montanus (A.D. 155), expanded by two prophetesses, and famed for its conversion of Tertullian, the church theologian. To combat the trend, the church turned to traditional patriarchy to bring order: "The Church gradually allowed the dominant culture to set the agenda." Enthusiasm about Christ's return gave way to an earthly eschatology, bureaucratic for men but ascetic for women. "This led women either to withdraw into the desert or convent and devote themselves to prayer and being examples of chastity, or to restrict themselves, in the case of deaconesses, to work with women or children."[52]

At Fuller Seminary, where Baptist pastor and scholar David Scholer teaches the New Testament, women are encouraged to see the cultural context of early church teachings. Women were illiterate, married, and in the home, while today female college graduates outnumber men and 45 percent of American women are not married. Whatever the milieu, the Scripture should liberate women's call, Scholer said. "Women pick up the attitude of the culture," he said. "They probably think, 'Well, I can do better in other forms of ministry. It's better to be chaplain.' "[53]

The debate over the role of women in evangelical churches continues to hinge on interpretations of the Bible and to a large extent on beliefs about female responsibility for the family. The division of views may be seen in evangelical magazines such as *Christianity Today* and *World*, where some seminary advertisements lack female faces and others include them. While women are not encouraged to ministry at Knox Theological Seminary in Fort Lauderdale, Florida, or Alliance Theological Seminary in Nyack, New York, for example, Fuller and Asbury Theological Seminary send a different message. And of course, evangelicals will always have to offer interpretations of their past history, when women often founded or led significant Christian enterprises. For example, the Moody Bible Institute, now a center of teaching men's sole leadership, was founded in 1873 as a school of "Bible work" by Emma Dryer and enrolled women until the 1940s.[54]

While Anglicans, Catholics, and Southern Baptists bring their disagreements over the role of women in ministry to large public forums for rule making or official decrees, evangelicals tend to localize their discussions. Their disagreements play out in local churches, theology schools, or small denominations. As a result, "special purpose" groups have sprung up across the evangelical landscape to rally the cause of either women's ministerial equality or keeping male and female distinct in their church roles.

After the *King James Version* of the Bible, the *New International Version* has pulled rank as the evangelical favorite. In 2001 when a "gender-neutral" *NIV-Inclusive Language Edition,* with text changes such as "God created *human beings* in his image" and "if any brother *or sister* sins against you" was published, orthodox and progressive advocacy groups, each with a cadre of noted theologians on its side, sprang to action. The chief opponents of the revision were the orthodox magazine *World* and the Council on Biblical Manhood and Womanhood, formed in 1987, while Christians for Biblical Equality, also founded in the late 1980s, endorsed updating Scriptural texts.[55]

Evangelicals agree to disagree by buying the Bible they like or joining the church that speaks to them. Willow Creek Community Church, nearly the largest in the nation, accepts women's ordination as a matter of biblical community. "Authentic community implies full participation of women and men on the basis of spiritual gifts, not on the basis of sex," said Gilbert Bilezikian, the seminary professor who helped Bill Hybels found the church. Laurie Pederson, a Willow Creek elder, said Christians don't have to agree with their stance: "If you can't embrace this teaching, practically speaking, you'd probably be happier at some other church." A church that allows only male leadership is the charismatic-rooted Calvary Chapel, a Southern California megachurch that, like Willow Creek, formed its own association of churches. There, if women question St. Paul's ban in the Bible, "they have to talk with God about that," a Calvary minister said. "He wrote it."[56]

Evangelical believers like Lisa Huber, an American Baptist from Michigan, get caught in these choices. An associate pastor at a Los Angeles church, she finished her master's of divinity at Fuller. "One of my primary gifts is preaching and speaking," said Huber, who lost a boyfriend over that call. "He just did not think women should be in a place of teaching authority over men. He was a very conservative Christian. So we ended our relationship."[57]

All of Christian ministry is affected by the larger context of American society, as the span of the twentieth century illustrates. While women finally gained the right to vote in 1920 under the Nineteenth Amendment, for a whole range of reasons the total equality of the sexes still is resisted today, even by many women. When the theological dimension is added, reasons to object apparently are intensified. Though women have entered nearly all other occupations, said Charlton, "Only ordained ministry [is still] understood to be declared by God to be off-limits to women."[58]

A kind of belligerence has also attended the cause of women's ordination. Recall again Anne Hutchinson, who in Puritan Boston declared that the male clergy "possessed no gifts of graces," which led to her expulsion in 1637. Women's ordination was apiece with the anti-slavery movement. A "revelation from God" compelled Joanne Lee and Harriet Tubman to free slaves, said black lay minister Marcia Louise Dyson today. "We want black men to be empowered. Then why can't women be empowered?" she said[59]

In antebellum America, Elizabeth Cady Stanton, who was reared a Presbyterian, advocated for women's rights. After her Seneca Falls women's conference of 1848 achieved only a symbolic victory, she openly criticized Christianity by publishing *The Woman's Bible*. Instead of being a minister, Francis Willard, a child of Chicago Methodists, led the Women's Christian Temperance Union and as a byproduct helped win the women's vote. Yet she also handed on her "radical" cause by urging all "younger women who feel a call, as I once did, to preach."[60]

Today also, women's ordination is taken by many as a harbinger of other social changes. When academics predicted a "culture war" on the horizon in the 1980s, a central indicator was the liberalism of female clergy compared to women in the pews. As Episcopal Bishop Iker puts the case, "Name me one woman bishop who is opposed to the gay agenda." One survey of clergywomen confirmed this apparent willingness to jettison the status quo. "I just assume that if you're a woman, you have to always be on the side of the oppressed," a responding female minister said. Those conducting the survey concluded that women who seek the pulpit will invariably, and quite consciously, carry the baggage of history: "Ordained women are naturally controversial and symbolic, and they are aware of it."[61]

4

The Catholic Priesthood

THE LONGEST PAPAL DOCUMENT ever written is on the priesthood. Issued by the prolific hand of John Paul II in 1992, *Pastores Dabo Vobis* (I Will Give You Shepherds) runs more than two hundred pages. At one point it says that becoming a priest is beyond words—"an *inexpressible dialogue*" between a man and God.[1]

At the U.S. Conference of Catholic Bishops in Washington, D.C., Father Edward J. Burns assists dioceses in their priest recruitment and thinks about who is having that discussion. Despite a priest shortage, with just 60 percent of the nation's forty-six thousand priests "active" in parishes, "You don't become a priest by default," Burns said. The Second Vatican Council (1962–65) also counseled "due strictness" so that men are not entering merely after losing a girlfriend or a job: "God will not allow his Church to lack ministers if the worthy are promoted and those who are not suited to ministry are guided with fatherly kindness and in due time to adopt another calling."[2]

The priesthood offers a list of daunting obligations: to be celibate, to obey a bishop, to make a lifetime commitment. Even with God in the conversation, these are demands that must bring "peace" in man's soul, said Burns, from Pittsburgh. "Peace is a fruit, a by-product of knowing God's will. You listen to that."

In Chicago, the University of St. Mary of the Lake, Mundelein Seminary, distributes a flyer on hearing that call to the priesthood. "When discerning your vocation the road ahead will always remain a bit foggy," it says. "Mystery and the unknown are part of everyone's future." At Mundelein, the nation's largest Catholic seminary, photographs of generations of priest-graduates tell the outward story of the God conversation. A decade after its founding, the seminary began hanging the class

61

portraits on hallways of the faculty building. The first, for 1931, shows fifty-six smiling young men. By around 1982 the faces are older and far fewer in number. "You see the drama," said Father Thomas Baima, the provost. "Right in the 1980s we make a shift."[3]

The historic seminary—set by a 150-acre lake and on a wooded campus of red stone buildings around a domed church—decided to open itself to dioceses around the country. From that point in the 1980s the class portraits grew in size. The "shift" also included the training of laity and deacons. Vatican II exalted the priest as "configured to Christ" and different "in essence" from others. But it also established ordained married deacons and lay ecclesial ministers.[4] Mundelein opened institutes to train both, spurring a "friendly rivalry" and enrollment contest between seminary and institutes. In 2001 the seminary seemed ahead, renovating space for 218 seminarians—the largest class in years. "We're having to expand," Baima said. "It's one of those happy problems."

Less than a year later, the American priesthood had little to be happy about. Beginning in January 2002, the sexual abuse scandal that rocked the Archdiocese of Boston spread across the Catholic Church in America. More than two years later, 700 priests and deacons accused of abuse had been removed from ministry. Moreover, a study conducted for the American bishops by the John Jay College of Criminal Justice concluded that 4,392 of the 109,694 priests serving in the United States from 1950 to 2002 had faced "allegations of abuse," totaling 4 percent of all priests in that half century. The allegations were made by 10,667 individuals, a far higher number than the estimates made by aggressive news reporting in the wake of the Boston scandal.[5]

Even before the John Jay College report came out, a rogue gallery of serial abusers was seared into the public's mind—James Porter, John Geoghan, and Paul R. Shanley of Massachusetts; Rudoph Kos of Texas; and Gilbert Gauthe of Louisiana, whose high-profile conviction in 1985 was the first public hint of the problem. The problem reached as high as some of the bishops. Before 2002 was over, Bishop Anthony O'Connell of Palm Beach had resigned for abusing a seminary student, and Archbishop Rembert Weakland of Milwaukee had disclosed his $450,000 payment to a man over an affair—both incidents of the past.

But it was the case of Geoghan, a Boston prelate and predatory homosexual with a wide grin, that tore open Pandora's box. When Geoghan went to trial in January 2002 for fondling a ten-year-old, a federal judge ordered the Boston Archdiocese to hand over personnel records to the *Boston Globe*. The Shanley case in December opened 2,200 more pages of files, and Boston's Cardinal Bernard Law, during his third emergency visit to Rome, resigned. From those documents, the photo of a young, smiling Father Robert V. Meffan made the *Globe*'s front page. Meffan was seventy-three now but made no apologies for his sex with teenage girls. "What I was trying to show them is that Christ is human and you should love him as a human being," he told the *Globe*.[6]

The John Jay College report painted a sad picture across the Catholic Church in America, but the Archdiocese of Boston received the overwhelming brunt of the controversy. There, a sixteen-month grand-jury investigation lasted until July 2003. The Massachusetts Attorney General Thomas F. Reilly issued no indictments. But he soundly blamed church leaders of a clerical and "institutional culture" that had ignored victims who alleged abuse since the 1940s. "When they had a choice between protecting children and protecting the church, they chose secrecy to protect the church," he said. A few months later Geoghan was strangled to death by inmates in the prison and the archdiocese reached an $85 million settlement with victims.[7]

Boston was also a landmark of the financial problems the scandal had only begun to cause in American dioceses. Under new leadership in 2004, the Boston Archdiocese began closing 65 of its 357 parishes (18.2 percent) due to low attendance, a shortage of clergy, and financial strain. In July of that year, the Archdiocese of Portland became the first to declare bankruptcy. The archdiocese faced 130 claims that sought more than $160 million, and as elsewhere in the country lawyers flocked to file victim lawsuits. "The pot of gold is pretty much empty right now," Archbishop John Vlazny said of his Portland Archdiocese.[8]

Despite such dark days for the priesthood, especially for a hierarchy that apparently had turned a blind eye, most Catholics doubtless presume that the "inexpressible dialogue" with God is continuing among men called to be priests. For the foreseeable future, the concern about ministry and the shortage of priests will seemingly be bound up in three topics: priestly identity, human sexuality in a clerical culture, and the role of an expanding lay ministry.

Also for the foreseeable future, the impact of the Second Vatican Council, and its milestone status for three generations of American Catholics and their priests, will be the broader context for discussion of ministry. "After the council, there was a period of great upheaval," said Monsignor Paul J. Langsfield, ordained in Washington, D.C., in 1977.[9] From the council forward, many liberals wanted more change and a small but vociferous group of church reactionaries rejected the whole idea of reform.

Yet even the most orthodox assertions about the priesthood, whether made by Pope John Paul II or the 1993 *Program of Priestly Formation* for American seminaries, draw on Second Vatican Council statements. A battle for the priesthood was indeed waged at the council, led by the liberal Dutch journal *Concilium* and expressed by Father Hans Küng of Switzerland. "In a pluralistic and democratic society, what sense is there in the polarity between office and people, 'above' and 'below?' " he said in his book *Why Priests?* He argued that a "universal priesthood is strongly emphasized" in the council documents, a break from the Council of Trent, which declared "anathema" anyone who questioned a priestly hierarchy "established by divine ordinance."[10]

Many Catholics would view Küng as over-polarizing, even "Protestantizing," the council's direction. American theologian and Cardinal Avery Dulles argues that the liberals deliberately "organized a movement to put a progressive spin" on the council, which was not too hard to do. John XXIII wanted the council to deliver "medicine of mercy rather than of severity." As a result, Dulles said, "One looks in vain in its documents for clear statements of what it rejected. It is easy to get the impression that it tolerated almost everything." But priestly powers were never handed over to the laity. And "the primacy of the Pope, as it had been defined in Vatican I, remains intact."[11]

Yet with allowances for more lay governance, the image of the priest in the United States definitely changed. After the Second Vatican Council "the picture of the priest is him surrounded by laity at a committee meeting," said Sister Katarina Schuth of St. Paul Seminary School of Divinity in Minneapolis. "It used to be a priest sitting at his desk or talking with other priests." Canon law still holds priests responsible for their parishes. "There are things only a priest can do," Schuth said. Even with lay collaboration, "the old role of the priest doing everything is still there, but the number of priests is not there."[12]

Both priests and parishioners have lived through the eras before, during, and after the Second Vatican Council (1962–65). For many, those changing eras best explain the complexity of Catholic ministry today.

Before the council, Catholics knew a traditional church in America. As this generation of Catholics left ethnic enclaves and stepped up from the working class, they still worshiped under the aura of the First Vatican Council (1870) and the Baltimore Catechism (1885). Mass attendance was 75 percent (with half taking Communion), and the Church had one priest for every six or seven hundred members. These Catholics—who still make up a fifth of today's U.S. Catholic Church membership—extolled their clergy and often designated a son for such service. While every priest was fairly versatile to fulfill all his duties, his theological standing in the church was chiefly in a sacramental role (what researchers, to the chagrin of many Catholics, call "the cultic model"). As seen by his flock the priest "was highly educated and wise, and had unquestioned authority," said Archbishop Daniel Pilarczyk, who entered seminary in 1948. "The specifics of his personal life were shrouded in mystery. He seemed happy, and he seemed to live better than most of the parishioners."[13]

A greater number of Catholics today (about a third), however, know an

American church from 1960 onwards. It was a time of mainstreaming and liberalizing, with the "medicine of mercy" being applied in experiments and innovations. For Philip Murnion, ordained in 1963 and once the leader of the National Pastoral Life Center in New York City, liturgy and social justice became one fabric: the council, civil rights and anti-poverty movements "inspired us to believe we could reshape both church and world," he said. They were the "conciliar cadre," or what researchers now call the "servant-leadership" priests, more activist and less sacramental. Back then they "wed personal conversion with social transformation," Murnion said. "Things have changed."[14]

That change has been attributed to the 1978 arrival of the doctrinally conservative John Paul II. The first global and media-age pontiff, he cast his message on the latest of three U.S. Catholic generations still alive today. Now in their twenties and thirties, this group was reared in well-educated and affluent homes and makes up fully half of today's church population. They relish mysteries and sacraments and side with social justice. Yet they have imbibed the ethic of choice, not authority—a generation with individualistic views on "truth and the role of conscience" and that favors "more lay participation." They back the idea of allowing priests to marry (by 71 percent) and the ordination of women (by 60–70 percent).[15]

They have heeded the Second Vatican Council's ecumenism, but as a result see less contrast between Catholics and other Christians. They also value personal experience over tradition. Combined, more lenient attitudes have led to "lower levels of commitment that are likely to persist throughout the lives of today's young Catholics," said one study. The two older generations of Catholics alive today, this study said, are honestly bewildered and challenged "to understand the post-Vatican II" generation; how "to make room in the church for them" is their sincere question. Sociologist James D. Davidson, a middle generation Catholic, said: "My kids think that guitar and vernacular have always been the way the church has conducted Mass. They assume that the priest has always faced the people." Since his own childhood, when Mass attendance was at 75 percent of all Catholics, Davidson has seen participation drop to 54 percent in the years when he reared a family; and it has moved down further to 37 percent today.[16]

The council also stands out as a milestone in the changing fortunes of the number of priests in the United States. From 1930 to 1980, for example, the priestly ranks doubled to nearly 60,000. After that, however, the decline was steady, settling at 46,000 priests today. Between 1970 and 1990, the losses might be considered staggering—but with a caveat. The United States still has the best ratio of priests-to-parishioners in the world, and as

Mass attendance declines, the ratio may even improve. Still, after the Second Vatican Council "something was happening that produced fewer seminarians and more resignations at the same point in time," said Davidson. Of Catholic clergy active in 1970, around 13 percent of priests ordained in dioceses ("diocesan priests") and 16 percent of priests ordained in religious orders ("religious priests") had left their posts by decade's end—a total of nearly 8,400 ministers, most of whom were younger men. Others estimate that 20,000 priests have packed up and left since the 1970s.[17]

In some ways, the church has never had enough priests. The high birthrates and expanded parish programs to serve more people have made the Catholic growth story a "success." But that has made the clerical pool seem smaller than ever (unless priests are compared only to "active" Catholics, a decreasing number as well). "Relative to the number of lay people, there are fewer priests today than in 1900," said one study. Sociologist Dean Hoge, who surveys priests, said there are not enough clerics "to keep the Catholic Church going as we know it." The priests themselves have naturally expressed "a desire for a national-level conversation among bishops [about] creative long-term solutions," said the hierarchy's 2000 report, *The Impact of Fewer Priests on the Pastoral Ministry.*[18]

According to *Fewer Priests*, "In the next ten years, 87 percent of the dioceses anticipate assigning more deacons and lay ministers to assist in parish management." Twelve percent of the nation's 19,179 Catholic parishes did not have a resident priest. The busiest priest worked somewhere in the thirteen states of the West (23 percent Catholic), with its booming Latino population and Sunbelt migration. He served an average of 1,752 Catholics, compared to a priest in the twelve-state Midwest (24 percent Catholic) who shepherded 1,016 parishioners. The ratios in the sparsely Catholic South (with sixteen states that are 19 percent Catholic) and densely Catholic Northeast (with nine states that are 34 percent Catholic) were about the same—just below the national average of one priest for every 1,257 Catholics.[19]

Under new church canons, meanwhile, priests were finding ways to fill gaps on their rural and urban beats, where the term "minimum priestly presence" was coined. Bishops worried that a single death or retirement could "mean ending priestly presence in an entire county." As a result, said *Fewer Priests*, 2,386 priests had become modern-day circuit riders by serving more than one parish. Some 271 priests had formed teams to jointly oversee several parishes, and in 437 parishes in the United States someone besides a priest is in charge.[20]

At the turn of the new century, all of this might have been manageable if not for the relentless issue of aging; mass retirements loom on the horizon. As described by *Fewer Priests* in 2000, diocesan priests were fifty-seven years old on average. Priests in religious orders averaged sixty-three. Retirements had already sidelined 20 percent of the priesthood into the "inactive" category. Of the active clergy (22,394 diocesan priests and 14,336 religious priests), two-thirds were fifty or older. Just 298 of them were younger than thirty—roughly the average age for new ordinations.[21]

The number of priests available for the future will hinge not only on the number of ordinations but also the rate of resignations, retirements, and deaths. By some estimates, since the 1960s the number of active clergy has been declining about 9 percent each decade for diocesan priests and 20 percent for religious priests—a 12 to 14 percent total drop each decade. While four in five dioceses have vocational recruitment programs, and indeed new priests are always being called, the overall number of ordinations is dropping by 4 to 6 percent each decade. In perspective, *Fewer Priests* noted, more than one thousand men were ordained in 1960, while just half that number took holy orders in 2000.[22]

The replacement level produced by seminaries meanwhile has been at only 30 to 40 percent. "That is, for every 100 older priests who retire, die or resign, you get 30 to 40 new ones," said sociologist Hoge. The resignations of young priests are of particular concern. The exact numbers are unknown, though one high estimate puts resignations at 15 percent. "Projecting current trends would predict a resignation rate of about 10 percent or 12 percent," said Hoge, using a lower figure. "So we did a study on this group."[23]

Among young newer priests, that study found four reasons for resignations. Most common (30 to 40 percent) was that a priest became "disillusioned," usually by "rocky relations with other priests, discovery of irregularities in the church, or discouragement with the hierarchy." The next most common reason was for a priest to fall in love and seek marriage (20 to 30 percent) or give up on celibacy (20 to 30 percent) even though "a woman isn't pulling him out." Finally, a smaller number (5 to 15 percent) were homosexuals and "wanted an open and long-term relationship with a man. . . . [and] rejected the option of living the double life as a priest."[24]

Despite this focus on the struggle of new priests, studies of priest morale have shown it to be remarkably high, especially as their years in service go by. Even after the sexual abuse scandals broke, the *Los Angeles Times* found exceptionally high morale among priests in 2002. Yet when asked about the "most important problems facing" the church, their top picks orbited around the modern priesthood: the shortage of priests (25 percent), problems with the hierarchy (20 percent), child abuse by priests (18 percent), and restoring the credibility of priests (13 percent).[25]

Priests' morale has been fleshed out in other studies, including a comprehensive one conducted by Bryan Froehle, head of the Center for Applied Research in the Apostolate (CARA), a research group at Georgetown University. He found that the vast majority of priests had never "seriously thought about leaving the priesthood" in the past five years. Almost no older priests entertained such thoughts, though the idea of an exodus did become more common as the survey moved toward the youngest priests. Over forty years of surveys, nearness to retirement signaled higher satisfaction, said Froehle, "again and again and again." And overwork correlated with complaints. Nearly all parish priests (91 percent) say, "I am on call 24 hours a day." While Protestant ministers "trade off" between competing pastoral and administrative duties, priests "trade up," he said. "Catholic priests simply do more."[26]

Nevertheless, a lot of very happy Catholic clergy populate the American landscape. The resignation study, in fact, found ample cases of enthusiasm and staying power. "I love what I do, and I love presiding at Eucharist," said one priest, ordained at age forty, a parish associate priest and parochial high school teacher. "I love the sacramental life that's present to people in those moments of union. Being with couples preparing for marriage, celebrating their love. Even being with people to share their pain and sorrow." Another priest, ordained at age twenty-seven, said: "People are so supportive. I mean, you get your occasional anonymous critical letter that you should probably just throw away. But people are so supportive." For all the foreboding about the priesthood, in fact, a literature that profiles the interesting lives of clerics may be making a comeback, ranging from the 1998 title *Enormous Prayers: a Journey into the Priesthood* to a more recent book that praises the humanity of clerical life: *Priests: Portraits of Ten Good Men Serving the Church Today.*[27]

On the eve of the Second Vatican Council, Protestant clergy in America were struggling with the new ambiguity of their role in society, and some looked on the priestly profile with envy. "In contrast to many ministers and rabbis, the Roman Catholic priest knows what he is doing and why he is doing it," said one Protestant assessment. Despite that encouraging evaluation, a few decades later the identity crisis was having an impact on Catholic parishes as well. In the Archdiocese of Baltimore, the number of priestless parishes has grown and churchgoers are feeling the loss. "They say to me, 'When are we going to get our own priest?' " said one nun who was in charge of a parish. "I tell them, 'You have to get used to it. You can't have your own priest.' "[28]

To bolster priestly ranks, the Vatican gave the topic a special emphasis, calling a world synod of bishops at which John Paul II's *Pastores Dabo Vobis* echoed the Second Vatican Council's likening of a priest to *alter Christus*, "another Christ." At the time the American bishops were already updating the *Program of Priestly Formation*, and they said it was further "enriched" by the papal words. In all, they wanted to emphasize a "clear doctrinal understanding of the priesthood [to] foster a secure priestly identity," an understanding that continued "Christ's mission as prophet, priest, and king." After the synod other efforts were made to strengthen the priestly identity in America, especially as the increase in lay ministry raised the specter of more confusion. To address that problem, eight Vatican offices with "specific" papal approval issued a fairly blunt *Instruction* in 1997 on "non-ordained faithful" collaborating "in the sacred ministry" of priests: "The blurring of roles and identities," it warned, "is a factor in the drastic decline of priests and seminarians."[29]

In the fall of 2002, when the "Priestly Identity in a Time of Crisis" conference convened at Catholic University in Washington, D.C., the generational differences among American prelates were on the front burner. Two concepts of priesthood—one as sacramental (a.k.a. "cultic") and the other a communal-oriented "servant" model—have been used in surveys since 1970. When a fourth survey was conducted around 2000, it appeared that priests had come full circle. American priests had moved from a cultic role in the 1950s to a servant-like role after the council. But now they had been moving back to a cultic role as a new corps of young conservative priests revived an allegiance to the sacramental approach to ministry.

The sacramental model, dominant in the 1940s and 1950s, stressed "that the priest is a man set apart," Hoge explained. Servant leadership came into favor after the council; it underscored "a greater collaboration with the laity," reducing the distinction between them "so the priest was a leader of the community." At the new century, "the cultic model is becoming more dominant among priests." When council-era priests die, "a total transition will have taken place." The key survey question offered the statement: "Ordination confers on a priest a new status or a permanent character which makes him essentially different from the laity in the church." While 52 percent of the young priests in 1970 had agreed, it was 95 percent for new priests today. Younger priests in 2000 felt as strongly about that as did older priests in 1970. While a third of today's older priests felt being "set apart" was "a barrier" to full Christian community, just 15 percent of young priests felt so in this new era.[30]

Working as a priest in New York, Philip Murnion had advocated the servant model. He tied it to the progressive impulses of the Second Vatican Council, which produced clergy who feel at odds with taking on too much self-regard and status as an *alter Christus*, a concept still at the heart of the council's theology of the priesthood. "Priests recoil from such talk when I raise it in priest sessions," Murnion said of an overly sacramental *alter Christus* status. "They fear reverting to special claims of privilege. . . . They desperately want to avoid the situation in which the grace of charism devolves into the entitlement of clericalism."[31]

At Mundelein Seminary, provost Baima said older priests around the country puzzle over the new generation. "The question comes, 'Why are the seminarians so conservative? We used to be so liberal.' My answer to them is, 'The seminarian today is no different than at any other time. We bring to the seminary the issues that the culture, in our age, struggles with.'" The age is marked by moral breakdown and the leveling of religious authority, he said, not the older Catholic concern about work and justice in ethnic ghettos. As the seminary's Patrick O'Malley, an older prelate, said in a morning homily on St. Joseph, "All our parents were from the working class." In the past St. Joseph was a workingman who prayed for laborers. But in this new era, when priestly identity is so important, Joseph as the father of Jesus is an exemplar for ministry: "We could ask for no better model for priesthood."[32]

Heightening the image of the priest is helping younger recruits, by some reports. With an unclouded priestly image, "Young priests have a sense of who they are in the midst of all these [lay] ministries that are arising," said one prelate who worked with priests in the Minneapolis-St. Paul region. "The clearer their understanding, the less likely they are to be in conflict in their collaboration." Older priests in Minnesota would ask him, "How do I get along with these young guys?" He told them, "Please talk to each other." Still, he said, "There are subjects of disagreement and even dislike. . . . It's a big problem and getting worse." Indeed the tension is sometimes palpable, according to other clergy. Some older priests call their callow successors "the young and the righteous." Some newer clergy, such as Opus Dei priest C. John McCloskey, said of the older conciliar crowd: "Their time is over."[33]

Every diocesan priest, regardless of generation, is beholden to a bishop, and in Catholic theology that priest-to-bishop commitment not only involves a vow of obedience but a relationship with a father figure and friend. "Support of the bishop is key to the sense of satisfaction, and support of the bishop is key to whether or not a priest is considering leaving the priesthood," Froehle said. Indeed, another survey asked priests if they would like to elect their bishop—who is in fact appointed by the pope; 62 percent of the older generation approved, while 22 percent of the younger priests did also. This relationship between the priest and bishop works itself out case by case in every diocese. And at times it has surfaced as a national issue, first in the 1960s over birth control—and today over the bishops' handling of the sex abuse crisis.[34]

In 1968, a large number of American priests had dissented over *Humanae Vitae*, the papal decree against artificial birth control, and some of their bishops had to dismiss them or curtail their protests. Soon after the 2002 abuse scandal in Boston, a similar protest was seen: Fifty Boston priests, and more elsewhere tacitly, called for Cardinal Law to resign. During the *Humanae Vitae* conflict, in fact, the most prominent association of national clergy in America, the National Federation of Priests' Councils (NFPC), was formed to defend the rights of priests. Today, twenty-five thousand priests—roughly half the U.S. clergy corps—are affiliated with it by local councils. As the headlines about sexual abuse crashed down on all priests, the organization acquired a new life as the defender and advocate of its clergy constituents. "What I hear from priests is, 'Help,'" said NFPC President Robert J. Silva.[35]

Inescapably, the scandal at its worst called into question the lives of all priests. "I told my parish that I would no longer wear a collar in public," said one Midwest priest, a minister for thirty-two years. The John Jay College report showed that 4 percent of priests had been accused over the past fifty years, and the allegations were "consistent" (averaging 3 to 6 percent) in all fourteen regions of the Catholic Church in the United States. As to generations of priests involved, the majority of the accused clergy (68 percent) were ordained between 1950 and 1979. One more question remained, but it was hard to answer or use as an excuse: Since all "caring professions"—counselors, teachers, youth club leaders, babysitters, and social workers—have abusers, was the 4 percent in the priesthood "normal" or exceptionally high?[36]

Whatever the margin, the U.S. bishops declared they would not compromise on the safety of children. They needed to assure the public of a draconian crackdown, so at their Dallas assembly in June 2002 they adopted what the media called a "zero tolerance" and "one strike and you're out" policy toward accused priests. At the time, Cardinal Avery Dulles warned the bishops of alienating their rank and file brothers. Yet the bishops were in an impossible situation, said one Catholic writer, for they were now "criticized for not cracking down on priests, then criticized when they did crack down." Despite the hierarchy's dilemma, the crisis tended to put canon lawyers on the side of priests. Priests had to become "aware of the importance, perhaps even the necessity" of claiming their rights, said Sister Sharon Euart, a canon lawyer for the Baltimore Archdiocese. "Many priests, we have discovered, simply do not know what rights they have by virtue of their ordination."[37]

The bishop-priest relationship in ways had complicated any strict ecclesiastical remedy to the decades-long sexual abuse problem. If a man is "once a priest always a priest," how can the bishop send him away or turn him in to the police? Indeed, Italian church law counseled against tarnishing a priest's reputation no matter what. Yet after the Boston scandal, this topic was forced into an open debate. On the one hand, theologians came out acknowledging a permanent priesthood. Or as Silva said, "We believe that ordination makes a man a priest and that that's something he is forever." Even when he does something "very, very wrong, . . . he is still one of us," Silva said. "We can't just cut him off."[38]

At the same time, and in apparent contradiction, some bishops assured the public that "certain actions can be so contrary to remaining in service as a priest that the basic relationship between a priest and bishop can be severed forever." The severance from priestly ministry, called laization, has traditionally been by the free choice of the priest or solely by decree of the pope. A new situation had arisen, however. So after some resistance, the Vatican approved measures for bishops to apply the severance without a Vatican inquiry or papal decision (though a priest still has the right to appeal an outcome to Rome). For better or worse, the process is very slow. One of the most notorious abuser priests, Paul Shanley, was not defrocked by the Vatican until May 2004, two years after the Boston scandal broke. Victims groups, of course, decry such foot-dragging and argue that priestly rights had been the obstacle for too long. "A priest's reputation, while important, absolutely pales in comparison with a child's safety," said abuse survivor leader David Clohessy.[39]

Many priests were happy to see their corrupt brethren purged from the ranks. But all in all, the onus was falling on priests in general. When the NFPC held its 2003 national meeting in Kansas City, Missouri, its agenda was to protect the priesthood as a lifetime calling. Accusations had blurred the distinction between hard-core abusers and priests with a deeply regretted foible. Silva, a priest from Stockton, California, agreed that guilty priests should not go back into ministry. Yet the church should "find someplace within its community where these priests can live, do something productive and be held accountable." Priests and bishops "are not adversaries," he said. And yet bishops were releasing names of priests "all over the place." For one reason or another, two-thirds of U.S. priests felt the bishops mishandled the crisis, according to a national poll.[40]

As with John Paul's long letter on the virtues of the priestly calling, the American media would also spill record amounts of ink on the priesthood, but as a scandal story. A year before the Boston calamity, Father Donald B. Cozzens, a former vicar of priests in Cleveland, noted the gravity of the exposé: "Some argue that there is nothing comparable in modern times." After the Boston case, Thomas Doyle, the U.S. Vatican Embassy priest who in 1985 produced an alarming internal report on the abuse problem—which he said the bishops ignored—told outdoor protest rallies that the crisis sprang from the hierarchy's autocracy. Concealing the abuse problem, he said, was akin to some of the worst deeds in church history, equal to the "horror" of the Inquisition and far worse than the "indulgence scam" that sparked the Reformation.[41]

Cozzens worried that the top bishops would learn the wrong lesson. For them "the scandal was simply another example of human frailty, the old 'the flesh is weak' wisdom." Cozzens believed that this view overlooked the possible guilt of the church structure, or clerical culture. By emphasizing human frailty alone, it detracted attention from "an all-out effort at understanding the larger network of forces that were supporting and contributing to the crisis." More starkly, former priest and psychiatrist A. W. Richard Sipe said, "[The scandal] is primarily a symptom of an essentially flawed celibate/sexual system of ecclesiastical power."[42]

The John Jay College report and the National Review Board set up by the bishops offered their insights into the causes as well. "Dioceses and orders simply did not screen candidates for the priesthood properly," said Robert Bennett, chairman of the twelve-member board. The entry of "dysfunctional" men into the priesthood, not celibacy or homosexuality, was primarily to blame. The bishops, meanwhile, said they had wrongly followed medical and psychiatric advice that sexual abusers were reformable. The report contradicted that belief by showing the large number of repeat offenders. While a majority of the accused priests (56 percent) faced allegations from just one victim, a group of just 149 priests accounted for 26 percent of all the known allegations.[43]

For all the negligence, the hierarchy had tried to do something. "Between 1985 and 1993, the American bishops were dragged kicking and screaming into dealing with sexual abuse by priests," Catholic writer Peter Steinfels summarized. "This window of transition came far too late and took far too long, but it did occur." In 1985, the year of the Gauthe case in Louisiana and the Doyle report, the bishops began grappling with the topic internally. By 1992, with the Porter case in the headlines, they publicly adopted active measures: a national plan to curb abusers, respond to legal authorities, and care for victims. A new openness may have been inaugurated by such measures: The John Jay College report showed that while the 1970s was the worst decade for instances of reported abuse, two-thirds of all complaints over a half century came after 1993, with a dramatic third coming after the mass publicity of 2002. Still, Steinfels was accurate enough to say that, thanks to the bishops over the previous decade, "very, very few priests having credible past allegations in their dossiers have remained in or been returned to standard parish duties."[44]

And at least the Archdiocese of Chicago, as early as 1992, decided that its bishop needed disinterested help in the task. Hence the archdiocese set up the nation's first independent lay panel to police the problem. After 2002, all the dioceses promised to set up lay units as a check-and-balance on the internal clerical handling of cases. The Chicago effort had, for a decade already, trickled down to its parishes and to places such as Mundelein Seminary. At Mundelein "we've been very careful about the recruitment, screening, formation, and evaluation of our future priests," provost Baima said. "We have to err on the side of caution." Yet the "inexpressible dialogue" with men has continued. During the most intense year of the scandal, enrollment at Mundelein rose to 224 seminarians. And while the Chicago Archdiocese hit an ordination low of just six new priests in 1996, it rose to fourteen in 2003. "We have more than doubled," Baima said. "If we were a Wall Street investment, that would be considered pretty good."[45]

In recent years, moreover, the *Program for Priestly Formation* has begun to emphasize what some priests call "human formation," a code word for handling celibacy in the all-male priesthood. "Priestly life should also include a healthy balance of physical exercise, study and leisure," it said, and priests should "develop discerning habits" with regard to entertainment. It acknowledged that sexual abstinence seemed "unintelligible" to America's "widespread tolerance of sexual behavior contrary to Catholic teaching."[46]

Yet the abuse scandal showed that celibacy was not being handled well, especially by homosexual priests (see Chapter 10). After the Second Vatican Council so many priests left the priesthood to marry that the ratio of homosexual men increased and perhaps attracted others. In 1987, theologian Richard McBrien asked quite publicly whether the priesthood was becoming a gay profession. Two years later priest-sociologist Andrew Greeley wrote that the American church "is developing a heavily homosexual priesthood." After Boston, it "became clear that the vast majority of cases were not cases of pedophilia—the abuse of prepubescent children— but homosexual abuse of adolescent boys, sometimes referred to as 'ephebophilia,'" said Catholic writer Russell Shaw. It was a difficult trend to admit. Silva of the NFPC said honestly, "We have to return to a place where straight guys can enter the priesthood. Things are out of balance."[47]

For years, celibacy has been the red flag for discussing recruitment of priests and their later misbehaviors. In his 1992 *Pastores Dabo Vobis*, John Paul II acknowledged that celibacy had been contested down through church history. But he also quoted the Second Vatican Council, which did "not wish to leave any doubts in the mind of anyone regarding the Church's firm will to maintain the law." When the Baltimore Archdiocese plunged into discussions in 2001 about fewer priests holding sessions for its 162 parishes, Monsignor Michael Schleupner asked participants to list possible reasons for the shortage. "One issue that all of us here would name is celibacy," he said.[48]

It is a topic that seminarians are often ready to discuss. At Mount St. Mary's Seminary in Emmitsburg, Maryland, Robert Villa-Candellaria took his deacon vows of celibacy at age twenty-nine, with priesthood a year away. The theological vision of the priest brings him through. "We give witness to the afterlife," he said. "People see celibacy as something very strange. Of course, it's something many people cannot conceive: 'How can you, a man in a seminary, not want to have a woman and children and a future?'" He said that the physical world will pass away: "Our lives, at the spiritual level, have eternity as the main focus."[49]

In the face of unflattering reports on priestly psychology, Greeley launched a spirited defense. At issue was a 1970 study commissioned by the U.S. bishops that profiled the nation's priests. While the report concluded that priests were quite "ordinary," it added that 57 percent were "psychologically underdeveloped." Greeley said: "Apparently, then, 57 percent of American males are psychologically underdeveloped." He concludes this because in the 1970 survey, "Priests compared favorably with men of the same age and educational attainment on maturity, self-actualization and the capacity for intimacy." He cited a similar 1992 study that "found slightly higher scores on priests' capacity for intimacy."[50]

At Mundelein Seminary, Gary Pennings, a former emergency room specialist turned priest, said society's awkwardness about the celibacy vow he took reflects a wider problem of keeping all human vows. "If there's a crisis, it's a lack of commitment to commitment," he said. "The biggest vocations crisis we have in the Catholic Church is marriage." The divorce rate among Catholics is on par with rates across the United States. Pennings said commitments to marriage and celibacy are mutually reinforcing. "Priests are a witness to commitment, just as couples with a life-long Christian commitment strengthen priests."[51]

The number one solution to fewer priests "would be to obtain more priests," the bishops have said rhetorically. "Much of the difficulty is due to the fact that there are smaller families, diminishing feeder systems, a contrary climate in today's culture, etc." Their report on *Fewer Priests* reviewed all possible ways to make the best of the shortage—which include new networks, consolidation, new immigrants, and finally the services of ordained deacons and lay ministers.[52]

Surprisingly, by 2000 ordinary Catholics had not noticed the scarcity. Young people were least mindful of it, and only 23 percent of all Catholics recognized the pinch. *Fewer Priests* reviewed the options: assign priests to oversee more than one parish; allow non-priests to oversee parishes; allow priests to form teams that serve several parishes; allow parishes to share staff; recall priests from retirement; reduce the number of Masses and consolidate parishes; and celebrate more Masses via closed-circuit television. And "in a number of dioceses in the East and the Midwest, parishes could probably be consolidated." To find out what American Catholics thought, the bishops polled the pews on these options. Half of all Catholics would "support merging parishes as a way to meet needs."[53]

Amid such preferences for purely programmatic solutions, some Catholic writers have tried to remind the faithful that, perhaps, priestly vocations could be revived. That inference is drawn from *Personal Vocation: God Calls Everyone by Name*, a book by writer Russell Shaw and theologian Germain Grisez. They write that if more ordinary Catholics seek a daily "vocation" mindful of God's will for their lives, the priestly call may come through more clearly and more often. It is a matter of increasing the human pool of religious sensitivity. Pope John Paul II dubbed it a "universal call to holiness." And meanwhile, it might even improve the quality of spiritual life for the laity, who struggle with the demands of life as much as priests do. If more Catholics—even *all* Catholics—worked at "discerning, accepting, and living out their personal vocations," Shaw argued elsewhere, more "would discover that their personal vocations did in fact include callings to the priesthood or religious life."[54]

Monsignor Schleupner, speaking to meetings in the Baltimore Archdiocese, also urged prayers for more vocational sensitivity. But he pulled no punches: "We're at a completely new juncture in history." Besides making sure there is one priest per parish, "There will have to be other remedies to promote quality pastoral care" in the absence of priests. If declines in the priesthood continue, by 2015 the number of priests in Baltimore will drop from 196 to 143. This projection is calculated on a retirement age of seventy and the presumed ordination of five new priests each year. By 2011 the average age of Baltimore archdiocesan priests will be sixty. In Baltimore City, Mary Halpin attends a tri-parish—three parishes that share two priests. She honors her priests, but wonders how so few earthly rewards can attract more. "When you can't retire until you're seventy, you can't get married and you have to work ninety hours a week, I wouldn't buy it," she said. Monsignor Nicholas Amato of the Baltimore Archdiocese takes the "grass is always greener" attitude toward his duties. "I love the world, too," he said after a career in public school teaching. "But it doesn't deliver what it promises."[55]

One alternative that received a lot of press attention was Rome's 1980 decision to allow married Episcopal clergy into the U.S. priesthood. While the tumult in the Anglican and Episcopal Churches would have seemed to produce a clerical "crossing the Tiber" to maximum effect, just eighty Episcopal clerics—most of them Anglo-Catholic or "Anglo-Papalist" already—have made the journey. They were predicted to be "few and rare" by U.S. Cardinal William Baum amid the initial excitement. "They are not the thin edge of the wedge, preparing the Western Church for married priests in general." So far he is exactly right. The Catholic bishops in Britain, not seeking to strain relations with the Church of England, did not ask Rome for the "pastoral provision," though by other means there are a small number of married Anglicans now in Catholic holy orders. Some other parts of this bridging of Rome and Canterbury are little known. The Holy See, for example, allows "Anglican-use" parishes, where Episcopalians on the cusp, including clergy, can receive Catholic sacraments in the setting of Anglican worship.[56]

A little-known discussion begun at Vatican II holds out a proposal called *viri probati*: allowing the ordination of older, stable married men finished with family commitments to be ordained full priests. They would be commissioned for emergency situations, such as a total lack of priests. "This discussion has continued quietly for the last forty years," said one expert. "It will be revived early in the next pontificate, and bishops in some areas, at least some parts of Western Europe, will press it upon the new pope." Such a step would be allowed only on an experimental basis at first, and only in response to appeals by bishops in need. American Catholics have increasingly "favored expanding ordination to married men and women," according to one study. From 1987 to 1999, according to Gallup polls, acceptance of married priests grew from 63 to 71 percent; between 1974 and 1993, approval of women priests jumped from 29 to 64 percent. Yet of any possibility for change in the celibacy rule in the Western church, *viri probati* seems to be the one slim possibility.[57]

There is, of course, a large number of priests in the United States who have left their calling and married. Many active priests would welcome these married men back to the priesthood. On this topic a generational divide is clear, as today's newer priests are less accepting of such ecclesiastical amnesties. Back in 1970, 78 percent of younger priests favored such leniency, compared to half in favor today. The older-younger gap also shows up on optional celibacy (that is, marriage): 73 percent of older priests accept it today, compared to just a third of young priests. Another national survey found that 56 percent of *all* priests said marriage should be a personal choice for diocesan priests, though just 12 percent would marry if the rules changed. More than half (52 percent) of this priest sample, moreover, believed the church should welcome back resigned priests.[58]

Priests from abroad have always served Catholics in the United States, particularly priests of Spanish, Irish, and German extraction. Immigrant priests are likewise bolstering Catholic ministry today. *Fewer Priests* said that one in six active diocesan priests (16 percent) is from overseas. Another survey found that 32 percent of seminarians are born outside the United States. While a young American may not see upward mobility in the priesthood, young men in Eastern Europe, Africa, or the Philippines may see it as a new beginning in the United States, even for the extended family—for whom a happy cultural adjustment is never a guarantee.[59]

But of all solutions to the priest shortage, *Fewer Priests* reported, "Catholics most favor an increasing use of deacons and lay ministers." The priests themselves are divided by generation on this as well, with the older (81 percent) in support of more full-time lay ecclesial ministers, and the young less interested (49 percent). Again said Hoge, "The people least in favor are the youngest."[60]

The Second Vatican Council fathers revived the deacon status as a stage before priesthood, an ordination "not unto the priesthood, but unto the ministry." Young men seeking priesthood first enter the deacon stage, with its vow of celibacy, "works of charity," and limited work with the sacraments. And the council fathers said, "Should the Roman Pontiff think fit, it will be possible to confer this diaconal order even upon married men, provided they be of more mature age." In 1968 U.S. bishops received permission to establish the post of permanent deacon, including married men serving part time—to help "where there are fewer priests," and also as an "official and sacramental presence" in secular life, cities, and rural areas. The deacon was "not solely to stand in for a priest," but was to be a teacher and charitable worker.[61]

By the turn of the twenty-first century, 13,000 men—the overwhelming majority married—had become deacons, with 2,500 more in formation. They lack the priest's power to consecrate the Eucharist, hear confession, or administer last rites. As married men with jobs they also lack the priest's available time each day. Today deacons are experiencing "anxiety" over an unclear identity. According to the U.S. bishops, having little time to teach or visit those in need, deacons are "focusing more on sacramental and liturgical ministries during a time of fewer priests." Some churchgoers view these married deacons as either "underqualified priests or overqualified laity"—a "fifth wheel" in ministry—prompting the bishops to worry about "the deacon's identity and acceptance."[62]

The new ministries allowed by the Second Vatican Council have played differently among the liberal and conservative factions that are so alive today in the American church. More broadly, John Paul II has made the worldwide Catholic hierarchy more conservative as American culture has made U.S. Catholicism more liberal, creating still more tensions over lay ministry. Into this breach comes yet another windfall of the Second Vatican Council: the allowance for a ministry position called "lay ecclesial minister," a full–time paid staffer with a graduate degree or certificate in Catholic doctrine. Thirty thousand now work in parishes, and that many more are in the academic pipelines. "Within a few years there will be sixty thousand and growing," said Davidson, the sociologist. "The expansion of lay ministers and declining number of priests and sisters has led to a more decentralized church." Or from the vantage of another commentator, it may have led to a new kind of clericalism: "the emergence of a clericalized, white lay elite composed mainly of women."[63]

This corps of influential lay staff—a prominent parish dynamic in U.S. Catholicism—will be increasingly relied upon by three-quarters of all dioceses, the bishops said. More than eight in ten dioceses expect to see their presence grow in the next decade, taking over education, catechisms, and youth work in particular. Visiting various dioceses, Davidson said, he had seen lay people "participating in decisions that my mother never could have dreamed of. De facto, this is happening whether everybody in the church agrees with it or not." During the abuse controversy, when some American laity asserted themselves in calling for reform, John Paul II urged the church to "safeguard" the priest's role.[64]

In normal times, lay women are making many of the parish decisions.

They make up an estimated 82 percent of local church officials who are not priests or nuns. "We now have more lay ministers working in parishes than we have priests working in parishes," said Hoge, noting a future parish governance by "collaboration." These "non-priest professional ministers" now fill Catholic seminaries and other divinity schools, earning graduate degrees roughly on par with priests. Bishops know the promise and peril for priestly workloads and identities, but happily note "evidence that some vocations to priesthood, diaconate, and consecrated life emerge from lay ecclesial ministry."[65]

While most priests are happy about the help, others bear a deeper burden: They lack close friendships. "You know, there are 7 percent of priests, [and] a little higher for just diocesan priests, who said they have no close friends at all," Froehle said. For some sociologists, such as Robert Putnam with his thesis about more lonely Americans overall, this may be a cultural feature not exclusive to the priesthood. Still, according to Froehle, loneliness puts priests at "risk" for leaving the ministry. And while many priests take advantage of support groups for solidarity and relaxation, the doctrinal divides, abuse scandals, and homosexual subgroups have not helped collegiality, said Cozzens: "Priests don't trust one another like they used to."[66]

In recent years, Chicago commuters have seen a new series of billboards bearing a giant clerical collar: "If you're looking for a sign from God, this is it. Consider the priesthood." Spots for the priesthood run amid sport broadcasts on Pittsburgh television, ministry is touted in advertisements on MTV showing in Rhode Island, and be-a-priest slogans have mingled with "March Madness" college basketball tournaments on Baltimore broadcasts.

If shyness once prevailed, the point of vocations today is to forthrightly ask young men if they want to be a priest. A campus priest had put to Father Baima the question that "every red-blooded Catholic boy" used to ask himself: Do I have what it takes to be a priest? "I initially told him no, but he knew me better" and persisted with encouragement, Baima recalled. Father Burns, who works at the bishops' vocations office, said, "It is imperative that an invitation be verbalized." Many men are caught between feeling unworthy and the trepidation of so dramatic a step. Once they want to investigate, he said, "I always say, 'Hold on to your seat, because you're going to go for a ride.' You're never quite sure where the Lord's going to lead you." What some clergy have called the "dark night" of the priesthood may be passing, as the scandal seems to have peaked, the media is satiated, and a new pope may open new discussions about the priesthood and ministry. A purification has gotten underway, said Kevin C. Rhodes, rector of Mount Saint Mary's Seminary. "Yes, they are men," he said of his fellow priests. "There are struggles. But I think the good, faithful, hard-working priests who live holy lives are the great majority. That's the really good news."[67]

5

Southern Baptists

IT WAS BIG NEWS in 1989 when Southern Baptist pastors held their annual assembly in Las Vegas, a first for the Southern Baptist Convention
and an event ripe with symbolism for the nation's largest group of clergy.
"No site for a convention had ever been so controversial," said one veteran observer.[1]

In ways, the choice of Sin City represented a geographical step outside
the traditional Southern Baptist domain south of the Mason-Dixon Line,
where their ministry had been shaped for generations. It also threw into
profile the Southern Baptists' emphasis on counting the number of souls
delivered from unbelief, not to mention the sins of gambling, drinking,
and prostitution. During the week of the clergy-laity convention, many of
the 20,423 delegates (called "messengers") knocked on 120,000 Las Vegas
doors, producing 470 "professions of faith" and 5,000 "prospects" to join.

The convention also demonstrated the robust politicking—both religious and secular—Southern Baptist clergy have become known for in recent decades. Las Vegas came at the midpoint of the "takeover" of the
Southern Baptist Convention (SBC) machinery by conservatives, a project
begun in 1979 and completed around 2000. Winning the SBC presidential
election each year was key to the battle between conservatives and moderates—also called fundamentalists and liberals—and the 1989 contest
was a crucial link in the process. Indeed, even picking Las Vegas was controversial because the mere obstacle of traveling there could swing the
election results. What was more, "Fear was expressed that the reputation
of the city might keep many conservatives away, while many moderates
might make a special effort to go and vote."[2]

As history would show, conservatives made an extra effort to show up
in the desert state with its neon city. They delivered 56 percent of the

ballots for their candidate and thus kept sway over the influential office of president, which is filled by a pastor and is renewable for a second year. By all calculations, the SBC presidency had become a greater political prize than ever before in Southern Baptist affairs. Over time, the president's appointive powers could result in handpicking all leadership personnel in a vast Southern Baptist bureaucracy, which at one point amounted to twenty national agencies for missions, publishing, schools, and budgets. Las Vegas was *so* political, in fact, that "many people came, registered, voted for their presidential candidate, and went home."[3]

The Southern Baptists are served by an estimated eighty thousand to one hundred thousand pastors, the largest corps of ministers in any American tradition. Besides such sheer numbers of clergy, Southern Baptists excel in other numerical ways on the American church landscape. They boast 16 million members worshiping in 41,000 congregations. Leaders claim that their missions here and abroad produce 100,000 new members and 1,500 new churches each year. One in seven U.S. seminary students attends a Southern Baptist theology school. While once a predominantly rural church, just half its churches and 36 percent of its members today dwell outside of a metropolitan area. Finally, the burgeoning army of SBC preachers may be attributed to the flexibility that often goes with the clergy call: Just half are seminary trained and four in ten are "bivocational," holding a weekday job and preaching on weekends.[4]

Only a fraction of the Southern Baptist clergy attend each annual assembly, which usually includes a greater percentage of lay delegates. Still, those massive gatherings for fellowship and church business are perhaps the epitome of large, participatory, clergy events. They are spectacles of church politics in action, especially as internal disagreements have become not only more ideological but increasingly overlap with nationwide secular politics. While church politics is a realm apart from the secular electioneering and legislating of the American political system, in recent years, Southern Baptist pastors have earned a reputation for becoming masters of both. As a result, they have become a unique window on the nature of clergy involvement in American secular politics.

While this shows its face in all ministerial traditions, in modern times Southern Baptist clergy stand out. They have become objects of political fascination after helping to shift the South from a Democratic to a Republican stronghold. If conservative Protestant clergy had once been considered "otherworldly," the Baptists' role in the new Religious Right has reversed the conventional wisdom about staying out of worldly politics. The recent activism by Southern Baptist clergy, in fact, has boosted the total amount of evangelical politicking to a level that may now exceed liberal clergy, who have kept up their political activism since the 1960s.

It was a gradual process for Southern Baptists, but it came to full fruition in the epic of the Reagan conservatives and the era's great battles for the White House. The shift toward more political involvement began as early as 1968, when resolutions at the Southern Baptist annual conventions began to take on heated political issues. Resolutions that had typically been filled with kindly gestures and tributes turned into politically charged stands on social topics. The change in tone, said one study of the resolutions, revealed "a once apolitical denomination becoming politically aware—in some cases militantly so."[5]

Not surprisingly, the Southern Baptist clergy's "political activity grew markedly" as well, especially during presidential elections from 1980 to 2000. All clergy like attention, and this southern majority got its share. "Southern Baptists have been subject to much attention from the Christian Right, which hopes to move them away from traditional church-state separation and, often, political passivity, to more conservative involvement," according to *The Bully Pulpit*, a 1998 study that surveyed eight thousand clergy in several denominations. Indeed, in Las Vegas, Jerry Falwell, an independent fundamentalist Baptist who now moves in Southern Baptist circles, announced the disbanding of the Moral Majority, a political group launched in 1979. "We've accomplished everything we set out to do," he said.[6]

Across the second half of the twentieth century, Southern Baptists and their clergy have recorded a remarkable ascendance in national politics. Harry Truman was a low-key Southern Baptist, Jimmy Carter a Sunday school teacher, and in the 1990s Arkansas Governor Bill Clinton of Immanuel Baptist Church in Little Rock became president on a ticket with fellow Baptist Al Gore. When the Republicans took over Congress, soon afterward, it was led by Southern Baptists Newt Gingrich and Trent Lott.

Democratic Party leaders of Baptist vintage had been legendary in the South, but a Republican realignment began changing that in the 1980s and 1990s. "The breadth of the Democratic collapse was staggering," so "rapid and comprehensive [was the] desertion of an established majority party by an entire region," remarked two political scientists. Partly as a result, Southern Baptist influence increased nationally and pastors developed a taste for Republican activism. "Southern Baptists and Republicans have exported a Southern brand of gloves-off politics and religion to the rest of the nation but not without trouble in the ranks," said Oran Smith in *The Rise of Baptist Republicanism*.[7]

The "Baptist battles" or "battle for the Bible" had begun in 1979, when conservatives strategically rallied messengers to elect the SBC president— and kept winning for the next two decades. The contest peaked in 1985 when 45,519 messengers poured into Dallas to conduct the largest legislative event by a religious group in history. The 1989 assembly in Las Vegas

was another small turning point, another conservative show of galvaniz-
ing the vote, but this time outside of the South. In previous decades, conservatives in small congregations had felt alienated from the national
scene, which was said to be controlled by the consensus of the moderate
"old-boy" network. But that changed under a get-out-the-vote mobilization by "a new generation of leadership, many serving as pastors in the
growing megachurches of the Southwest."[8]

Looking back, the vying parties disagree: Was it a "great corrective" to
return the denomination to biblical "inerrancy" for the sake of evangelism? Or was it a "conservative takeover" to gain the plum jobs and restore
the older ways of the South?

Before this time, generations of Baptists had been bound together by a belief that "the Bible was their only creed." Colonial Baptist Roger Williams
had also handed down the idea of "soul competency," the ability of each
believer to discern biblical truth. That colonial emphasis on independence
of the Baptist conscience and local church was augmented in the 1920s by
something new: the oppositional temperament of Baptist fundamentalism. So when Southern Baptists decided in 1925 to centralize under a Cooperative Program, a funding bureaucracy, fundamentalists split from the
fold, declaring their cause a matter of religious freedom. Before they left,
however, they galvanized a movement to write down Southern Baptist beliefs for the first time.

The result was the 1925 Baptist Faith and Message. By mid-century,
controversies about how to train seminarians and a 1961 book, *The Message of Genesis*, sparked another revision of the Baptist list of beliefs. The
Genesis commentary was written by Professor Ralph Elliot of Midwestern Seminary and published by a church organ. But critics viewed it as
equivocal on the Fall of Man, diluting the concept of sin, the very linchpin
of evangelistic repentance and salvation. Such writings could undermine
"the life force of the SBC, especially of its number-oriented corporate bureaucracy," said Samuel Hill, a historian of the South.[9] So the Baptist Faith
and Message of 1963 naturally reiterated the words of its 1925 predecessor, that the Bible is "truth without any mixture of error."

Indeed, by the 1960s the Cooperative Program, buoyed by the postwar
economic boom, kept the Southern Baptist Convention at the forefront of
American church growth. It was erecting the world's largest system of
theological schools, focused on six seminaries. Yet the falling out between the conservatives and moderates began to brew into a strategic
clash by the late 1970s. Not only was moderate Baptist Jimmy Carter in
the White House, but it was also "the first no-growth decade" for the
convention.[10]

The backdrop for the coming tumult was also two decades of rocky race relations in a church that still dominated the eleven states of the former Confederacy. The voting rights struggle of blacks and then the 1954 Supreme Court decision to desegregate schools by busing shook all things southern. Many young Baptist clergy and seminarians were eager to remake the church, but local resistance was great. In 1961, thirteen Southern Baptist pastors had to leave their cities after signing a pro-integration "Affirmation of Basic Religious Principles." That summer—the season of the "freedom riders"—the convention forced its seminary in Louisville "to apologize publicly" for allowing Baptist minister Martin Luther King Jr. to speak. Already in 1956, the conservative W. A. Criswell of First Baptist Church of Dallas—an early megachurch—called integrationists "a bunch of infidels" who upset "the things that we love as good Southern Baptists" (but at the end of his life wished "with all my heart that I had not spoken on behalf of segregation").[11]

The liberal wing of the church had sided with a new kind of race relations, taking its cues from Truman, who desegregated the military and proposed the same for federal employment. Many moderates among SBC clergy had "passionately supported the changes brought by the civil rights movement," said Nancy Ammerman, wife and daughter of Southern Baptist preachers. There would be more around in the SBC today, she said, except that a "missing generation" of young Southern Baptist clergy left when the denomination opposed desegregation and voting rights for blacks. The divide over race is still mirrored in Baptist battles. When self-identified fundamentalist Southern Baptist clergy were surveyed in the 1980s, fewer than half (47 percent) agreed that civil rights moved "the country in the right direction." Nearly all (87 percent) of the self-identified moderates in the SBC agreed.[12]

Yet the conservatives had "much truth on their side" when they said social change would also liberalize religion, said Hill. "They warned that to open the windows would be to allow all manner of creatures to fly in." Ideas that overturned "old segregated structures brought to the South secular ways of looking at things." To defend the old-time religion, conservatives mobilized in journals and networks. They aggressively pursued the day when they could vote themselves into denominational power. Political activist Ralph Reed said the Christian Right, whether in secular or church politics, was not an offensive strike, but a "defensive struggle by people seeking to sustain their faith and their values." Indeed, the phrase "offensive-defensive" soon came into vogue.[13]

Clergy of all denominations invariably became caught up in the wider social tempest. In the last two decades of the twentieth century "it seemed impossible to find any political controversy that did not involve clergy—often on both sides of the issue," reported *The Bully Pulpit*. Yet Southern Baptist pastors in particular have come under new pressures in their congregational and secular roles. Southern Baptists "have a history of allowing their pastors to take an active part in politics," said Smith, but now they are "suddenly outpacing others" in that arena.[14]

Quite naturally, the Baptist Faith and Message had never addressed politics. It likewise had never spoken about the role of a pastor or the Reformation belief in a "priesthood of all believers." That is, until the topic arose at the 1988 annual convention.

The legendary Criswell's views were well known by then. "The pastor is ruler of the church," he said. "A laity-led, layman-led, deacon-led church will be a weak church." By 1988, however, his church party realized the difficulty of enforcing the concept of Bible inerrancy on individuals. So they turned "to resolutions supporting strong pastoral authority in the interpretation of scripture," said historian Arthur Farnsley. The key resolution, which won a majority vote, said the "priesthood of the believer" was an individualistic attitude sometimes "used to justify the undermining of pastoral authority in the local church." And it cited the Bible: "Obey your leaders; and submit to them."[15]

In ways, this motion from the floor set the mood for the entire assembly. During the SBC presidential contest, the moderate candidate railed against "a handful of high priests" for making the audacious pastoral claim. The conservative candidate praised the "courageous conservative" stance, for the resolution had reasonably argued that a man cannot "believe whatever he so chooses" and still be a loyal Southern Baptist. "Nothing separated the two emerging parties in the Convention more than this difference on pastoral versus individual authority," Farnsley said. The autocratic style, a trademark of independent fundamentalism, was most "visible in the so-called super churches" of the SBC, said Baptist historian Bill Leonard, a moderate. "But it's also quite prevalent in small churches that see it as a way to grow into super churches."[16]

By the time of the 1988 resolution, Pastor K. Randel Everett had been in full-time ministry for twelve years and was beginning his fourth pastorate, now at University Baptist Church in Fort Worth, Texas. A native of Arkansas and son of a Baptist preacher, Everett is among those who feel uncomfortable with a commander-like role for the senior pastor. His life story—not untypical for Southern Baptist clergy—may offer glimpses why.[17]

Growing up as a preacher's kid, Everett had only good memories. Tall and eloquent, he was a debater and drama club enthusiast in high school, thinking about a career in law or politics. But when he studied Ephesians one night with a high school senior group, " 'God turned a light on in my life.' God said, 'I'm calling you to be a pastor teacher.' " At his father's church a member motioned that he preach "the next Sunday night," and that was the start. "I preached on the whole Bible in about eighteen minutes. I threw in everything I knew," he said. "My image of a pastor was absolutely positive," he added. "Dad's friends would come over. So I met a lot of pastors."

During his first year at Ouachita Baptist University, a small country church ordained him, "a crazy thing for a church to do" since he was just eighteen. After college, where he had been sophomore class president in 1968, he was off to the largest SBC seminary, Southwestern in Fort Worth, where his father had studied. Completing a master's of divinity in 1975 (with a doctor of ministry to come), he was hired as senior pastor of the one-thousand-member First Baptist Church of Gonzales, Texas. It was no small ministry for a twenty-five-year-old with a wife and the first of two children.

Though just half of Southern Baptist clergy earn a seminary degree, they all must move from book learning to the reality of churchgoers' lives. And Everett moved over quickly. "In four years I did over two hundred funerals, and twice three funerals within twenty-four hours," he recalled. "I was overwhelmed. Every week, brand-new grief with a different family." Emotional hardiness, theology, and faith kept him going. "I could not have made it through if not for the resurrection of Christ, the resurrection of the dead, the eternal security of believers," he said. "I preach it as a certainty."

Under the Baptist system, the deacon board at each church generally decides how well a pastor is doing at this inspired and stressful job. Pastors average four-year posts, amounting to a massive turnover across the Southern Baptist Convention. As senior pastor of six churches in his ministry, Everett served four years at each. After two churches in Arkansas and two in Texas, he was hired by a megachurch, first in Pensacola, Florida, with five thousand members, and then in Northern Virginia, with three thousand. By comparison, some pastors "have been in really difficult situations," he said. "But when your church situation is easier, you might depend less on God. Your personal walk with Christ might suffer."

Throughout this time, Everett's "typical week" changed little. Freshest in the morning, he rose to pray and study, putting his routine aside "when people needed to see me, or an emergency health situation arose." The study was in part for sermons, which he gave Sunday morning and evening. Yet it was also to feed the pastoral soul, taxed daily by the needs of parishioners. "I tried to spend afternoons in administrative work, like staff meetings." The staff worked as a team on hospital visits, which he made once a week. Weddings and funerals were relentless. "And then, probably at a minimum, three nights were tied up with visitation, meetings, or church activities."

Modern clergy burnout has prompted counselors to urge a day off, despite protests of old-time clergy who toughed it out. Everett took a Thursday or Friday. "You never finish your job," he said. "Yet pastors have so many people praying for them, encouraging them. We get flak and criticism, but also a lot of affirmation." The best defense against burnout is a personal relationship with God and bonds to family, he said. But next best is escape: "Have a life apart from the church. If your whole life is the church, you'll probably burn out."

Having entered ministry in the 1970s, Everett had only known a time of Baptist battles. While in seminary, he was an enthusiastic worker at Criswell's First Baptist Church. "I revered him," he said of the "compassionate" one-on-one pastor. "I would have taken a bullet for him." Yet the irenic life of local worship evaporated on the national stage. Everett never took the invitation to join the conservative vanguard. "Some of the 'correction' was needed," he said. "But I've ended up on the moderate side, even though I'm very conservative." He felt that the cause had become judgmental and ruthless. In the purge of moderates, as some put it, only pastors "with blood on their hands" had a future. "With the SBC it was always winner take all," he said. "If you're with the winners, you get appointed to boards and agencies and even pulpit committees. And if you're a loser, you get boycotted."

Rather than impugn either side, Everett attributes his stance more to his own temperament, which "never liked a monolithic" approach to church life. "I don't think the pastor should wield all the power," said this former megachurch pastor. "I guess I had always challenged authority. I love debate. And probably if the moderates were in control of the SBC I'd be a fundamentalist."

In 2000, a conservative panel revised the Baptist Faith and Message once again. It praised pastoral authority, urged wives to "submit gracefully" to husbands, and barred women as pastors. All SBC personnel, seminary faculty, and missionaries were asked to sign or lose their jobs. "That does not reflect 'no creed but the Bible,'" Everett said. He agreed with the idea of using the Apostles' Creed as a line-by-line affirmation. "But when Baptists say we have no creed but the Bible, then it's which part of the Bible do you emphasize?" The parts about mercy or justice? The texts on salvation or ethics? Everett prefers to allow for differences, and to trust each soul's competence.

Over twenty-five years of feverish votes, taking sides, and loyalty statements, good feelings have soured among many pastors. Everett regretted this most, since the grassroots work of the local church—"visiting hospitals and conveying Christ"—is doing well enough despite the top-tier political infighting. "Used to be, the annual convention was a place to go see friends from seminary," he said. "In my dad's generation pastors pulled for each other more. Now we're divided into too many camps. Literally brother divided against brother."

At Southwestern Seminary, where both Everett and his father garnered the tools for ministry, a next generation of clergy is still serving a high-demand church. When Michael Drennan, a Virginia native, graduated in 2000, he got forty to fifty inquiries from around the country about his availability for open jobs. "A lot of churches are really looking for youth ministers now," said Drennan, who was thirty at graduation. A friend who graduated the next year had four or five inquiries on his voice mail each day. "They are all saying, 'We have seen your resume and would like to know if you could come talk to us.'" In these years it took about six months for a church to find its next pastor, which is quick by other Protestant church standards. The seminary was reporting four thousand requests for a pastor each year; the placement rate was 70 percent. "Ministry has a high rate of burnout and turnover," Drennan said. "So churches always have a great need of preachers."[18]

Before there were seminaries, the preacher was a working man. Baptists in the South held that "preachers were called immediately by God" without formal requirements, said historian Robert Baker. "Many a farmer plowing his furrow reproduced the experience of Isaiah by responding, 'Here am I, send me.'" Such "bivocational" self-sufficiency saved Baptists the overhead that burdened so many other denominations. But in time, said Baker, the great "corrective" that was needed to compete in a democratic, sectarian, and modernizing America was to have theologically trained pastors.[19]

The growth of the seminary system—from 2,666 students in 1950 to nearly 8,000 four decades later—created a new kind of clergy and clergy-supply system. "During the era of untrained bivocational pastors and small churches, the local pastor was 'called' from within the congregation or recruited from one nearby," said sociologist Roger Finke. Such local recruits had the "ability to keep in touch with the people." With the national training and deployment system, however, "the local church has gradually moved from an autonomous church, holding a loose affiliation with the national Convention, to a church increasingly dependent on the services of the denomination's bureaucracy." What is more, paying a full-time pastor is still beyond the means of many Southern Baptist churches.[20]

For all these reasons, "bivocational" ministers remain a Southern Baptist mainstay: 40 percent of clergy hold jobs and preach on weekends. In recent years this career mix has become an "intentional" movement to grow churches. "If God calls men to be bivocational ministers, that means

He had a purpose in churches being bivocational rather than calling fully funded pastors," said Larry Lehr, a marketing coordinator and Oklahoma pastor. "The beauty of bivocational ministry is that people in the church have to be involved in ministry." Pastors can also focus on their strengths—preaching but not counseling, for example. Moving between two jobs can keep a pastor fresh, said Bruce Grubbs, a denomination employee and Tennessee pastor. "You can walk away from one and go to the other," he said. Often "churches are prideful" of full-time clergy. Yet he believes they are often underemployed in time and in earnings.[21]

The increasing conflicts in congregations has also added to the dramatic turnover in ministry. The Southern Baptists have been fairly open about this, reporting in 1988 a peak of roughly 1,400 "forced terminations"—or firings—of pastors in one year. Subsequent surveys, conducted out of pastoral concerns for clergy themselves, found the number settling to under one thousand in 2000. It was found that fired pastors had served, on average, for just three months.[22]

The primary cause has been "control issues regarding who will run the church," reported the LifeWay ministry of the convention. Other factors included "poor people skills of the pastor" and a "pastoral leadership style perceived as too strong." While some worry that a third of all Baptist clergy will experience "termination" in their ministry, an outside scholar notes wryly that "Since the relationship between pastor and congregation is said to be God's will, there is much (deeply ambivalent) laughter about God changing his mind so often." The LifeWay study also found that 45 percent of the recently fired pastors left Baptist ministry: "We would like to know why so many did not return."[23]

A survey by *Leadership* magazine, which caters to evangelicals, revealed that the trend extended well beyond Southern Baptist churches. A quarter (23 percent) of the clergy respondents had been fired or forced to resign. "Americans want leaders, but as soon as they get them, they have a compulsion to bring them down," said the magazine's David Goetz. "And I think that's true in the church." Many of these ministers, who most often cited "small factions" as their nemesis, reported that their church had fired the previous minister (62 percent) or the previous two pastors (41 percent).[24]

It sounded like what author G. Lloyd Rediger had labeled "clergy killer" churches—congregations controlled by small, dominant factions or deep, unresolved conflicts. "Clergy firings are very high compared with the national labor force, where 1.2 percent of all employees are involuntarily terminated," said sociologist Kevin Leicht, author of *Professional Work*. The ministers' firing rate "is even higher than coaches in the NFL, a notoriously unstable profession."[25]

On the list of common conflicts between a pastor and church, doctrinal and political disputes hardly made a showing. But pastoral assertiveness ranked third most common. The Southern Baptist pastor had once been the church administrator, answering to deacon boards, the congregation, or both. "To conservatives, however, the pastor is more the titular head of the church, a prophetlike figure," a larger-than-life person who uses deacons for prayer support but not for advice, historian Oran Smith said. Psychologist Wayne Oakes, who advised the North Carolina Baptist Convention on the firing problem, said the "too strong" pastor was a new problem. "Pastors are listening to some of the wrong voices," he said. Church growth conferences urge them to be strongly directive, which may work at a megachurch. But at a "rural North Carolina church with fifty to sixty members," said Oakes, "it's a totally different situation."[26]

Yet the highly directive Baptist pastor is clearly playing a new role in building megachurches and in leavening secular politics. Of an estimated six hundred megachurches in the United States—those with at least two thousand members—one in five is Southern Baptist, according to church-growth expert John N. Vaughan. These have produced—or made better known—strong senior pastors, especially as pastoral staff may number twenty or more.

The Republican Party has not ignored these new suburban centers with their Moses-like commanders. In 1988, for example, political strategists for presidential candidate George Bush, Sr. targeted megachurches in two different ways. For the 1988 Super Tuesday primaries, GOP contender Pat Robertson—ordained a Southern Baptist but with a core constituency in the Assemblies of God—relied on charismatic megachurches to turn out the vote. Knowing this, the Bush campaign flooded them with partisan appeals in advance. This prompted the pastors to expel all politicking from the church foyer and parking lot, undercutting a Robertson edge.[27]

When Election Day 1988 approached, the strategy was different. The Bush campaign had compiled a list of 180 megachurches with 5,000 or more members, half of them Southern Baptist, and relied on their pastors to create a forum. "For a political candidate to reach a large number of people, and not be embarrassed, he can find a pretty good ally in one of those [megachurch] pastors," said Doug Wead, who led the 1988 outreach to churches. "They know how to communicate, how to use technology, how to organize."[28]

The American view of clergy and politics today is probably not much different than at any time in the past, honoring their rights as private citizens, but "leery of religious leaders becoming too involved in certain kinds of political activities." Clergy themselves admit to certain theological constraints on politicking. Evangelical pastors have felt their mission of teaching personal salvation "constitutes the principal impediment to political" engagement. The more liberal mainline clergy are "reluctant to invoke religious authority to support their political viewpoints." In both cases, said one study, "ministerial political leadership seems self-limiting."[29]

Though prominent in setting the tone for the politics of peace, life issues, and social justice today, Catholic clergy in the United States brave their own constraints. They work under a hierarchical teaching authority that prefers broad principles over specific policies. Their "seamless garment" social ethics joins stopping abortion with expanding welfare and helping immigrants. As a result, they are difficult to be "mobilized for politics because their issue agenda does not line up with the positions of either major political party."[30]

In the mid-1990s about a fifth of churchgoing Americans reported hearing political sermons from church pulpits. Catholics and mainline Protestants reported it least (12 percent), while both black churches and white evangelical congregations heard such messages the most. While the black sermon topics ranged from religious issues such as school prayer to economic ones like national health care, evangelicals stuck mostly to topics of piety and morality. The three most common topics were prayer in school (66 percent), pornography (59 percent), and homosexuality (45 percent).[31]

At the turn of this century, a "Religion and Politics Survey" conducted by a team of sociologists asked Americans: "Do you think it is ever right for clergy to discuss political issues from the pulpit?" Only four in ten (37 percent) supported the proposition, but that is no small part of a voting population. "Sunday worship service appears to be regarded as sacrosanct," said sociologist Robert Wuthnow, who led the survey. More acceptable was for clergy "to preach on broad social and moral issues that can be related to biblical themes" rather than hinge on political specifics.[32]

One of the strictest tax rules regarding churches bars ministers from endorsing candidates from the pulpit, for which they could lose tax exemption for their church. Still, clergy as public figures use many other forums to smile on candidates. In this sense "public endorsement of candidates is actually quite common among ministers," said political scientist Corwin Smidt. While clergy in general "do not engage in heavy campaigning" for candidates or laws, they do "campaign more than the mass public." Pastors in poor neighborhoods are more politically engaged than their colleagues in wealthier parts of town. And most significant, "When clergy perceive their political views to be the same as those of their congregations, they are more likely to be politically engaged."[33]

This uniformity of thought between minister and congregation has surfaced as a key explanation—indeed the Holy Grail—of the new clergy activism. The first major studies of clergy in politics, conducted in the 1960s, looked at what was *then* the so-called "new breed." They were younger mainline clergy who marched for civil rights, backed the government-expanding War on Poverty, and denounced the war in Vietnam. The more politically active and theologically liberal clergy were, the more they endured conflict with their congregation. Many opted for activism over a pulpit and left the ministry altogether.[34]

The "new breed's" legacy endures in many liberal Protestant denominations, and these clergy—Presbyterian, Disciples of Christ, and United Methodists—still show high rates of political involvement. Yet, now as before, these "challenge-oriented" clergy will rarely bring their diverse following into a single way of thinking about the will of God. For moderate-to-liberal ministers, in other words, it is typically harder to claim divine authority for a political statement. Their diverse and well-educated churches easily "dismiss their pronouncements as mere 'opinion,'" said historian Ted G. Jelen. One study of liberal and conservative Reformed clergy found that the former were excited by the idea that "clergy of different faiths need to cooperate more in politics"; the latter held that "there is only one correct view" on most political topics.[35]

Evangelical Bible quoting gives those clergy "a powerful justification for making political pronouncements." Put another way, while some clergy claim absolute truth, others search with deep questions. As one study put the case: "Clergy from the 'truth' perspective should find it much easier to make direct and explicit calls for participation on a political issue than should clergy from the 'questioning' perspective." Moreover, if the middle-class churches of the 1960s resisted the activist "new breed" liberal clergy, evangelical churches today have come to the point where "political activity is *expected* of clergy."[36]

This ability to focus hearts and minds on a simpler political target goes with being "evangelical." Calling oneself an evangelical is also to adopt an activist "religiopolitical identity," according to the Wuthnow study. And thanks to Southern Baptists, most evangelicals are in the South, where "evangelicals are significantly more likely than non-southern evangelicals" to back religious intervention in politics. Baptist majorities in southern states might naturally feel political entitlement, a sense that "their religious leaders deserve to have more power than they presently do."[37]

Yet the final mystery about the new evangelical and Southern Baptist political activism is why they gave up their formerly passive ways. Political scientist James Guth, who has interviewed Southern Baptist clergy for three decades, said they were "long regarded as politically passive." They were loyal but inactive Americans, living in social enclaves that reflected their values well enough. In addition to that, they had overwhelmingly adopted pre-millenarian theology. A smaller core also adhered to an intense dispensational view: belief that this was the final "dispensation" in history, evidenced by global events, before Christ's return to judge a recalcitrant world. The world of politics was not only a dirty game, but it was being played, in Dwight L. Moody's pre-millennial analogy, on a "sinking ship." So why did they convert to getting out the vote?[38]

Guth and his collaborators believe that evangelicals have adopted a new "social theology" to match their end-times theology. This new "civic gospel" was not the social justice agenda of the liberal new breed but a vanguard for moral reform. Though Christ might return any moment, "true Christians" still had to stop non-Christians from taking over America: "Clergy who were not only orthodox but also dispensationalist fomented early Christian Right activism." So also is Southern Baptist activism "the province of the most theologically conservative clergy." The most active SBC clergy hail from larger churches where "parishioners approve of their political activity." At a personal level, moreover, neither age, upbringing, education, geography, nor even theology explains much about the new activist pastors. They are driven by "political interest, partisanship, and ideology."[39]

Their shift to the Republican side between 1980 and 2000 began in increments but then snowballed. Half of SBC clergy were Democrats in 1980 and fewer than three in ten had "strong" Republican loyalty. The change began to show up in 1985, when six in ten SBC clergy (62 percent) said the rise of the Moral Majority was a "good thing." During the U.S. presidential elections of 1992 and 1996, two in ten belonged to at least one conservative Christian political organization. They most often affiliated with policy groups such as Focus on the Family. But those tied to the get-out-the-vote Christian Coalition were the most politically active. By 2000, 61 percent of SBC clergy reported contact "from party or candidate groups." Half of the clergy by then claimed "strong" Republican affiliation. The 2000 result: "Almost nine in ten ministers" (86 percent) voted for George W. Bush on the Republican ticket. "It is hard to imagine more political cohesion in a large, national church," said Guth.[40]

Historically speaking, the Southern Baptist clergy accomplished one other thing: They helped evangelical ministers close the gap between their rates of political activism and the rates still found among liberals from the 1960s. This is significant because most conservative clergy still are not politically active, with the Assemblies of God as emblematic. Their clergy are more Republican, but their "ministers are quite inactive."[41]

While the activism gap has been closed in what Guth and others call a clear "two-party" system of clergy, each side has its distinct preferences for political activity. The conservatives lag behind the liberals, for example, in joining other groups, organizing church activities, or contacting public officials. They "compensated with superior performance" in decrees and direct action, said *The Bully Pulpit*. While 58 percent of conservatives "preached a whole sermon on a political issue," fewer liberals (47 percent) did so. Similarly, the two sides compared 79 to 69 percent on taking "public stands on political issues" and 71 to 44 percent on publicly endorsing a candidate.[42]

In presidential elections in particular, the Southern Baptists showed "extraordinary activity beyond voting." Compared to more liberal clergy, they were on the hustings in the 1988 presidential election (37 percent of clergy) as much as the Presbyterian Church (USA) clergy (36 percent) and the Disciples of Christ ministers (41 percent). Nearly three in ten (27 percent) participated in getting out the vote in the 1992 national primaries, and six in ten (59 percent) in the general election. By 2000, 63 percent of SBC clergy who voted Republican claimed an "active role" in the election. Overall the "steady increase" was concentrated among the "orthodox, fundamentalist, and dispensationalist clergy," and among clergy under age thirty-five, suggesting a more politicized SBC clergy in the future. Indeed, by 2000, the SBC clergy with "less experience" as pastors were *"more* active politically." What *The Bully Pulpit* concluded in 1998 still holds: The nation has reached "a rough parity in political competition between the two historic 'parties' in Protestantism."[43]

For over twenty years, Southern Baptist ministers have been a significant doorway into the world of clergy politics. But it would be wrong to say politics is foremost. In Southern Baptist circles, the top priority is reserved for evangelism—and numerical growth.

When, in 1917, Southern Baptists began expanding outside their eighteen-state stronghold in the South, they fiercely debated what justified such an "invasion" of the North. Two main reasons were to provide "programmatic"—that is, systematic, regular, well-organized, and packaged—services to members who moved north, and to evangelize numerically. Having reached all fifty states by 1972, the next great shift of the rural Southern Baptists was to colonize the suburbs. But the convention had not yet penetrated the nation's fifty largest metropolitan areas, where 60 percent of Americans lived, and that was the next mission agenda. Thanks mostly to urban evangelism in the 1990s, nearly half of all new churches and missions were for immigrants, especially Hispanics and Koreans.[44]

So when the annual convention met in the heartland of Atlanta in 1999, cities were the hot topic. The 1990s, unfortunately, had seen almost no growth in membership. And for the first time since 1926, the convention experienced a year that *lost* members, a 1 percent drop in 1998. The news was not much better in 2004; the convention was told that the number of new baptisms had declined in each of the past four years, raising worries about "a denomination that's lost its focus" or even one that was "declining." While some conservatives have attributed the years of slippage to changes in counting methods, departures of liberals, or closings of rural churches, moderates point to "doctrinaire fundamentalism."[45]

Whatever the case, the Atlanta convention of 1999 pushed to reverse the no-growth trend, a push led by its new president, Paige Patterson, an early protégé of Criswell. Patterson inaugurated a three-year Strategic Cities Initiative, which aimed to open hundreds of new congregations, establish megachurches, and bring hundreds of thousands of evangelistic volunteers into the urban heart of several target cities. As it turned out, it was a bold vision with modest results, but Patterson gave the convention a new determination at the helm, and a somewhat unequivocal stance. In his first year as president, Patterson said it would not bother him if moderates simply left the SBC. "I think probably integrity demands it," he told the *Atlanta Journal–Constitution*.[46]

But the moderates stayed, setting up alternative mission agencies and theological seminaries and complaining that the "conservative–caused" conflict seeped down to the congregation level. Some one to two million Southern Baptists are die–hard moderates. Their pastors control state conventions in Texas, North Carolina, and Virginia and many Baptist state newspapers and nearly all the Baptist colleges and universities. Enrollment at the SBC theological schools has dropped, with both sides pointing fingers for the declension. The enrollment debate came to a head in October 2001 when the Baptist General Convention of Texas voted to cut its annual contribution of $5 million to the seminaries. The Texas moderates, flexing their muscle, concluded that the six schools espoused "doctrinaire fundamentalism" and were foundering in recruitment. The action on the seminary front came as general Southern Baptist giving to the Cooperative Program was also declining.

By now the moderates had formed associations such as the Baptist Alliance and Cooperative Baptist Fellowship to organize churches and pastors for parallel missions and educational work. The Texas funds were earmarked, in fact, for four moderate-led seminaries, which enrolled about 600 students in 2001 (compared to about 6,400 at the six historic seminaries). They included George W. Truett Theological Seminary in Waco, Texas, and Baptist Theological Seminary in Richmond, Virginia, founded in 1991 as the first breakaway. "There are [conservative] churches out there that would never think of coming to us for a pastor. We don't fit each other's expectations," said W. Robert Spinks, a pastor and officer at the Richmond seminary. He said that growing numbers of moderate congregations likewise "do not trust the product" at Southeastern, where he and many of the Richmond faculty worked before a new board ousted them in favor of conservatives.[47]

By swinging the historic seminaries to a more fundamentalist stance, said sociologist Ammerman, conservatives solved the problem of "keeping bright young conservatives in the fold." They typically drifted to the moderate persuasion after going to graduate school. Many moderate clergy and SBC faculty have joined other Baptist, evangelical, or mainline Protestant groups. "Their old recruitment, training and placement system has been broken up," she said. "It still is hard for people who are outsiders to the [conservative] 'new SBC' to figure out where to go to college and seminary, who their mentors should be and who will sponsor them as candidates for pastoral positions." With all the splits it is no longer easy to typecast a typical Southern Baptist minister: "The term 'SBC clergy' covers a lot of territory."[48]

Since ending his last pastorate in 2001, Randel Everett has become part of the diverse landscape of longtime Baptist pastors. He had been thinking intensely about missions, especially to a culturally diverse and urban modern world. He noted that there were two hundred Baptist unions, or associations, around the world, and much of the excitement was happening in multicultural urban centers and in places such as Asia, Africa, and Latin America. Most of the debate between the conservatives and moderates, he said, was over "who can build the best Edsel." But the conservative SBC in assembly was not seeing it that way, for in 2004 it voted to sever ninety-nine-year-old ties with the Baptist World Alliance, charging the alliance with becoming "anti-American" and liberal on the Bible and female preachers.[49]

Well before then, in 1998, Everett was tapped to be president of a new seminary, which had its sights on the global picture for world Baptists. It was called the John Leland Center for Theological Studies, named for an early Virginia Baptist preacher who worked with James Madison to promote religious liberty. With Baptist roots, the graduate school is recruiting among all evangelicals, styling itself as a would-be "Fuller Seminary of the East," after the Los Angeles institution that is the nation's largest. "Some of our young students are really dynamic, and asking much better questions than we asked," Everett said. "They don't ask the moderate and fundamentalist questions. They ask about community and authenticity." Being global-oriented, they don't mind being in alliance with a variety of Baptists around the world.

With sufficient attention to current SBC literature, they may also ask about the new theological dispute that has broken out among conservatives themselves: Are Baptists strict Calvinists or Arminians? Calvin

(d. 1564) had argued that God alone chose who would be saved, while Jacob Arminius (d. 1609), a Dutch theologian, rebutted that every person may seek the promise of salvation, thus putting human desire, experience, and effort into the equation. This dispute over God's exact role in soul winning "has been a relatively genteel one, as Baptist battles go, but is not without its passions," said one Baptist historian. While the Calvinists, who organized in the early 1970s as part of the conservative resurgence, cited the Baptist "founders" in the South, the non-Calvinists looked to the 1925 Baptist Faith and Message (BFM), which said all people may receive the grace of salvation. By the time of the 2000 BFM, however, there was a "distinct Calvinist slant to the statement," especially regarding the absolute predestination, or foreknowledge, of God.[50]

Strict Calvinism poses a problem to evangelism, some critics say, because it presumes many people are already lost—thus rendering some evangelism futile. Non-Calvinists hold that an experience of God can prepare any heart for salvation. "Strict Calvinism minimizes individual Christian experience," said Russell H. Dilday, a former seminary president and moderate, explaining why some missionaries will not sign the 2000 statement. The evangelical magazine *Christianity Today* also felt that the 2000 statement was a move toward Calvinist dogma: "Shutting down the debate by convention fiat runs a serious risk." Two seminary presidents in particular are Calvinist standard bearers: R. Albert Mohler, whose school in Louisville, Kentucky, has gathered Calvinist faculty, and Mark Coppenger of Midwestern Seminary in St. Louis, Missouri. This debate over predestination might simply be academic, but in a tradition so dedicated to evangelism it is likely to emerge as one of the new "stress points confronting the SBC." Among conservatives at least, the united front around Bible inerrancy is more important than divisions over who God will or will not save.[51]

Whatever God's disposition in such matters, the Atlanta convention of 1999 set out an evangelistic agenda beginning in 2000: send witnessing teams to Chicago and Phoenix the first year, Boston and Las Vegas in 2001, and Philadelphia and Seattle the year after that. While the assembly in Atlanta had drawn just 11,352 messengers, fewer than expected, some Baptists still felt that the candor was refreshing. "We're late in coming to the cities," said Charles Lyons, a Chicago pastor who said his urban neighborhood was "as much a mission as any foreign country." Frank Lewis, a pastor from Las Vegas who had moved to Nashville, known as the "Southern Baptist Vatican," stated the challenge of the SBC's mission: "We can't put southern churches in the north or west. And we can't put rural churches in the cities."[52]

Even the firebrand Patterson, who leans Arminian in evangelism, said that reaching the cities "will take more than an affirmation of belief in the inerrancy of the Bible." It would take faith and work. Patterson, now a seminary president, was elected in Atlanta to his second year as convention president. It was yet another symbol of how completely the conservative clergy had ousted the moderates. "The war is over," Patterson said after the election.[53]

6

The Minority Challenge

IN HIS LAST SUNDAY SERMON, Martin Luther King Jr. told listeners at the Washington National Cathedral that the worship hour of America fell short. "We must face the sad fact that at eleven o'clock on Sunday morning when we stand to sing 'In Christ there is no East or West,' we stand in the most segregated hour of America," he said.[1] Since King spoke those words in 1968, four days before his assassination, little has changed about Sunday worship in the United States.

While the majority of churches are hardly multicultural, minority congregations may still be the most homogeneous, with all the racial, ethnic, and cultural implications this homogeneity has for the work of their clergy. The story is best told by the three most prominent areas of minority Christian ministry in America: the black, Hispanic, and Korean churches.

King dramatically raised the prominence of the minority minister in the United States. Yet as a Baptist preacher, academically trained and ecclesiastically connected, he represented only one approach to ministry. He took the stance of the civil rights preacher, as he was portrayed on a 1957 cover of *Time* magazine. When in 2001 a *Time* cover featured the second black minister in the magazine's history, the ministry approach was quite different. He was Pentecostal Bishop T. D. Jakes, who rose to prominence on his best-selling book about God's healing for abused black women. A native of West Virginia who had dug ditches to support himself and was self-taught in the Bible, Jakes went on to build a sixteen-thousand-member megachurch in suburban Houston, a haven for music, praise, and personal sanctification.[2]

In the forty years between King and Jakes, the minority population in the United States has not only grown but diversified. Today, blacks,

Hispanics, and Koreans make up more than a quarter of all Americans. Their clergy account for 15 to 25 percent of all the nation's ministers, encompassing the spectrum of styles.[3] Some minority clergy today can be heard preaching that faith is a private affair and others that it is a social revolution. Some extol degrees in divinity while others say the anointing by the Holy Spirit is sufficient for ministry. Some make their churches a place to preserve group identity, and others make it a staging area for social action and even assimilation.

The economic, racial, and educational obstacles faced by minorities has produced a larger share of self-taught, apprenticed, or bivocational ministers for blacks, Hispanics, and Koreans. Yet their presence in North American accredited theological schools has been rising. In the decade after 1992, minority faculty at North America's 243 seminaries grew from 9 percent to over 14 percent. Minority enrollment in the 205 U.S. seminaries has also risen. Black students make up 11.6 percent of seminarians, while Asian enrollment is 7 percent. Hispanic enrollment remains low at 3.5 percent; however, Catholic seminaries report 13 percent.[4]

Of the three minority groups—black, Latino, and Korean—clergy in the first two work in the most difficult environments of poverty and family breakdown.[5] While 8 percent of white Americans suffer poverty, the rate is more than three times as high (26 percent) for blacks and Hispanics, both of whom have younger populations as well. Asian-American poverty is half that of blacks and Hispanics. These two minorities also have been vulnerable to the general decline of two-parent families in the United States. With a family unit defined as a parent and child, the number of white American families with a married couple at home has dropped to 82 percent. But for Hispanics, only 68 percent of families have two parents and for African Americans it is still lower at 47 percent. The duress on Korean ministers is small by comparison.

The nation's one million Korean Americans mostly arrived in the massive migrations of the 1970s and 1980s, an urban middle-class group seeking economic opportunity and escape from political turmoil in South Korea. Half the immigrants were already Christian. But over time, nearly eight in ten (77 percent) of all arrivals joined a Korean-language church, creating one of the nation's most intensely churchgoing groups. Yet for that first generation, the barriers of language and culture proved insurmountable, and many experienced "downward mobility." The church became an even more important place for personal and ethnic support.[6]

In all these ways, when minorities feel less empowered, clergy can assume a prophetic role, which has played out differently in black, Hispanic, and Korean groups. Black sermons in particular are rarely without a theme of oppression, even in middle-class churches. "That will always be a part of our preaching," said Dorothea Belt Stroman, a black minister in the United Methodist Church. "We can't act like it never happened."

Each minority also brings a distinct "sacred cosmos" to the Christian experience. Many Hispanics and Koreans bear it by direct acculturation, as one in four Latinos is foreign born and seven in ten Korean Americans were born abroad. Minority theologians, in fact, will often distance their work from Western influence on Christianity, pointing instead to a more supernatural cosmos of their own ancestral cultures.[7]

The "acids of modernity" have thus had less effect on the religious life of minorities. They have consequently been receptive to Bible literalism, religious festival, and Pentecostal enthusiasm. Their cultures, in fact, are also changing world Christianity. The number of believers is growing in only three places: Africa, Latin America, and Asia.[8]

Since the nation's black clergy emerged as leaders during slavery, they have been an unparalleled mainstay of ministry in the United States. Yet in more recent times, the civil rights movement divided their paths in new and significant ways. First, the call to activism brought out all the conflicting perspectives on the role of the black pastor. And second, by the very success of the civil rights movement, black Americans—part of a growing middle class—have found other avenues to leadership besides the ministry.

When Martin Luther King called for civil disobedience, a senior generation of black Baptist clergy opposed him. A struggle for control over the National Baptist Convention ensued, ending with King and the activist clergy forming a breakaway National Progressive Baptist Convention in 1961. Still other black ministers, however, became restless over "the passive, patient, long-suffering strategies" of King. When the Selma, Alabama, protests in 1966 produced the "black power" movement, the National Committee of Black Churchmen formed to issue a church "Declaration of Black Power." Theologian James Cone later articulated that more militant theme in his *Black Theology and Black Power* (1969), which urged ministers to become a vanguard of class struggle.[9]

But still a fourth powerful voice was heard in the 1960s. It was the growing influence of the largest black Pentecostal denomination, the Church of God in Christ (COGIC). The church grew dramatically as entrepreneurial clergy opened urban congregations that lured young people to join mass choirs. During this same period, the civil rights movement produced its own musical highlights, such as the a cappella Gospel music of the Freedom Singers, whose songs became famous at the student sit-ins in Nashville. But the Pentecostals, who preached self-help rather than street demonstrations, turned music into a powerful commercial and cultural force. The music filled sanctuaries and inspired men such as Jakes to found their own churches.[10]

When a sampling of top black clergy met in Detroit for the "State of the

Black Union: The Black Church" forum in 2003, diversity was in full display. Chicago Pastor Jeremiah Wright, who served in the predominantly white United Church of Christ, declared that the black church had become "a kaleidoscope," not a monolith. He praised the activist young ministers and divinity students who surrounded King, but said they were a breed "you do not find overwhelmingly in the pulpits" today. Theologian James Cone continued on his liberation theme: The church must save the body as well as the soul. "The black church has to be political," he said. Christians bear witness to a crucifixion, which is a gospel of struggle and "failure" in the eyes of the world. But now, he said, "the black church is concerned with saving its own life because it's so interested in the gospel of success."[11]

Gardner Taylor, first president of the Progressive Baptists, said the African church began as a protest to slavery but now is a place where black folks draw identity in an alien society. "The church began in oppression," he said. "When we get too far away from that we lose perspective. We lose the sense of the church's energy and its power." Yet one Pentecostal minister begged to differ. Marvin Winans, pastor of Perfecting Church in Detroit, said too much emphasis on politics and race undermines the church's universal role. "To think that the black church is simply something born out of slavery is incorrect," said Winans, a COGIC minister and successful recording artist. "The church was born out of God."[12]

From Boston had come Eugene Rivers, a Pentecostal preacher, ex-gang member, and Harvard University graduate. While the church is "losing a lot of young black men," he said, it prefers to "get high" on the Holy Ghost: "We worship worship. We praise praise." The cover of *Newsweek* had featured Rivers in 2000, reporting on his projects to end street violence in south Boston. "We have a black underclass," he told the forum. "And we have a growing megachurch phenomenon which is not, in too many cases, connected to the lived reality of poor black people."[13]

The conference was a showcase of talented men and women who had entered ministry. Their work was carried out, however, at a time when careers in politics, sports, entertainment, and business were held out as the main illustrations of black success. Yet the religious calling had preceded them all, for the church was "the first institution blacks controlled." They were prominent evangelists in the Great Awakenings, and an estimated half of all black leaders before the Civil War days were clergy. The independent black church grew exponentially during Reconstruction, spurring ministers into electoral politics and "public offices from local school boards to the U.S. Congress."[14]

At the turn of the century, W. E. B. Du Bois praised the preacher as "the most unique personality developed by the Negro . . . A leader, a politician, an orator, a 'boss,' an intriguer, an idealist." Du Bois had also predicted, however, that their leadership role would be eclipsed by a new moneyed class: "farmers and gardeners, the well-paid porters and artisans, the businessmen—all those with property and money." In his day, King once more gave the position of minister prominence. But after passage of the 1965 Voting Rights Act, secular opportunities called. The number of black elected officials soared from 100 in that momentous year to more than 8,000 in 2000.[15]

Yet the political opportunities have had two significant effects. Black talent began to bypass the step through ministry and move directly into politics. And by 2001, nobody in the Congressional Black Caucus had a clergy background. Through the 1980s and 1990s, *Ebony* magazine's annual roundup of the "100 Most Influential" listed "fewer ministers and more politicians," said political scientist Ronald Walters. With the increasing cost of higher education, talented young blacks saw a greater payback in secular careers than in the kind of divinity degree earned by King.[16]

At the same time, however, lifetime clergy were urged to play an increased, if temporary, role in civic leadership. The Black Clergy and Politics Survey of 2000, for example, found that nearly a tenth of the pastors had been elected to something, suggesting "that hundreds of black clergy have served in elective office over the last thirty years." The increase "during the 1990s was fairly dramatic," moreover, for a third had held office in that decade.[17] Yet, for higher office and certainly national office, the secular route seems to have become the dominant avenue for black leadership.

These modern trends bring to mind an early debate over black advancement. Earlier in the century, African-American leaders disagreed on whether leadership should be achieved by a more elite path, open to the few, or a general one, followed by the many. Du Bois had urged that a "talented tenth" of blacks excel in the liberal arts and thus play a role in politics and culture. In contrast, Booker T. Washington emphasized that ordinary blacks should learn industrial and trade skills. Early black clergy had also espoused the two roads, some adopting the educated formality of the Anglican or Presbyterian traditions, others responding to the warm emotionalism of the Baptist and Methodist frontier revivals.

Today the pattern continues, but with the non-elite forces having prevailed, since most black Christians and clergy today are Baptists or Pentecostals, followed by Methodists. From the start, blacks melded Christianity with African and Caribbean customs. The features of modern worship—the "whoop" and shout of the preacher's gravelly voice, the call-response between pulpit and pew, and the bodily "falling out" of worshipers—have roots in the slave churches. Well suited for frontier revivals, the cathartic worship struck some churchmen, such as Bishop Daniel Payne of the African Methodist Episcopal Church (AME), as "ridiculous and heathenish." Despite disdain from some, those African traits were polished into an array of modern-day arts of worship. "When it comes to rhetoric," said one Southern Baptist, "the best Anglo preachers on their best days don't preach as well as a good black preacher on his worst day."[18]

After the Civil War, the black clergy adopted the "ideology of separatism" espoused during the Reconstruction era. They formed their own church organizations, founding the eight black Baptist associations of today and expanding the black-founded Methodist Episcopal churches, of which there are now three. An exodus from white churches fueled the growth. By 1860, for example, nearly two-thirds of blacks in the southern Methodist Episcopal Church had left. Still today, however, United Methodism has the largest remnant of black clergy and communicants.[19]

The new African-American churches grew most rapidly in the rural "black belt" of the South. They served 80 percent of all black churchgoers, at least through 1900. The next few decades swiftly reshaped black society and the nature of ministry. Beginning around World War I, blacks began a great migration to northern cities. Between 1870 and 1970, seven million African Americans were part of "the largest internal migration America has experienced." The clergy moved also. This created an "absentee pastorate" in rural churches and the new and complex world of the urban church.[20]

The first migration, between 1910 and 1930, involved 1.2 million blacks. It coincided with the rise of Pentecostalism, which was predominantly an urban phenomenon, especially in the so-called storefront churches. The migrants were channeled into an "assigned place" in the cities, so churches were restricted geographically, often to older edifices bought from departing Protestant or Jewish congregations. For blacks also, "much of the socioeconomic class divisions began with urbanization." The clergy followed the stratification in worship styles and in economic rankings.[21]

As late as the 1980s, however, a true picture of the African-American pastor could not emerge, so informal and unreliable were the data. As historian C. Eric Lincoln explained: "Poor record keeping has been one of the major sources for conflict in church disputes and schisms." Through the 1980s Lincoln and his colleague Lawrence Mamiya partly filled the void with the first national survey of rural and urban black ministers, reported in *The Black Church in America*.[22]

As the great migration would suggest, only 20 to 25 percent of black churches are now located in rural America. Their clergy are more likely to serve more than one congregation. The rural ministers usually have to supplement their incomes. They mostly live in cities, traveling out for worship times to churches whose "buildings range from dilapidated shacks to elaborate modern structures." Ever since the civil rights era, these rural churches have expanded their activities and no longer act as insular institutions. Now, half of them actively work with a civil rights organization. They tend to have stronger Sunday school and youth programs than churches in the cities. And their legacy is great: They were centers for slave rebellions, civil rights protests, and mobilization of the black vote.[23]

The migration produced "a transfer of membership from rural" churches into the new urban congregations. The cities also produced "a small but steadily growing population of unchurched blacks, mainly composed of black men." Key city churches became a base for black politicians, yet they still focused mostly on meeting spiritual needs. Nearly nine in ten (88 percent) of the nation's urban black congregations met "in regular church buildings," while the rest (12 percent) used "storefronts, rented halls, and individual homes." With the growth of suburbs around Atlanta, Nashville, Philadelphia, Washington, D.C., and Baltimore, many of the urban churches bought land and moved to where the black middle class was making its home.[24]

Whatever their station, the clergy ranked preaching and teaching as their highest priorities, and the better educated ministers tended to sponsor the more "innovative programs." Rural and urban clergy alike overwhelmingly endorsed the "civil rights protest role" of ministers and the "social prophecy" role of the church. What is more, the civil rights theme has widely influenced black preaching, with two-thirds of clergy employing it regularly. In the same ferment, other black thinkers, often in seminaries, produced new political theologies of black consciousness, black power, and liberation. Their visions, however, never seemed to touch older ministers, though clergy under forty and Methodists in particular were open to the more radical outlooks.[25]

Central to the new consciousness was the black Christ, an image marshaled to create political solidarity in the churches. More than twenty years later, however, "those who imagined Christ as black were not more likely to believe that churches . . . should be involved in politics," according to a study. Less than a third of African Americans viewed Jesus as black. A larger share (63 percent) believed that "Christ was beyond color." In their own talks with clergy, Lincoln and Mamiya concluded that the new liberation theologies had "been unable to move beyond the middle-class origins," even as supposedly "bottom-up" movements. The "older tradition of liberation"—self-help, work, education, saving, and buying property—remained widespread.[26]

Both views still percolate in black ministry today, as a study of ten Philadelphia pastors active in community development showed. All but one of the pastors held traditional or fundamentalist theologies. But they diverged most on diagnosing social problems and proposing solutions. One group, inclined toward coalition building, advocacy, and "disruptive strategies" against an unjust system, reflected in the rhetoric of justice, war, sin, and holy power. The other group of "traditional" clergy, who produced the more concrete successes, worked solo. They used pastoral leverage with city hall or local businesses. The rhetoric was entrepreneurial, using the themes of negotiation, integrity, and leadership: "They did not see the system as quite so alienating."[27]

The growing sophistication of black clergy on such economic projects was noted in *The Black Church* and, in more recent years, studies about the new faith-based welfare initiative. Yet the black clergy are aging, and while their incomes have risen, they still earn just two-thirds of what white ministers earn today. While *The Black Church* pegged their median age at about fifty-one, it has risen slightly since then as "newcomers" to ministry tend to be older. *The Black Church* also found that half of the churches had not called a candidate to ministry for the past five years. Still, a "very important finding" was that a very small number of churches produced high rates of clergy candidates. In particular, a precious 3.6 percent of congregations had nine or more people called to ministry in that half decade. These churches obviously focused on recruitment and were the places that theological schools should focus, the study recommended.[28]

The financial security of taking on a lifelong ministry has become no small matter for attracting new ministerial talent. There will always be glowing exceptions, such as a Bishop Jakes, who has a $1.7 million home and wears a large diamond ring. But what *The Black Church* found in the 1980s is far more typical: "Close to half the black clergy nationwide must work at another full-time occupation." New polls find the same is true today. Still, the number of clergy who earned at least $33,000 has risen in that time (in constant dollars) from just 12 to 27 percent. Medical and retirement benefits are more commonly provided by the church today, although, only a third to half of black ministers enjoy them. The secular jobs black clergy hold, however, have changed dramatically since the 1980s. The blue-collar and farm work once so common has disappeared. White-collar and clerical (72 percent) and service jobs (25 percent) have taken their place.[29]

The picture fits other reports of more second-career African Americans, often employed in government or the military, feeling called to minister. Of all American clergy who had secular careers before ordination, blacks are the oldest and most likely to have gone ahead without academic studies. Overall, however, theological training has risen. While *The Black Church* found just one in ten clergy graduating from "an accredited divinity school or seminary," 46 percent of ministers now report having a master's of divinity degree or higher. The current trend of entrepreneurial ministry, however, is strong, following the style of COGIC or Baptist churches and increasing the portion of second-career pastors. These "newcomers"—in ministry less than ten years—are half as likely (22 percent) to hold a graduate divinity degree.[30]

Such educational choices, of course, were a major topic at the Detroit forum on the state of the black church. Pastor Wright was derisive of untrained ministry. "I cannot be a doctor if I don't go to med school," he said. "But all I got to do is turn around my collar and 'hallelujah,' and I have the anointing and I have fifty thousand Negroes following me." Pastor Winans had a respectful reply. "I believe we should be trained," he said. "But can you imagine what educational institutions will charge for us to receive eternal life or the knowledge of Jesus Christ? How much tuition would it cost us to be filled with the Holy Spirit? How much would they charge us to be healed from our diseases?"[31]

If ever these twain should meet, some believe it will happen in a new fusion being called Neo-Pentecostalism, a spirit-filled style of religious expression bursting out in the more formal denominations, such as the AME Church.

That story begins with John Bryant, the restless son of an AME bishop, who was ordained to lead a church in Cambridge, Massachusetts. Before taking the position, he had served a year in Liberia with the Peace Corps and come in contact with "the 'spirit dimension' of Africans," which included healing, ceremonies, and "inexplicable" occurrences. In Massachusetts, the regional COGIC bishop tutored him in "the doctrines and techniques" of that Pentecostal tradition. "Bryant felt that his own denomination had emphasized 'the Father' and 'the Son' of the Trinity and had largely neglected the Holy Spirit," said historian Mamiya. The church in Cambridge became known as the "rocking church" for its use of drums and electrified Gospel music, which "helped to attract black young people."[32]

In 1975, Bryant transferred that approach to a historic church of the denomination, Bethel AME in Baltimore, which for generations had worshiped in a tall gothic sanctuary in the heart of an inner-city neighborhood. After his first year there, Bryant commissioned a purple-toned and abstract mural on black consciousness for the wall behind the pulpit. Then he introduced drums and electronic Gospel music. When he moved on in 1988 to become a bishop, his protégés spread Neo-Pentecostalism to AMEs in other cities, such as Los Angeles.

The pastor who succeeded Bryant, Frank M. Reid III, was no less active. He mounted a vigorous but unsuccessful campaign for Maryland political office, and the church bought suburban property. Zoning disputes have slowed the possible move to build a new megachurch, but not ruled it out entirely. What differs about this new church movement, supporters argue, is the pastoral leadership: accountable and wise in finances, and innovative with programs that touch not only poverty and parenting but the spiritual lives of the middle class and youth. Some senior clergy remain skeptical. "The good thing it did was get people back into church," said AME minister Leon Lipscomb, a thirty-year veteran of the pulpit. "But the shouting doesn't last. You have to sustain them with a good theology." For his part, "My job is to challenge them to think."[33]

Whether people are drawn by theology or by enthusiasm, the larger the numbers, the greater the chance, perhaps, of achieving what Bethel has accomplished: 40 percent of its participants are men. The plight of the black church today, Lincoln has argued, is the lack of male attendance, averaging only 20 percent. "The young professional woman's problem is there's nobody there," he said. "The females are in the church. The males are outside the church. It's about as acute as a class difference." Unemployment and imprisonment have cut into male participation rates. But Baptist minister Carl Tilgham believes the church has lost what the black Muslims have found—an aggressive effort to build male identity and moral beliefs. "With black folks, it's up front and personal," Tilgham said. "You don't come tiptoe. You want to get loud, I can get loud with you." He cited the appeal of the Nation of Islam and other sectarian groups. "Muslims don't play," he said. "Jehovah's Witnesses; they don't play. See, Christianity has taken this 'lite love' thing. We lowered the standards."[34]

In the years before he died, Lincoln had joined an experimental church in Durham, North Carolina, called Reconciliation United Methodist. The pastor was black, his associate white. The congregation drew American Indians, Hispanics, East Indians, and Koreans. Worship styles were being worked out and so were the stigmas of races. "The black church has to make a determination about whether it is going to remain an ethnic or racial group, or move toward a common communion with other churches," Lincoln said in 2001. A year later, a decades-long project of "pan-Methodism" to unite three historic black denominations and the United Methodist Church was finally voted down. "We all want to be what we are," said African Methodist Episcopal Zion minister George W. Maize. "We need some model to become unified without losing our identity."[35]

In 2003 the U.S. Census Bureau announced that Latinos had become the nation's largest minority, surpassing African Americans. Like Father Miguel Solorzano, a Catholic priest in Houston, nearly seven in ten Latinos living in the United States are from Mexico. More Latinos simply means more Catholics to minister to, said Solorzano, spokesman for the National Association of Hispanic Priests.[36]

Despite predictions that Protestant evangelism would erode the Catholic identification of Latinos, immigration has kept it at a high plateau for years. Yet more than any other minority group, Spanish-speaking Catholics struggle to find enough ministers from within their own ethnic enclaves. At the turn of the century, nearly 4,000 U.S. parishes (20.6 percent) reported a "majority Hispanic presence," yet just 2,900 Hispanic priests—500 of them born in the United States—are on hand.[37]

"A few years ago there was an effort to bring priests from Latin America to minister here," said Father Solorzano. "But the main goal is to get Hispanics born in the U.S. into the American seminaries. That is the great challenge." For the Catholic Church funding is not a great problem, as the institution is eager to support college and graduate school training for the priesthood. Solorzano, who finished college in Mexico, completed his seminary training in America on scholarships.

The main obstacle to recruiting young Mexicans to ministry is their lack of immigration papers, inability to speak English, and need of a high school diploma. "While they are illegal aliens, we cannot even sponsor them," Solorzano said. "It's easier to get somebody from Mexico than to get somebody who has been here since he was nine, and who is now seventeen, but entered the country illegally." But then again, "Immigrants from Mexico are not thinking of entering seminary. They are thinking of the American dream, like work, make some money, help their relatives."

North American Catholicism, streamlined under the Second Vatican Council (1962–65), has focused its religious life on Christ and the Eucharist. In this context, Latin devotions stand apart. Their hearts have turned to the Virgin Mary. What draws them most are the festivals of national saints and family rites of passage. "Our culture requires us to celebrate," said Ana Maria Diaz-Stevens, coauthor of *Recognizing the Latin Resurgence in U.S. Religion*. "Everything that is important to an individual is important to the group." Always lacking priests, she argues, Spanish-speaking immigrants pioneered lay ministry in North America (though European immigrants claim likewise). "The Hispanics," she said, "prepared the way for that kind of change in Vatican II."[38]

The church has called a significant number of Hispanic married men to be deacons. But Solorzano said nothing easily substitutes for a real priest. Parishioners "would rather receive communion from the hands of a priest than from a Eucharistic minister," he said. "Even on Ash Wednesday, we see the lines: everyone would like to get the ashes from the priest." Still, Hispanics reportedly make up more than half of all students in Catholic institutes offering certificates in theology for lay parish leadership.

Solorzano said the growing number of second-career men entering the priesthood is also promising. He is most enthusiastic, though, about a teaching movement for young people, the Neocatechumenal Way, founded by an artist-musician in a Madrid slum during the Second Vatican Council. Applied in the United States, the concept is to create a nurturing environment akin to a religious order or community, but without formal structures. "They invite the teenagers to consider the priesthood," Solorzano said. "So for those who say, 'Yes, I would like to think about it,' they go to a regional meeting once a month." The project, which John Paul II called "an itinerary of Catholic formation, valid for our society and our times," is active in a quarter of U.S. dioceses and more than 150 parishes.

Participants encourage each other through college, hopefully as a prelude to seminary, said Solorzano: "Vocations among Hispanics are growing in these new movements."[39]

Other movements are also speaking to Hispanic Catholics. By one estimate, a fifth of all Latino Catholics (5.4 million) are "Catholic charismatics" who combine "gifts of the Spirit" with parish liturgy and prayer groups. The charismatic movement has circulated in U.S. Catholicism since the 1960s and was approved during the Second Vatican Council. Along with the festivals of saints, it has proven to have great Latino appeal. "The expression of our religiosity is mostly in the form of external manifestations," said Father Mateo Perez, and is "experienced more at a level of emotion than at an intellectual level."[40]

The parallel to charismatic Protestantism has not gone unnoticed, said Assemblies of God minister Esdras Betancourt, who once headed a Hispanic division for the National Association of Evangelicals. "They sort of imitate the Pentecostal church in how they worship," he said. "The main difference is they will have a Mass by a priest." Such types of worship intensity can make a big difference in church participation as well, according to some studies. While just 24 percent of Hispanic Catholics may be called "committed" because of regular churchgoing, evangelical levels exceed that greatly: "Church attendance rates are substantially higher among Latino Protestants than among Latino Catholics."[41]

U.S. Catholic bishops have often noted the sheep stealing of the evangelical sects. But when it comes to Pentecostalism, that force is consuming all brands of American Protestantism as well: "In short, 28 percent of all Latinos are Pentecostal or Charismatic." Part of the appeal is the localism and lack of structure, said Marcos Rivera, pastor of Primitive Christian Church in New York City: "Denomination in the Latin mindset is not that important." The Pentecostals have grown on such strengths as proselytism, indigenous clergy, church plantings, prayer groups, healing ministries, pastoral and lay leadership opportunities, and roles for women. Indeed, all the churches have proved beneficial for immigrant women, who find them a moderating influence on the "machismo" role of Hispanic men, which often undermines fidelity in the family.[42]

Historians have long described how immigrants turn to religion for identity, but also to their religious institutions as places to take on social roles denied to them as minorities. While recruitment of Hispanic clergy has proved difficult, the opportunity to take leadership still is attractive. Betancourt, the Assemblies minister, said the real obstacle to turning out skilled pastors is financial. "We don't have any problem getting people interested in ministry," he said. "Our main problem is getting money to train them." Membership growth in the Assemblies for a decade has been from Hispanics, he said. When leaders emerge, "They train all the way from correspondence courses to two-year Bible school, four-year Bible school, or on to seminary." Some are recruited by mainline Protestants who want a Latino ministry, and an estimated 5 percent of these new Hispanic evangelical clergy are women.[43]

Ministers such as Edwin Hernandez, an Adventist with a doctorate in religion, believe that education beyond the Bible institute is the key to minority success in the United States. "A better-educated clergy will bridge immigrants with the mainstream," he said. But at that academic tier, Hispanics say it is hard to feel culturally at home. The nation's accredited theology schools today enroll about 2,400 Hispanics, or 3.5 percent of all seminarians. Hispanic faculty amount to about 100, or 2.7 of all the teachers. "Wherever a Latino is present in the institution, students are attracted," Hernandez said. But still, "theology is for the most part taught from a European, White Anglo-Saxon perspective. There's a rich tradition of U.S. Latino theology, both Protestant and Catholic. But these views and biographies are not in the curriculum."[44]

Hispanic clergy most often provide a spiritual message, extending from individual to family and church, but stopping short of any call for social action. Only a fifth (22 percent) of all Latino churchgoers, for example, have ever heard the minister or priest urge them "to engage in activities" relating to social, educational, or political topics. Even though they are not hearing the message in church, Hispanics—who still have very low voter turnouts—say they want to get involved. Hispanic pastors and priests "have not capitalized on their parishioners' desire to become more active in public life."[45]

Hispanic religious culture is already influencing the majority churches in America, providing the margin of growth for several denominations, including the Southern Baptist Convention, which sees its main growth in Latino and Korean start-up churches. As Betancourt likes to put it: "The Hispanics are spicing up the church. They are the salsa picante, the hot sauce. Salsa picante is outselling catsup."

Yet their presence is not as permanent as that of past immigrants. Nor do they accept the past notion of entering a "melting pot" on arrival in America. "Hispanics are characterized by a strong sense of individual nationalism," said Father Perez, arguing that they see the United States as "a halfway house, a retreat center, a hideout or a [re-supply] center, a temporary stopping-off place in life's journey." Compared to the past, fewer Hispanic immigrants are becoming U.S. citizens, either because of legal obstacles or lack of interest. While 74.2 percent of Hispanics arriving before 1970 became citizens, according to the census, the rate has dropped to 23.9 percent for the 1980s and 6.7 percent for the 1990s. "They may live and work here, but their heart tells them that home is where they came from and where the rest of their family is," Perez said. This has "strong implications for ministry."[46]

Hispanic churches are more dedicated to "preserving" ethnic heritage than other U.S. congregations, according to surveys. The largest heritage at stake is Mexican, which accounts for most Latinos, followed in number by Puerto Ricans (9 percent) and Cubans (4 percent), and the rest are mostly a plurality of Central and South Americans. Despite the nationalist tendencies, and even differing social classes, Hernandez said that those barriers are being overcome as immigrants join mixed Hispanic churches. Even then, however, the strengths and weaknesses of ethnic insularity continue to be an issue. An ethnic church reinforces family identity and morals, he said, which helps youth avoid delinquency. Yet ethnic and linguistic isolation may also undermine an immigrant's chances of social advancement. In Hispanic immigrant churches, the second generation "walks in a dual world, bilingual and bicultural," Hernandez said. They feel the tug-of-war between isolation and assimilation most. "In many cases, you have literally two congregations in one."[47]

The Korean-American clergy, whose estimated 3,500 churches serve the nation's one million Koreans, are experiencing the same generational dynamic, but perhaps even more dramatically.[48]

In 2003, many Korean-American Christians celebrated their centenary in the United States, begun when Koreans joined a small Methodist mission in Hawaii for migrants who worked in the sugar cane fields. Yet nearly all Korean Americans today arrived during migrations of the 1970s and 1980s, which were followed by a dramatic drop-off after 1990. As a result, Korean immigration is likely to have been a "one generation phenomenon" that produced two distinct groups: parents who speak Korean and children who speak English.[49]

When the centenary was celebrated, the two sides of minority ministry—the ethnic particular and the Christian universal—were played out by Korean believers. United Methodist Bishop Hae-Jong Kim hoped the event would "not be just a 'Korean' celebration but a churchwide one" in which all believers, meaning even the predominantly white church, would take notice. But this was also a particular piece of Korean heritage to be marked. Without white participation, Koreans in United Methodism joined a drive to raise $60,000 for a Korean mission center in Mongolia.[50]

While the first Koreans entering American Christianity joined in the Hawaiian sugar cane fields in 1903, the first continental Korean church was a Methodist one in San Francisco in 1905. The second was a Presbyterian church in Los Angeles, founded the following year. Today, about half of all Korean-American Christians are Presbyterian, 20 percent are Roman Catholic, and 14 percent are United Methodist. The remaining 16 percent are spread somewhat evenly across Baptist, holiness, Adventist, evangelical, and non-denominational groups. They are all working out what it means to be Korean in particular, but Christian in general, in the

United States. And with the emergence of the first English-language ministries at the end of the 1980s, the stage is set for "proto-congregations" to
emerge as fully assimilated churches.[51]

Koreans are "so well organized religiously" that their ministries have
gained significant attention in wider American Christianity. More than
seven in ten Korean Americans affiliate with an immigrant (Korean-
speaking) congregation. Their theological tenets have been measured as
more conservative than the beliefs of Hispanics and African Americans.
While half of the immigrant generation was Christian when it departed
for America, another 30 percent (who were non-Christians) joined
churches after arriving. Given the high esteem awarded to senior pastors,
the churches "enjoy a surplus of pastor candidates." A 1990 survey of Koreans in Chicago found one ordained Protestant minister for every sixty-
nine adults, typifying the "abundant supply of Christian ministers from
the home country." Young Korean Americans "aspire to clergy careers,"
helping keep many U.S. seminaries at full enrollment. And phenomena
such as the Yoido Full Gospel Church in Seoul, which claims to be the
world's largest, have been a harbinger of Pentecostal revivals in the
United States.[52]

While Korean Americans struggle with questions of assimilation and
generation change, their church ministries have been the talk of U.S. denominations. Presbyterian leader Louis Weeks, president of Union Theological Seminary in Richmond, Virginia, describes their contribution using
the New Testament concept of many gifts, or members, in the body of
Christ. "Different parts of the family have different functions," he said.
"And I, for example, have come to know the Korean-American church
quite well, and there you have an almost fundamentalist view of Scripture.
And also zeal for ministry. But they are not judgmental on other parts of
the family." Weeks is also enchanted by their tradition of unison prayer,
which emerged during Christian revivals in Korea a century earlier, particular at dawn prayer meetings. "It sounds like glossolalia [speaking in
tongues]," he said. "It's absolutely wonderful to participate in that."[53]

Those characteristics point to the history of Christianity in Korea,
where the faith was first brought by Catholic missionaries but then
planted in new ways by Protestants at the turn of the twentieth century.
Just before Japan occupied the Korean Peninsula in 1905, annexing it until
1945, Christian revivals had broken out around Pyongyang, a large city
that became the capital of North Korea. Whereas the Japanese suppressed
the church, the communist invasion that prevailed in the North destroyed
it. Christian refugees flooded to the South into Seoul and formed its
urban middle class. During the economic and political turmoil of the
1970s, this skilled and mostly Christian population migrated in waves to
the United States, which had opened its doors to Asia under a new 1965
immigration law.

Faced with language barriers and a range of cultural obstacles, Korean Americans soon became frustrated with the economic challenges they encountered. Immigration nearly stopped after 1990. An emerging democracy in South Korea opened up new economic opportunities there, while financial prospects remained dim in the United States. "It is not surprising, therefore, that they have turned to religion" in America, said an immigrant Korean-American student. As a social institution, the immigrant church became the primary center of shared experience, ethnic identity, and opportunities—especially for males from a Confucian culture—to fill leadership posts. In one study of diverse Korean churches, 23 percent of the membership held staff positions such as minister, elder, deacon, and exhorter. In Korean churches that were Presbyterian, the lay position of elder was so highly esteemed that only 15 percent of congregants had held it, usually a wealthier and more theologically conservative gentleman. In the predominantly white Presbyterian churches in the United States, elder is a widely held position, a role served by 50 to 60 percent of a congregation at some time.[54]

Over the century, however, the great mission denominations that aided Koreans—now the United Methodist Church and the Presbyterian Church (USA)—have become much more liberal. Koreans by comparison are far more conservative, sharing a theological "proclivity toward personal salvation" but not Christian social activism. Korean clergy have thus taken a variety of stances toward the national bodies. In 1976, they founded the independent, orthodox, and single-language Korean Presbyterian Church in America. In 2001, this Presbyterian body reported 305 churches, 54,000 members, and 570 clergy.[55]

The United Methodist Church has about 100,000 Korean-American members who are served primarily by 540 Korean clergy in 420 Korean congregations, mostly Korean speaking. Korean clergy also might receive a "cross-racial appointment" and serve in a predominantly white or black church. What is more, a fifth of these Korean Methodist ministers are women, still frowned on by many Korean immigrants. To avoid the denominational advocacy of women in ministry, in fact, many Korean congregations have sought autonomy within the Methodist and Presbyterian systems. Others have affiliated with the more conservative Southern Baptist Convention, independent Bible fellowships, or the orthodox Presbyterian Church in America, which does not ordain women.[56]

Often Koreans rent space for Sunday afternoon worship. It is also the case, as in 1997 with Broughton Presbyterian Church in New Jersey, that a dying congregation hands over its building to a vibrant Korean one. The fast-growing Korean churches have brought forty thousand new members to the Presbyterian Church (USA), a liberal mainline church that lost a million members over three decades. Koreans have also played a role in opposing some calls in the denomination to liberalize both theology and views on homosexuality. "Rather than saying we are conservative, we say we are more biblical," said Pastor Chong An Lee, leader of the New Jersey congregation. Another pastor from New Jersey, where a high concentration of Koreans that work in New York live, said, "American Presbyterians lack that explicit evangelism—the idea of spreading the gospel."[57]

Korean academics, some of whom are active in churches, have studied the growth. Part of the ethnic appeal, they report, is the chance for members to "expand their social networks." This had made Korean Americans adept at "congregation hopping." Half of Korean churchgoers have belonged to their congregations for no more than six years and a third no more than three years. Once committed, Koreans invest undivided attention in a congregation, with no outside affiliations. Yet the "rapid turnover," often involving long drives to new locations, is part and parcel of immigrants expanding their social and business networks as a family's needs change. Korean churches tend to be small. And they are fractious enough to regularly produce new churches with new pastors. In nearly all cases, older men who speak only Korean lead the church. And by one account, a Confucian ethic of teaching maintains: "Pastors at Korean immigrant churches preach the Bible message every Sunday, and church members are expected to accept the message as the will of God."[58]

While the founders of the immigrant churches are aging, the so-called 1.5 generation is in its thirties and forties and the "second generation" is college age. The collegians, often unable to understand the Korean sermons, have either joined a "silent exodus" or looked for new avenues of ministry. Most common is to start an English ministry, supervised under an elder or senior pastor. That was a step taken as late as 1989 by the large Young Nak Presbyterian Church in Los Angeles, which bears the name of the famed Pyongyang church that was central to early revivals in northern Korea. At the Presbyterian Church of Minnesota, associate Pastor Jin S. Kim is taking this new direction, but with some resistance. Born in Korea, Kim emigrated in 1975, graduated from Georgia Tech, and earned his ministerial degree at Princeton Theological Seminary. "We want to avoid the ghettoization and cultural isolation so common among Korean churches," he said of his English ministry.[59]

By some estimates, it will take twenty-five to forty years for the traditional immigrant churches to change over to some form of English-speaking congregation. In that slow transition, moreover, two generations of clergy have already emerged. The younger often have more advanced degrees and speak English. Many churches prefer an immigrant pastor, forcing the young clergy to branch into new kinds of ministry. Regardless of denomination, except Roman Catholic, the second generation is evangelical. It uses contemporary "'Vineyard' style" praise music. And it cooperates with parachurch groups such as Campus Crusade, InterVarsity, and Young Life. Just as St. Paul had accommodated Gentiles in the face of

Jewish law, said one second-generation pastor, the immigrant leaders should start making "major cultural concessions in order to effectively minister to Americanized Korean Americans."[60]

Fortunately for the second generation, evangelicalism, with its strict moral norms, matches the traditional Confucian standards of their upbringing. Being evangelical also is a bridge to American culture, including opportunities for women and more negotiating room with Korean parents, who otherwise demand "filial piety," namely acquiescence. A similar cultural adaptation in South Korea itself, according to some, allowed the evangelical explosion of the 1960s to happen, typified by the Yoido Full Gospel Church of Pastor Paul Y. Cho. The historic Korean belief in "hananim"—or "God in heaven"—is unique in Asia and a good fit with Christianity. Yet just as important, some believe, was the Korean reliance on shamans: for centuries these ceremonial and dramatic individuals mediated with the gods or spirits to aid people in the "fulfillment of material wishes."[61]

To succeed in Korea, Christianity "had to be 'shamanized,'" said one Korean sociologist. The South Korean theologian Jing Yong Chung said: "Korean Christians' attendance at church, and their enthusiasm for dawn prayers and generosity in offering to the church are all intimately linked to their desire for this-worldly wish fulfillment." The Korean church, to be sure, has always been a center for social and political struggles. The Hawaiian cane workers sent wages to the liberation movement against Japan. In 1992, church leaders helped bring the peace after riots in Los Angeles destroyed $500 million in Korean property. Yet Korean faith mostly fosters pietism. So a shamanistic Christianity, with its pleading to God for good fortune, has, "catered to this-worldly, materialistic, fatalistic, magical, and even utilitarian tendencies of Koreans." Korea's fastest growing churches have featured sermons on healings and blessings. When the Gallup organization surveyed South Korean Christians, half said heaven is in this world, not the next.[62]

When Cho began his church with five members in 1958, he was part of a burgeoning Pentecostal and missionary movement. "From the beginning of any church," he said later, "missions should be a priority." His contemporary ministry at a church claiming six hundred thousand members has preached the "threefold blessing of Christ": health, prosperity, and salvation. When Holy Spirit revivals in the 1990s drew thousands to churches in Toronto and Brownsville, Florida, some of the leaders cited Cho's predictions of an outpouring. Cho had also studied America's "health and wealth" gospel, drawing him into this state-side controversy as well (see Chapter 7). Yet Korean culture offered something unique. Missionaries had long observed it, and contemporary observers still note how Korean shamanism's "image of a spirit-filled world seems to add to the appeal of pentecostal or 'full gospel' streams of Christianity."[63]

Historians have also noted how immigrants to America will assimilate almost anything—except their religion. Their religious identity, in fact, becomes stronger. The young leaders say the next church must offer Korean Americans "distinctiveness," a core faith and ethnic pride but also a comfortable foot in American culture. Korean churches could well evangelize non-Koreans as well. While some lament a "silent exodus" of the young, the vitality—and confidence of Korean Christian identity is abundant. As the president of the elders' board at the New Jersey congregation said: "We are closer to God. That's why attending a Korean church is better than American churches." One young Korean American, appreciating his ancestral traditions, added: "The more you believe in God, the more Korean you tend to be."[64]

When Martin Luther King Jr. appeared on the 1957 cover of *Time*, he was just twenty-six, the son of a Baptist minister in Atlanta and a recent graduate with a Ph.D. in religion and philosophy. At the time, the reformist ideal for American race relations was integration, especially for public services and political rights. Yet a leading analyst of that day, the black sociologist E. Franklin Frazier, said in *The Negro Church in America* that its "backwardness" blocked the very assimilation that blacks would benefit from.[65]

In the decades since, that "myth and metaphor of the melting pot," especially for racial minorities, has been largely rejected. Minority ministry today operates in a variety of possible approaches to multi-racial America. There is far more integration than in the past, but probably a predominance of practical and amicable separatism. Minority ministers, speaking to the stresses of their constituents, lay out hopes in heaven and on earth. Many live in what one Korean writer called "an ambiguous vision" of ministry—one that focuses "on the needs of Korean Americans while theoretically welcoming people of all races."[66]

7

Spirit Filled

WHEN THE JESUS PEOPLE arrived in Spokane, Washington, around 1972, the local clergy were not altogether pleased with this new kind of ministry. After bursting on the California scene in 1967, the movement had made its way up the Pacific coast to the Northwest. The guitar music, long hair, and "One Way" symbol attracted high schoolers to "happenings" at Manito Park, near the city center.

"Thousands of kids would gather," recalled John Odean, a Spokane native who was "born again" during the activity. Downtown shoppers were "being accosted" with a little newspaper, *The Truth*. "It was driving city hall nuts," Odean said. Mainline churches, such as his own, frowned on what looked more like counterculture than religion. "They wanted nothing to do with these hippies. Back then it was, 'We save 'em, we shave 'em.'"[1]

Looking back three decades later, Manito Park may be seen as part of a "re-invention" of ministry in the United States. While Spokane caught the tail wind, Southern California was taken by storm. Odean, who went to Los Angeles for an acting career, saw it for himself: good weather, informal dress, Neo-Pentecostal enthusiasm, rock music, and interest in the Bible's end-times prophecy. When evangelical leader Billy Graham said it was the hour of the "Jesus Generation" in 1971, he may have been thinking of more than the Jesus people. It was also a threshold time for historic Pentecostalism, a new force in the country, and one that Graham had embraced, with no small controversy, by giving the keynote address at the 1967 opening of Oral Roberts University, founded by a faith healer in the classic Pentecostal tradition.

The new spirit-filled movement would shape modern ministry on several fronts for the next few decades, and it showed its impact in the western United States with the Jesus people movement and in the South and Midwest with new currents and developments in classical Pentecostalism and faith healing.

On the West Coast, Odean and his generation of baby boomers became the "twice dropouts" who left behind their parents' beliefs and then secular culture to "re-invent" ministry. By dropping out of traditional religious systems, they showed how ministry could adapt to local culture, and they developed a new system of recruitment and training for ministers. In contrast, Pentecostal clergy in the South and Midwest retained their traditional systems but in the 1970s revamped their message into the "health and wealth" gospel, converting many clergy to the idea that a minister's wealth was testimony to God's blessing. In time, the new forces of megachurches, contemporary music, and enthusiastic worship began to influence all of American ministry. The new emphasis on concert-quality worship and programs meant ministers needed to hone new skills and master new technologies.

When Odean arrived in Los Angeles, the "Jesus freaks" still had one foot in beach culture, while the other foot stepped toward organized religion. As one historian said at the time, "Many of the Jesus People have joined existing Classical Pentecostal or Neo-Pentecostal churches or have established similar structures of their own."[2]

A single congregation seemed to be at the center of this transition: Calvary Chapel in Orange County, California. Founding Pastor Chuck Smith had classic Pentecostal roots, but at Calvary he was evangelically innovative. From Calvary another new movement branched off, called the Vineyard Church, which began as a local Calvary affiliate but became the nucleus of an entirely new denomination; its ministers wanted to keep an emphasis on "gifts of the Spirit" such as healing and prophecy. The two parted ways officially in 1982, and Odean stayed with the Vineyard group. But both left a great legacy of changes in today's ministry. "Most of the contemporary Christian music started through Vineyard and Calvary," Odean said.

The Spokane native attended his first Sunday service at a Calvary-affiliated congregation in Southern California in 1977. It was, in fact, the first congregation to bear the Vineyard name. Before Odean arrived, it had congregated at the beach, specializing in saltwater baptisms in the roiling surf, and then it began to hold Bible studies in Hollywood homes. Now in a church building, the Vineyard congregation had three hundred worshipers the day Odean walked in, worshipers who included Debbie Boone and at one point Bob Dylan. "All these people were standing up," Odean recalled. "Their arms were raised and they were singing to somebody out there, very intently. They were very much like me, people in the entertainment business."

Nearly a half-century has passed since those Los Angeles happenings.

Calvary and Vineyard, which both gave rise to associations of churches, produced some of the nation's largest and most-innovative congregations. The original Calvary was one of the earliest modern megachurches, developing from a giant revival tent to a hacienda-style complex that looks like a high school campus and shopping center combined. In 1981 it became the second largest church in the country, drawing 12,500 people a week, and in 2000 Chuck Smith claimed that nine of America's twenty-five largest churches were Calvary associates. While Calvary remains an association of independent churches, Vineyard Christian Fellowship became a denomination, reporting 529 churches and 122,000 adherents in 2000.

The other legacy of both churches was their ability to train effective ministers without seminaries. The older, apprentice-style training they implemented appealed to a wide variety of talented baby boomers, such as Odean. For this shift in American religion, sociologist Donald Miller has called Calvary, Vineyard, and others of this stripe the "new paradigm" ministry. He likened the shift in American Protestantism to the Reformation. Others parallel it to the Second Great Awakening, when common folks usurped the elites and preached for themselves.

Compared to other churches in the American marketplace, sociologist Miller argues, the new paradigm is "doing a better job of responding to the needs" of people. "They are successfully mediating the sacred." A generation had grown up where paid ministers in robes led somber services in historic buildings. But baby boomers asked different questions, so the new paradigm became an attractive alternative, said Miller: "Who needs paid mediators—especially ones who parade around in archaic clerical clothes?" In their Hawaiian shirts and sandals, Calvary and Vineyard clergy, for example, "are indistinguishable from the audience."[3]

For John Odean, a people person with theater arts skills garnered in his hometown, Vineyard's informal track to ministerial leadership was a natural process. As Odean took on duties around the Vineyard congregation, he listened to Chuck Smith's sermons on tape, went to hear Jack Hayford preach at his charismatic Church on the Way, and enrolled in a correspondence course. "I went down to the Calvary pastor's school one evening a week," Odean recalled. "In my first stab at teaching, I just read everything Chuck Smith had said, and they thought it was me." Then one day, after a year on the Vineyard staff, its pastor put the Sunday worship in Odean's care. He relates the experience to performer anxiety: "Most of my life I've been one of those people where they hand you something, and you never let them see you sweat, and you just step into it." Yet his plunge into ministry was no different than that of many young men at Calvary Church.

Sociologist Miller said these baby-boomer ministers attracted their peers by sharing the same values, and foremost was being anti-institutional. Baby boomers liked to design and manage their own local activities, not follow a national program from a church headquarters.

Though of an older generation, Chuck Smith had also shunned institutional religion. "I did not fit within the denomination," he said. "So I was wanting out." What he saw in denominations was leaders surrounding themselves with weaker subordinates. Talented peers were pushed to the margins or underemployed. Smith thus concluded: "The more spiritual a man is, the less denominational he becomes."[4]

Naturally, Smith stands by the educational system that flowed from the Calvary experience. He pioneered a method of teaching the Bible chapter by chapter. It takes about a decade to teach the entire Bible verse by verse. "We're on our fourth time through," Smith said of his four decades in ministry.[5] "We've been over a year in the book of Acts and we're not quite halfway." Each of Smith's sermons is taped to provide hundreds of "Word for Today" lessons. Students who listen to them while commuting or working are "in a seminary of sorts," Smith said. "After a few years here, they are ready to go out and share with others the things they've learned." They follow the same format. "You will see how these fellows, without any formal Bible training, reproduced what they experienced here. You'll see these burgeoning churches."

Sociologists such as Miller and ministers such as Odean take away various lessons from the Calvary and Vineyard church legacies. According to Miller, mainline denominations could take a lesson from new-paradigm churches on building fellowship, generating it around activities rather than dull committee meetings. Mainline denominations could also allow local churches to groom their own ministers, a "radical decentralization of clergy training" seen in the new paradigm. "Let the clergy who want a graduate education go to a major university and study philosophy, church history, or theology," Miller said. "Seminaries, in contrast, should be professional schools where people are mentored and taught while they serve within a local congregation."[6]

From inside the new-paradigm churches, Odean draws another kind of lesson after twenty-five years in ministry, mostly on the East Coast overseeing Vineyard churches. While the authentic "spirit" of a ministry must stay the same, the presentation must change with culture. The fusion of the 1970s had worked well, but in 2000 the "power" of God may need another cultural form, said Odean. When Chuck Smith founded his church in 1964, he "had the wisdom" of opening up to the youth and taking on a hippie youth director, Lonnie Frisbee. In 1971, when *Time* featured its psychedelic Jesus cover story, ministries like Smith's were the happening thing. A photo inside showed him carrying a "young paralytic" into the ocean; from rock cliffs behind hundreds watched the "mass baptisms that have made his Calvary Chapel at Santa Ana famous."[7]

Now new cultural bridges need to be built. "Our kids wear Hawaiian shirts, sit on a stool, and strum the guitar," said Odean, a pastor and father of seven. "But there's no power. It's imitation." The dream of every minister is to foresee the next cultural shift, as illustrated now by the struggle to speak to Americans born since the 1970s. "But I doubt anybody has ever been smart enough to anticipate the next generation," Odean said. "We are at one of those times right now."

The idea of spirit-filled ministry is as old as Christianity, and the role of the Holy Spirit is a part of the theology of every church tradition. Yet in the United States at the turn of the twentieth century it was given a new life in the rise of Pentecostalism.

Such enthusiastic ministry had many proximate sources, from the ethos of Negro spirituals to the "holiness" movement, typified by the start of the Church of the Nazarene in 1895 to reform and purify middle-class Methodism. The modern outbreak of speaking in tongues was reported in Kansas in 1901, and evangelists took its message to the Midwest and Texas. But the culmination happened with the Azusa Street revival of 1906, where, in a former Methodist church in an industrial section of Los Angeles, an interracial gathering of revivalist preaching, prophecy, speaking in tongues, and physical acrobatics gained international media attention. The holiness preachers involved called it the "full" gospel, restoring all aspects of Christianity, including the gifts of the Spirit reported by the early church.

By 1912, Azusa Street had become an all-black congregation and the Pentecostal message was rebounding in other parts of the country, especially the South. During a 1914 meeting in Hot Springs, Arkansas, the predominantly white Assemblies of God was formed. For the next several decades the Assemblies became a seedbed for training spirit-filled ministers. They helped the denomination grow, but many of them also broke away to form independent ministries, an activity that was widely characteristic of Pentecostalism and its offshoot of faith-healing ministry.

The most vivid example of that independent streak, of course, was Aime Semple McPherson, trained and licensed by the Assemblies. She broke away to build her own KFSG (Kalling Four Square Gospel) radio ministry and in 1923 erected the massive Angelus Temple in Echo Park, an early megachurch. She was popular, charismatic, and feisty. "You cannot expect the almighty to abide by your wave length nonsense," she told the Commerce Department in a regulatory dispute.[8] In 1927 the ministry became a denomination, the International Church of the Foursquare Gospel, and in time opened its LIFE Bible College. It was here that Chuck Smith earned his degrees and went on to found Calvary Chapel in the 1960s.

All in all, Pentecostalism developed in many strains, some of them mainstream enough to take part in the founding of the National Association of Evangelicals in the 1940s. The entire spirit-filled movement was recognized by mainline Protestants as a "Third Force" in world missions in the 1950s. Yet if its theology of the gifts of the Spirit—from speaking in tongues to faith healing and prophesying—was most controversial in American Protestantism, its greatest influence was probably seen in its music. And for ministers today, music is becoming a paramount issue.

Early in the twentieth century, when such collections as *World Renowned Hymns* typified Protestant evangelism and Sunday worship, every minister knew well that music was sung to honor God. Yet the very power of music divided ministers over theology. It was a division as old as the Great Awakening. Back then, Calvinists distrusted human efforts, since only God saved souls. But other revivalists believed, like John Wesley, that human inspiration was part of conversion, so they exploited enthusiasm and music. As a result, "Preachers became more theatrical. Music began to play an important part in working on the emotions." Traveling evangelist Rodney "Gypsy" Smith's advise at the turn of the century was: "Always sing before you preach. The song is the gimlet that makes the hole for the nail to go in. Sometimes if you don't sing you might split the board."[9]

The enthusiastic side of American hymnody had been influenced by frontier revivals, holiness movements, and Negro spirituals. Spirituals, which had roots in the slave experience, featured the call-response of a preacher and audience and improvisational moans instead of words. The moans were predecessor to "the wail of the saxophone" in jazz and bent notes in blues guitar.[10]

For many blacks, however, the spirituals echoed bygone days of slavery. So they moved on to the more refined hymnody of "Dr. Watts's hymns" and later *New Songs of Paradise* by black Methodist pastor Charles Albert Tindley. Tindley's work is considered by some the modern roots of Gospel music, but the enthusiastic "body rhythms" of the music clearly went back to the days of slavery and before, for the songs and motion were filled with "improvisations characteristic of African music."[11] Black churches disagreed on their approach. But the "golden age of gospel" was nevertheless born in the 1930s when Thomas A. Dorsey, the son of a Baptist minister, pianist, and "ex-blues musician," breached the sacred-secular boundary.

Dorsey migrated from the South to Chicago, a trek taken by many early Gospel talents. He wrote such classics as "Precious Lord," arranged for soloist Mahalia Jackson, who arrived from New Orleans. By 1946 her contract with Apollo Records for "Move on Up a Little Higher" produced the first million-selling Gospel record. Jackson was reared a Baptist. But she was influenced most by the Pentecostal church next door. "We Baptists sang sweet," she said. But "the blues and jazz and even the rock-and-roll stuff got their beat from the Sanctified Church."[12]

The musical tradition among blacks and in black churches was well known to Elvis Presley, who was reared a Pentecostal. But white evangelicals still viewed rock-and-roll as the devil's music. That taboo was lifted in 2001, however, when the Gospel Music Association inducted Christian rockers Larry Norman and Keith Green into its hall of fame. Norman, a San Francisco guitarist, was reared around black churches and knew where Presley got his style. He cut the first Christian-lyric rock album, *Upon This Rock*, with Capitol Records in 1969. His broken forefinger, which he elevated at concerts, gave the Jesus people their "One Way" symbol. Norman witnessed to other rock prodigies, most struggling with drugs. One was Keith Green, who became the first worship leader for the Vineyard churches. As one music executive said: "Music had become the *lingua franca* of the Jesus movement."[13] And whether clergy liked it or not, by the 1990s any contemporary Christian praise music had become the *lingua franca* of growing congregations.

In Southern California, Calvary Chapel also yielded several accom plished music groups. It first produced the "The Everlastin' Jesus Music Concert." Then in 1973 the "Praise Album" was such a success that it helped launch Maranatha! Music, now a multi-million-dollar company that has spread copyrighted worship music across the modern churches in the United States. But the story of Vineyard is more interesting still. When it broke from Calvary to form its own denomination, its leader was a professional musician. The Vineyard music became part of the most ebullient charismatic, or Pentecostal, activity at the end of the twentieth century. And as to worship and ministry, some scholars speak of the "Vineyardization" of churches.

The new Vineyard leader was John Wimber, a talented musician and businessman who had put together the Righteous Brothers. After a Christian conversion through the Evangelical Friends (Quaker), Wimber became a traveling church-growth advisor and "pastor to pastors." When he joined the Calvary movement, he opened a church in Annaheim, California, the city of Disneyland, and gave it the popular Vineyard name already used by Calvary-affiliated fellowships in other cities.

What characterized the movement later called Vineyard Christian Fellowship, however, was a desire to evoke the Holy Spirit. These early Calvary turned Vineyard pastors wanted to relive the "signs and wonders" of the New Testament. No one pioneered this emphasis more than Wimber, who spoke of "power evangelism"—the Holy Spirit's power to heal, prophesize, and battle demons. When Wimber began teaching a course on "Sign, Wonders, and Church Growth" at Fuller Theological Seminary in 1982, it caught the interest of evangelical ministers nationwide. Faculty member C. Peter Wagner heralded the evangelical openness as the "third wave" of the Holy Spirit; first was historic Pentecostalism and second the 1970s "charismatic renewal" in mainline and Catholic churches. Strikingly, power evangelism employed the biblical "word of knowledge"— revelation to a pastor about someone's need or God's plan. For example,

after a sermon once, the self-deprecating Wimber, heavyset and avuncu-
lar, had a vision of " 'sevens' all around him." By the end of worship seven
people accepted Christ.[14]

These kinds of claims are what prompted Vineyard and Calvary to part
ways in 1982, though both were doctrinal conservatives and Bible literalists.
As Calvary settled into what Smith humorously described as "Bapticostal,"
Vineyard took "risks" with the Holy Spirit, said John Odean, "so that the
body of Christ should fully become what it should be." Wimber led this
drama. His teaching and song at the piano were always an attraction, and
his tours in England dovetailed with Holy Spirit enthusiasm at Anglican
churches such as Holy Trinity in London. In 1990, he took the risk of siding
with "the Kansas City prophets," a small and "elite" group of ministers
who claimed to discern secret sins and predict end-time upheavals, including earthquakes. Wimber quelled the controversy over their prophetic excesses, and as the excitement died and some of the "prophets" moved on,
Vineyard churches became home for many of the Kansas City following.

A Vineyard church in Toronto was also the scene of a raucous outpouring of the Holy Spirit, including a repetition of the "holy laughter" that had
showed up in London in the wake of Wimber's visits. The year 2000 was
approaching, and a few other dramatic revivals broke out, in particular at
the Assemblies of God Church in Brownsville, Florida, where reports of
tongues, prophecy, and healings drew hundreds of thousands.[15] The Vineyard movement had one other unexpected impact. Former University of
Colorado football coach Bill McCartney was born again at a Vineyard
church in that state. When he launched Promise Keepers rallies for men in
football stadiums, Vineyard worship teams led the way. The work culmi-
nated in the "Stand in the Gap" men's assembly on the Washington Mall
in October 1997, the largest religious gathering in American history.

It would be excessive to say that most modern ministry is prone to the
Vineyardization of worship styles. But when the success of black Gospel,
rock-and-roll, and the praise worship of Calvary and Vineyard are combined, researchers are not surprised to see enthusiastic worship dramatically increasing nationwide.

Organized religion has become "more enthusiastic than ceremonial,"
according to one researcher, Ian Evison of the Alban Institute. Church
growth expert Lyle E. Schaller said: "The unifying power of music helps
to explain why so many rapidly growing evangelical congregations devote most of the first fifteen minutes of that weekly worship experience to
music and prayer." And historians wonder whether music may be usurp-
ing doctrine. "Our new sectarianism is a sectarianism of worship style,"
said historian Michael S. Hamilton. People will "choose their churches by
the type of worship and music they feature," he said.[16]

It is no wonder that many clergy verify phenomena called the worship wars. Sunday is the one time each week when ministers are most likely to invigorate and unify the congregation. "Pastors rated music second only to prayer, and tied with the sermon, in importance," said one survey. Yet the cultural pressures on all aspects of modern worship are toward change, from music to use of audio visuals for sermons. "Worship can be a source of consternation, confusion, and conflict in congregations," said one study. Another survey agreed: "Changes in worship often prompt serious congregational conflict."[17]

The new tumult has developed along different lines, such as tastes for old hymns and new songs, between formal or informal worship. Small and large churches also handle the new forces differently: The large can afford music programs that younger people in particular expect. The 2000 report *How Do We Worship?* identified the polarization between "ceremonial" and "enthusiastic" in the activities of a given Sunday. Ceremonial worship included choirs, organ, printed programs, and Holy Communion, while the enthusiastic program highlighted applause, piano, hands raised, drums, or "amens." Enthusiastic worship was more prolific in churches outside New England—churches with more young people and poorer constituents.[18] And where enthusiastic worship took place, churches tended to grow.

In a second study, Faith Communities Today (FACT) correlated worship styles with the age, beliefs, and vitality of churches. Congregations founded before 1945 put more authority in creeds and doctrine, while those founded after showed "a profound shift in the location of religious authority" to the Holy Spirit. Churches founded since 1990, in fact, almost entirely relied on Holy Spirit-inclined praise songs. The surest sign of being a church with a Holy Spirit emphasis was use of electric musical instruments at worship. In their beliefs, these churches also de-emphasized "creeds and human reason."[19]

The nation's churches still report using mostly traditional hymns. But the tastes are rapidly dividing up the pews by age. Traditional fare is favored by worshipers over age forty. But "less than half" under that age relish the old hymns. Whatever a church's denomination—liberal, moderate, or evangelical—if it has shifted to praise music and, for example, "always" uses an electric keyboard it is usually "rapidly growing," though liberal churches are least likely to adopt innovation, said the FACT survey. "Smaller and declining congregations, especially in towns and rural areas, do not feel as receptive." They invariably lack the resources: "Developing topical events with contemporary music and coordinating drama is hard and demanding work—far different from picking three hymns to insert into the same liturgy with the assigned texts for the day," said David S. Leucke, a veteran of starting new churches.[20]

The future impact of "worship wars" on ministry is unclear, partly because their degree of real ferocity is still debated. To the extent that there is a war, clergy staying in charge of worship could be part of every minister's desire to keep "jurisdiction," said Gilbert Rendle of the Alban Institute. As the secular world takes away more of the clergy's domain, they may be "digging in their heels in an effort to claim a last bastion of authority in liturgy and worship."[21]

On the other hand, a 2002 poll by Barna Research Group found that while a quarter of Protestant senior pastors testified to "music related tensions," only 7 percent of those had a "severe" or "somewhat" serious worship war. Most conflicts arose over "blended" music—use of two or more styles in a service—and blended music is widespread in Protestantism, used in 30 percent of all worship services and at 43 percent of all congregations. Barna called the trend a "questionable attempt to please everyone at once," and cited data that people feel more "connected to God" when a single style of music dominates worship.[22] Whether or not there are significant "worship wars," clergy are having to grapple with the new role of music.

The way American ministry turned to the Holy Spirit *and* to music brought controversies galore, from the way Gospel queen Mahalia Jackson swiveled her hips Pentecostal style—to the chagrin of Baptist ministers—to how Vineyard ministers prophesied. The primary theological opposition has come from Calvinistic Protestants, who believe gifts of the Holy Spirit ended in New Testament times.

Within its own ranks, modern Pentecostalism produces its share of schisms, scandals, and political ventures as well. In the late 1980s, two Assemblies of God televangelists, Jim Bakker and Jimmy Swaggart, fell from grace, and both were defrocked. Religious broadcaster Pat Robertson, though ordained a Southern Baptist, had the Holy Spirit conversion and on that inspiration built his own powerful ministry in Virginia. Then in 1988 he made a bid as Republican candidate for the U.S. presidency, relying in particular on support from Assemblies and other charismatic churches to get out the vote in the Republican primaries.

Yet probably nothing has prevailed more, or touched more clergy, than the preaching of the "health and wealth" gospel, which, like so much innovation, had roots in classic Pentecostalism and the life of a former Assemblies minister. Faith healing, of course, dates to the ministry of Jesus, and in the United States, no one brought it to the fore like Oral Roberts, who was reared in the Pentecostal Holiness church and became America's best-known faith healer. After he settled in Tulsa, Oklahoma, in 1947, Roberts began television broadcasts and planned to open a university.

Roberts was an example for many in Pentecostal ministry, including Assemblies minister Kenneth Hagin, who experienced a healing himself as a young man and felt the call to preach. He was ordained in the Assemblies and then served as pastor of several churches in Texas. After hearing Roberts preach at a healing crusade in Dallas in 1948, Hagin became an itinerant evangelist. He organized a ministry and in 1966 moved to Tulsa. Two years later, he began publishing the magazine that gave his movement its name, *Word of Faith*. The schisms between the classic Pentecostal groups and the new charismatic evangelists and healers were legion. But in a crowded field Hagin stood out, and his Word of Faith theology began a distinctive enough movement.

Hagin zeroed in on a biblical passage from Mark (11:24) in which Jesus said, "Therefore I tell you, whatever you ask in prayer, believe that you have received it, and it will be yours." From this he elaborated what theologians have called a "faith formula" or "confession and possession" theology. Sardonic critics labeled it the "name it and claim it" or "blab it and grab" teaching. The ministry of Hagin enlarged on three main teachings, the first two—healing and financial prosperity—were conventional enough. But he added to these the power of "positive confession," or declaring that God has already provided the desired thing. While some historians see in Hagin's teaching simply a materialistic spin on faith healing, others claimed he has borrowed wholesale from New Thought belief such as Christian Science, which holds that illness and evil are illusions and that mind has power over matter.[23]

Hagin also expanded on the idea of generating "love offerings," the normal donations made by crusade audiences to cover costs of a program and a continuing ministry. Donations were given in the belief that God would answer a prayer request in return, and before long Word of Faith ministers who followed in these footsteps were doing well indeed. As with Pentecostal denominations such as the Assemblies or the Four Square Gospel, Hagin set up a central school, the Rhema Bible Training Center and a vast system of correspondence courses. The local congregation at the 110-acre Tulsa campus became a megachurch. And besides the magazine, which claimed 250,000 subscribers when Hagin died in 2003, his courses, books, and an audio tape ministry were said to have reached tens of millions, some of them becoming Word of Faith ministers.

Though the wealth of many Word of Faith ministers has become the chief public bone of contention, the rift among Pentecostal theologians and clergy was over its theological authenticity: Was it God's work or a heresy? "By 1980, the message had been challenged by many charismatics, because it eliminated tragedy from Christian theology and seemed to callously imply faithlessness on the part of all those who suffered," said Roberts's biographer David Edwin Harrell Jr. "The 'faith formula' controversy pitted some of the most successful independent preachers against a growing body of teachers and professors in the charismatic movement."[24]

Besides Hagin, a pantheon of Word of Faith ministers developed large ministries with home congregations, tours, and nationwide broadcasts.

Today, Word of Faith teachers such as Kenneth Copeland, Fredrick Price, Paul Crouch, Robert Tilton, Benny Hinn, and T. D. Jakes dominate televangelism, and they all wear their conspicuous wealth comfortably as ministers.

On questions of affluence, Word of Faith ministers have taken a range of stances. Price is fairly bold about the successful minister's right to his lifestyle. "If the Mafia can ride around in Lincoln Continental tour cars, why can't the King's kids?" he said. More subtle is Gloria Copeland, who co-ministers with her husband. "I think the message had been abused, but you can't throw the baby out with the bath water," she said. "In our personal lives, in our ministry, God has been so good to us. Every dream that Ken and I have ever held onto, based on the word of God, has come to pass." A repentant Jim Bakker, who spent prison time for bilking the faithful, said he "led so many people astray" with "the prosperity message," which was an "imposter" gospel. He returned to television ministry, "deeply grateful that God had not struck me dead as a false prophet."[25]

In ways, the Word of Faith approach to ministry is no more than Pentecostal positive thinking (or "Pentecostal Christian Science," according to a critic). Such approaches have proven to have wide audiences in the ministry of Norman Vincent Peale, Robert Schuller, or the motivational speaker Zig Ziggler, a Southern Baptist in good standing. And though Oral Roberts came from deep within classic Pentecostalism, his first book, published in the 1950s, was titled no less than *Formula for Success and Prosperity*. He went on to urge believers to make a "Decree List" of blessings they needed, and he promised that making a "Blessing Pact" to donate $100 to his ministry "would be the key to unlimited financial blessing for many."[26]

Roberts's efforts had brought spirit-filled ministry into the mainstream. He founded a university and joined the rolls of United Methodist clergy in the 1970s. The Word of Faith controversy finally came home in 1980, however, when he invited Price and Kenneth Copeland to speak at the Oral Roberts University Chapel. A faculty member shouted a disagreeing "No" during Price's preaching, and then Roberts took the pulpit to strenuously defend his two guests. The open confrontation is remembered as "Black Friday." Roberts was a tolerant soul by now, but he was also indebted to Price and Copeland for their financial gifts. And the theology was catching on; Roberts and Pat Robertson were "appropriately called 'friendly outsiders'" of the movement. Its chief opponent conceded that the faith formula was "without question the most attractive message being preached today or, for that matter, in the whole history of the church." Hence, ministers were falling in line.[27]

Some Word of Faith role models, in fact, built megachurches, wore diamond rings, lived in mansions, and toured in personal jets. Conspicuous wealth, indeed, is at the heart of T. D. Jakes's ministry in Houston, and it has become an inspiration to other black clergy. Earlier still, in 1989, Price opened the Faith Dome in Los Angeles as the nation's "largest church" building, with a capacity of more than ten thousand. In the travel department, Word of Faith ministers own a cavalcade of aircraft that include Bombardier Challengers, Cessna Citations and Golden Eagles, and Grumman Gulfstreams. Before long, the satirical Christian magazine *The Wittenberg Door* has reported that Copeland, a former pilot for Oral Roberts, was "telling the faithful that God wants him and his wife Gloria to *each* have their own Cessna Citation Ten super-jets." Meanwhile, "Grandma mails another check to bless the ministry."[28]

Though the Word of Faith movement peaked around 1990, and was thereafter slowed down by the televangelism scandals, it has been revived. It has new stars and is drawing in more ministers impressed by the theology and the financial opportunity. The strongest criticism still comes from within the spirit-filled fold, whose image suffers most from health and wealth excess. "A small group of people in our circle could ruin it for the rest of us," *Charisma* magazine editor J. Lee Grady said. Speaking of the "charismatic cartel," he cites ministers who require a $7,000 spending allowance for speaking engagements and others who preach a "24-hour blessing" for a $2,400 offering or promise a new house for giving "right now"—almost like a game show. "My Bible says that men who love money aren't fit for ministry," Grady said. Word of Faith ministers will not join the Evangelical Council for Financial Accountability, and it is no wonder, said the ministry ethics group Wall Watchers: "Such a high level of profitability is appalling for ministry."[29]

Despite the controversy over faith healing, televangelism, and the most high-profile leaders of the "health and wealth" gospel, ministry in America was perhaps most influenced by an afterglow called "soft Pentecostalism," the success of independent-style ministry, and the arrival of the new megachurches, many of which have charismatic origins. In Wagner's typology, the "second wave" hit mainline Protestants and Catholic and the "third wave" led evangelicals to recognize modern gifts of the Spirit. As historian Joel A. Carpenter said in 1997, "The pentecostal-charismatic movement is quickly supplanting the fundamentalist-conservative one as the most influential evangelical impulse."[30]

A prelude to much of this was the "charismatic renewal" in the Protestant mainline. While it had many sources, a significant one was the Full Gospel Business Men's Fellowship founded in 1951 by Demos Shakarian, a wealthy California dairyman who had funded Pentecostal evangelists since the 1940s. As a member of the Assemblies, he bridled at clergy control and so formed a lay fellowship, which first met in the "upper room" of Clifton Cafeteria in Los Angeles. Soon enough it was introducing businessmen and mainline clergy to "respectable" Pentecostals.[31]

An Episcopalian couple who had the Holy Spirit experience eventually contacted Dennis Bennett, a British-born rector of the prosperous middle-class St. Mark's Episcopal Church in Van Nuys. Bennett, too, spoke in tongues and then resigned when his scandalized congregation found out. Though his own church was too polarized for him to stay, he said: "No one needs to leave the Episcopal Church in order to have the fullness of the Spirit." This invitation for "Neo-Pentecostalism" to enter mainline denominations would spread with some divisiveness in Lutheran, Presbyterian, Congregational, Mennonite, Reformed, and Roman Catholic circles. "Four years after its inception, Neo-Pentecostalism was a clearly recognizable religious movement—affecting both clergy and laity," said historian Richard Quebedeaux.[32]

In time soft Pentecostalism added a new ecumenical spirit to American ministry, putting aside doctrinal differences to focus on prayer, spiritual gifts, and healing. Churchgoers began to adopt a worship style of uplifted hands, the *orans* prayer posture of the ancient church. Two Assemblies ministers, the brothers David and Ralph Wilkerson, became non-denominational in projects such as the Melodyland Christian Center in Anaheim, which held "charismatic clinics" for pastors. Teen Challenge was begun by David Wilkerson when he took the ministry to street gangs in New York City, a story told in the 1964 book *The Cross and the Switchblade*. The small book, in fact, sparked a charismatic movement at Duquesne University, a Catholic school in Pittsburgh, and in 1973 twenty thousand charismatics assembled at the University of Notre Dame.

One outcome was for charismatic clergy to join the growing trend of starting very large independent churches. During the mid-1960s, when the term "megachurch" had not yet been coined, the "largest" congregations in the United States were deemed so by the size of their membership lists. The top American churches were all Baptist: southern, black, or fundamentalist. Their memberships ranged from 5,800 to 17,000. What changed by 1981, however, was the rise in actual turnout at worship, since much membership is inactive. That was the year Calvary Chapel was second highest for the nation. The former tent church was now drawing 12,500 participants a week.[33]

While such large churches are not new in the United States, their sheer numbers are a novel development. There are probably more than six hundred. And while nearly half describe themselves as "evangelical," another quarter say they are Holy Spirit filled. What is more, three-quarters of all the megachurches are in the suburbs of Sunbelt "sprawl cities"—with a key exception being Willow Creek Community Church, not far from Chicago. Historian Hamilton has noted how such large audience congregations with full-service ministries had once before dotted the landscape, especially between the world wars. McPherson's 3,500-seat Angelus Temple, a classic Pentecostal church, had a stage rather than a pulpit in its

1920s heyday. "Angelus Temple was lit up like a Las Vegas casino," Hamilton said. "Searchlights swept the sky above the traffic jams."[34]

Hamilton noted that back then the large, non-denominational, and full-service congregations—some of which advertised "something for everyone"—were part of three kinds of movements. The first was the fundamentalist gospel tabernacle. Second was the "institutional church" movement: mainline city congregations that offered everything from a gym to an employment agency. Third was the liberal "community church" movement. Its members abandoned all denominational distinctions in favor of universally acceptable doctrines. All three movements are now "accounted as having ultimately failed," Hamilton said. Yet for God "they may have accomplished his exact purposes for exactly the right length of time."[35]

That assessment has also been offered for the current excitement of today's music-driven megachurches. All those past features have again been resuscitated in the newest cultural forms. Megachurch researcher Scott Thumma has limned the current crop also in three categories, more as styles than as movements. The "nontraditional" is represented by Calvary and Willow Creek, one with Pentecostal roots and the other Calvinist. Both have shorn themselves of Christian symbols. They cater to informality, have upbeat worship, and encourage lay ministry. Willow Creek made famous the "seeker service" for "unchurched Harry"—a non-offensive and entertaining Sunday event for baby boomers put off by organized religion and unfamiliar with Christian belief.[36]

Next is the "traditional" megachurch, typified by the large Southern Baptist or Methodist congregations in southern cities. Though the buildings may be typical colonial brick with white steeples—an "exaggerated replica of a country church"—the seating, classrooms, and parking accommodate thousands. "This form epitomizes religion in the South." A final style is "composite." It may well be a Pentecostal or evangelical church that opens a massive new structure but keeps crosses and stained glass. Whatever the external style, Thumma said, a few dynamic features are the same everywhere. "Once a congregation reaches a critical mass of around 2,000, its numerical strength alone becomes a powerful attraction." Some call it the "vortex effect."[37]

With size the megachurch no longer needs denominational resources. They adopt "a distinctive visionary identity or purpose" and are nearly all biblically orthodox. "Even the megachurches from moderate and liberal denominations often stand out as having a more conservative theology than do their counterparts," Thumma said. Leucke, the church planter, worries less about megachurches watering down doctrine to reach "seekers" than the need to be flexible in the long run. "The more worrisome consequence is that when the culture changes, as it will, Willow Creek may lose its effectiveness," he said. A Willow Creek or Calvary

Chapel, with their large resources, can surely adapt. But "what about the hundreds of imitators who lack the creative drive, flair and energy to adjust?"[38]

For all their celebrity, megachurches draw fewer than 2 percent of the nation's worshipers: about two million people. Yet they have become a major test case for the direction Protestantism will take in the future. One of the major contributions, however, has been to add to the informal training system of American clergy. The environment of a large church, with roles to play for many assistant pastors, has trained a new cadre, just as the apprenticeships and correspondence courses of the Assemblies of God, the Rhema Bible Institute, and the International Church of the Foursquare Gospel have done.

In ways the Assemblies, one of the earliest of the Pentecostal denominations, has been the way station for much of independent charismatic ministry today. Although candidates for ministry in the Assemblies of God may attend any of the denomination's Bible colleges or even its Barean University, many more—numbering in the thousands—learn by the Assemblies correspondence courses. To be ordained, students must take part in a successful two-year apprenticeship at a local congregation. The system has produced an abundance of clergy. Today, there are 18,607 active Assemblies ministers for 12,082 congregations. In ways, the system has proved the value of an apprenticed ministry that does not require graduate school. But it also has touched so many tens of thousands of people that no one knows what other kinds of ministry they may have gone into, according to Assemblies scholar Russell P. Spittler, who was a provost at Fuller Theological Seminary until his retirement in 2003.

Though Spittler earned a Ph.D. from Harvard in the New Testament, he argued the merits of an apprenticed clergy without an academic degree. "Some of the best ministers I have run into would fit that category," he said. "It's a strange thing to say, but true." Indeed, the Assemblies elected its first general secretary to have a graduate degree in 1993. And for sure, the Assemblies have generated ministers who have taken their work in all kinds of charismatic directions, Spittler said. "There are people who grew up in the Assemblies of God but eventually find themselves strictured by the various denominational specifications, so they bail out," he said. "The Assemblies of God, in some ways, is a colorful farm where they grow up and get these ideas and practices. Then they want to make more out of it."[39]

At Calvary Chapel, the leadership still extols the apprenticeship approach to ministry, both for its immediacy, efficiency, and ability to connect with the people it hopes to serve. And Willow Creek Community Church, which trains its own ministers rather than relying on a seminary, obviously sees ministry the same way. With time to assess the claim, church growth experts agree: There is nothing like a minister rising up from his own peer group. "Church planters tend to attract people of their own age," said Leucke, the pastor who has started churches. To reach a particular age group "the leaders need to be born into that culture."[40]

Yet the exchanges between the new charismatic and megachurch movements and the old graduate schools of historic denominations are going both ways. At the National Council of Churches—which represents the Protestant mainline, its historic creeds, a downplaying of Holy Spirit enthusiasm, and an emphasis on graduate school seminary—the hope is that the two sides can value the distinctiveness of each.

"The megachurch is the most dynamic edge of the American religious landscape, and it is not through evolving," said Eileen Lindner, a Presbyterian minister who is head of research for the National Council of Churches. "It is diversifying perceptions of clergy and lowering the [academic] bar of the pastor as a pastor-theologian." Still, she sees the need for more interaction between the old and new forces in Protestantism. "The venerable institutions are not paying enough attention to megachurches, but neither have megachurches explored the resources at the seminaries," she said. "I suspect that part of the unfolding reality of the megachurches will be a deeper quest into doctrine, belief, and history, and to me that spells the academy." Or put another way, she said, "At some point megachurches will say, 'Gee, we want to find a way to fast that takes its cues from the desert fathers, not from L.A. Weight Loss Centers.' "[41]

At the Vineyard Christian Fellowship denomination, the academy is being valued anew, said John Odean, a twenty-five-year veteran of the ministry. "Back in the Jesus movement, everybody expected his return any moment," he said. Believers gave up on social security, insurance policies, and college: " 'Cause what's education? He's going to be back this year, next year, five years tops." The Bible still holds the world in tension because "no one knows the hour," but that does not deny the merit of seminary-trained clergy. "What we've been trying to design is schooling that allows ministers, such as myself, to do what God has called us to do, and yet get a little bit better," he said.

One Vineyard pastor, for example, serves a church and is also earning a master's of divinity at Regent University Divinity School, which has a charismatic and scholarly focus. At the university, which was founded by religious broadcaster Pat Robertson, this pastor "can study Greek but not be bored out of his mind," Odean said. "The other students say, 'How come you're loving it.' He says, 'Well, you guys aren't going to use this for four years. But I'm going to use it this Sunday.' " For all the freedom of the Holy Spirit, however, academic mastery is hard to dampen in ministry. That was clear in 2003, when Regent's divinity school declared a small revolution in Pentecostalism. With bona fide accreditation, Vinson Synan, the university's dean, announced, "Regent will now become the first Spirit-filled seminary in the world to offer a Ph.D. in divinity."[42]

8

Organized Religion

EVERY MINISTER LONGS for a "purpose-driven" church. Whatever that purpose might be—providing meaning, reaching others, helping families—it is the force that attracts membership. Members bring resources. Those contributions drive the church's programs and pay the minister's salary. As one study of declining churches in changing neighborhoods concluded: "The most crucial resource is membership."[1]

The formula for a thriving church could not be simpler: bring members. Yet that aim is buffeted by countless other factors, making the overall story of churches today one of rags and riches. At times like this the "Purpose-Driven" slogan, invented by Saddleback Community Church in Orange County, California, has become famous. Saddleback, founded by Southern Baptist pastor Rick Warren, draws fifteen thousand participants. Its "Purpose-Driven" methodology has become so successful that the very term "Purpose-Driven" is copyrighted. Pastors flock to Purpose-Driven Ministries conferences to learn how it is done: "We've trained more pastors than all the seminaries combined," said Warren.[2]

The fates of church institutions will clearly determine the fates of most ministers, both spiritually and economically. Some will retire on par with CEOs and other professionals. Others have left ministry for lack of income to raise a family or pay seminary debt. "Most pastors don't enter ministry for the delightful opportunity to raise money," said one clergy counselor. Yet for those who stay, the majority "have bare minimum salaries and few fringe benefits," according to a national study.[3] Income has increasingly become a factor in how ministry will endure and draw new talent. Church income can depend on style of governance, the neighborhood, the congregation's size, and ability to recruit people. Few ministers can ignore this financial ebb and flow of the churches in charting their own futures.

Two styles of church organization prevail in the United States, the congregational or the hierarchical and "connectional." Though Saddleback is affiliated with a denomination, the Southern Baptist Convention, it operates under congregational governance. With a large membership, a local church can pay a senior pastor generously. Under a connectional system such as a Roman Catholic diocese or the United Methodist annual conference, bishops and administrators regulate clergy income. While the connectional system appoints or approves clergy, congregational churches face the laws of supply and demand when they seek a new pastor. As a result of these two forces—one free market and the other regulatory—the top tenth of clergy earners in America have a salary six times more than the bottom tenth, according to one study.[4]

Whatever strengths the two polities may have, a church must also survive in its local environment, which is always changing as jobs and people move, neighborhoods age, and immigration to the United States continues. As illustrated by Saddleback, suburban churches are typically the most successful in growth and resources. But these are only some of the nation's pulpits. Clearly, most aged churches in older habitations, whether urban or rural, face the greatest challenges today. "Older, smaller, town and rural churches are less likely to claim a sense of purpose and vitality," reported the 2001 study, Faith Communities Today (FACT). Nancy Ammerman's *Congregations and Community*, a study of twenty-three churches struggling with changing environments, reports that church adaptation and even growth are possible. But that will require changes that can spur conflict inside the church.[5]

The FACT survey found that of churches working in the worst environmental conditions, only 12 percent conceded having "low vitality." What churches draw on for their energy is either the obvious excitement of growth or the more internally generated pride in a tradition and heritage. Growth is, of course, the most powerful "center of cohesion." Black churches thrive on both the memory and hope of growth. Mainline Protestants have a rich heritage but lack youth. "Large, newer and growing congregations most clearly report feelings of being vital and alive," said FACT. But again, regardless of size and environment, churches with some kind of clear identity and expectations of their members—in behavior, beliefs, outreach, and tithing—reported higher vitality.[6]

When the nation's largest congregations were listed in the 1960s, Adam Clayton Powell Jr.'s Abyssinian Baptist Church in Harlem ranked fifth with ten thousand members. There is no rule that says a megachurch cannot thrive in an urban setting. That 1960s listing, of course, excluded some of the nation's largest Catholic parishes, with tens of thousands of registered members in downtown New York, Boston, or Chicago. Today the largest churches are found in the suburbs. "The only people who like big churches are pastors," said Warren, half in jest. Many churchgoers like them, too. They have fluid social settings, a multitude of activities, and even anonymity. Many pastors believe that large churches own the future: They "are more able to put on high-quality programs and sponsor spiritually enriching worship."[7]

But the small church still prevails. Half of all U.S. congregations, for example, draw fewer than one hundred people each week. Half of all clergy, in other words, serve just 11 percent of all churchgoers. "This is probably the most profound reality facing congregations today," the 2000 Congregational Life Survey reported. According to one formula for Protestantism, it takes a congregation of two hundred to pay a full-time pastor's salary. That fact is leading many smaller congregations to a possible financial "train wreck," said United Church of Christ minister Barbara Zikmund Brown. "People still like a church of 200 members, a pastor-centered church," she said. "But fewer and fewer can afford to pay what a well-trained clergy person ought to get."[8]

While in the Protestant tradition people travel to a church of their choice, "Catholics are members of a church by where they live, not where they attend," writer Peter Steinfels said of the nearly nineteen thousand U.S. Catholic parishes. A quarter of these have at least three thousand registered parishioners—perhaps the original megachurches. Yet many Catholic parishes are also small. A quarter have Mass attendance of just 10 to 274 people a week. They share company with the many small Protestant congregations.[9]

Part of Saddleback's "Purpose-Driven" methodology is to circulate new members through Christian education—the diagram is like four bases on a baseball field—until (at the home plate) they start "sharing Christ" to recruit more members. Growing membership is crucial to the vitality of every congregation. Yet it is not only hard to do but some congregations prefer to keep the status quo. According to the Congregational Life Survey, few churchgoers bring guests to worship. "In an entire year, most people did not invite even one person," the study said. Most growth in one church is transfer from another: a win-lose situation. One third of worshipers have been members of their current church for five years or less—suggesting high mobility. The flux has its benefits: "With the inflow of new people comes the potential of new ideas and new energy." Still, just 7 percent of new members are real "converts" who never attended a church. While some non-believers are converting, however, the non-believing segment of the U.S. population is growing much faster.[10]

The lack of men in the pews (just 39 percent) continues to be a salient feature of church life. When husbands attend with wives, or when young men and women seek each other's company at church, social vitality usually increases. For churchgoers, "the majority experience the congregation *only* by attending worship service." That suggests how crucial that Sunday experience is, not only in deepening faith and loyalty to the church but also for encouraging financial giving. The other contact point for people with their church has become the small group, which provides intimacy and generates loyalty to the congregation. Yet "less than half of all worshipers (44 percent) are involved," the Congregational Life Survey found.[11]

As the nation's clergy reach out to newcomers, their institutions are undergoing dramatic changes. In Protestantism it is being called "decentralization." Large denominational structures are downsizing. Local churches and even clergy rely on them less. The result is that less funding is sent to "church headquarters." What sociologist Robert Wuthnow calls the "restructuring" of religion, meanwhile, is based on a growing loyalty of churchgoers to "special purpose groups" that cross denominational boundaries. Usually that loyalty is on the basis of a conservative or liberal stance in the "culture wars." Still, some research shows that a majority of mainline Protestants still "hold the center," ensuring a future role for denominations. Meanwhile, according to Warren, much ministerial talent is bypassing the denominational path. "Today, the sharpest guys I know are starting churches," he said. They are not trying to save old ones.[12]

The restructuring in Catholicism is driven by the shortage of priests and nuns, perhaps even more than by Second Vatican Council reforms calling lay people into ministry. "Leadership has traditionally been in the hands of priests and nuns—that is, of people who underwent an intense, shared religious formation and who, because of celibacy, lived almost entirely within the framework of Catholic institutions," Steinfels said. Now the shortage and aging of priests and nuns is requiring reform. "Leadership is steadily passing into the hands of laypeople, and certainly at many levels of church life this change will be permanent."[13]

U.S. Catholics put an estimated $7.5 billion in the offering plate each year. The parish then gives 5 to 15 percent to the diocese. But with fewer priests and nuns to work for "free," salaries of professional lay staff will increase budgets—and less may go to diocesan headquarters. "Each diocese is dramatically different in its financial condition," said Pat Schiltz, dean of the University of St. Thomas Law School in St. Paul, Minnesota. "Some are extremely wealthy, with big savings and stock accounts. Others are very poor."[14]

The Catholic Church is guaranteed growth by Hispanic immigration and birthrates. Parishes with many Hispanics "have more than four baptisms for every funeral," a high ratio of newcomers. Though Mass attendance is down from the 1940s, twenty million Catholics still gather at the altar every Sunday. A new financial challenge, however, will be to gain their financial trust after the sexual abuse scandal: Hundreds of millions of dollars were drained into lawsuits and legal settlements. "There is, I suspect, a real need for more accountability to the People of God in matters such as the use of funds donated by the laity," Avery Dulles, an American cardinal, said in 2002. Yet he believes that only the orthodox wing of laity will be able to preserve Catholic vitality. "In a secularized society such as ours, consistently orthodox Catholics will constitute a minority [even] within their religious community," he said. As the majority accommodates secular culture the minority carries "the greater promise for the future."[15]

Protestant ministers judge their institutional futures in two ways, either by sobering experience or by a hopeful revivalist theology. More than half (56 percent) believes American church attendance will grow or stay the same through 2012. "The most popular [single] view is that church attendance will decline," a view held by 44 percent of ministers, especially Lutherans and Baptists. Conservative Protestant ministers are most optimistic, especially about their own worlds of ministry: 70 percent of evangelicals predict growth in their own denominations, as do 80 percent of Pentecostals. Yet the pastors who predict *overall* growth in American Christianity, the survey concluded, "are apparently expecting something new—something that, by all available measurements, isn't currently happening in the U.S. and hasn't happened for many years."[16]

Mainline clergy, faced with denominational declension for three decades, are more realistic: 54 percent expect further losses. Regardless of those denominational trends, members of local mainline churches seem confident enough about their futures, according to sociologist Wuthnow. "Many more mainliners think their churches are growing than think they are declining," he said. Indeed, more people may be attending though not actually joining. Whatever the case, "the notion that mainliners suffer from self-doubt, inspired by lack of growth in their numbers, seems unwarranted."[17]

In their quest for members, thousands of ministers have gone to church-growth conferences since the 1970s, and sampled ever newer methods of evangelism. An early harbinger was the Institute for Successful Church Leadership at Robert Schuller's Crystal Cathedral in Orange County, California. Pastor Warren had attended it and so did Bill Hybels. Hybels went on to found in 1975 Willow Creek Community Church, which along with Saddleback is now the emblematic suburban megachurch. Today, the Willow Creek Association trains church leaders to develop "seeker-sensitive" churches, just as Saddleback's Purpose-Driven Ministries trains in its methodology of introduction, fellowship, commitment, and then outreach.

Also joining the new tool set of ministry is an import from England called the Alpha Course. While not unusual in its content, its approach has proved remarkably successful at introducing people to the basics of Christianity. Those rudiments were first set out in a series of lessons by the pastor at Holy Trinity Anglican Church in west London around 1980. A decade later, these were expanded and given a dynamic, intellectual, and almost hip flavor by former lawyer and Cambridge graduate Nicki Gumbel, the associate minister at Holy Trinity, which stands in a neighborhood called Brompton. At first the Alpha Course was geared toward people unfamiliar with Christianity. But with its growth, it now invites churchgoers who want to deepen or discuss their faith.

With Gumbel at the helm, the course became an entire experience: ten weeks of eleven lectures and a weekend retreat. Each talk was delivered at midweek in someone's home, preceded by a potluck dinner and followed by informal conversation or small groups. Others learned to give the Gumbel lectures. But the course primarily spread by use of videotapes that featured his quality presentations. At some point in the series, guests are invited to the weekend retreat, where the concept of the Holy Spirit is introduced. That emphasis has prompted some to link Alpha with the charismatic movement, and one course is on "Does God still heal today?" But Gumbel has said, "I've resisted all labels."[18] Other lecture topics include: "What is the point of life?"; "What happens when we die?"; "How does God guide us?"; "How do we deal with guilt?"; and "Why did Jesus die?"

Alpha's casualness, plus the way it built networks through friends, fueled its popularity and launched it in the United States in 1995. "Basically, it spreads by word of mouth," Gumbel said on his visit then. Hosted first by Episcopal churches familiar with Holy Trinity's evangelical tenor, other churches joined in, and the Catholic Archdiocese of Baltimore sponsored its first Alpha for Catholics in 1999. In Austin, Texas, St. Barnabas Episcopal Church was formed around the Alpha Course in 1997, creating a congregation of two hundred fifty members in one year. "It really is for intelligent seekers who don't yet belong to a church," said Jeffrey Q. Black, the minister.[19] The course was endorsed by Archbishop of Canterbury George L. Carey and presented on British television in 2001 by Sir David Frost, the son of a Methodist minister.

By 2004, Alpha USA claimed that one million people had already attended one of their five thousand regular courses offered in North America. Its methodology spread by way of a mass-published course outline by Gumbel, titled *Questions of Life*, and regional training conferences. Training sessions include, for example, a "Model Alpha Evening" and "Integrating Alpha into the Church." As Gumbel put it, "Running Alpha without going to a conference is rather like driving a car without taking lessons." Church liberals, especially in England and Canada, have called the Alpha Course a throwback, citing its more literal interpretation of the Bible and rejection of homosexuality. Secular wags in London have called converts "HTB positive," for Holy Trinity Brompton.[20] But the course attendance continues to grow, including in the United States.

All of these methodologies—from the Purpose-Driven church to the Alpha Course—more or less fall into what has been called the modern "church-growth movement." The movement is about saving souls, but also about filling pews and reviving churches. By its very emphasis on growth, however, the world is taken not so much as a mystery as a marketplace, a place of calculated advertising and selling of one belief system or another. It's a concept that some Christians reprove. "The most pervasive logic or vision for ministry today is shaped by the market and the values of consumerism rather than by the Gospel of Jesus Christ," one Methodist bishop lamented.[21]

For good or ill, the open market is where ministries have to sway shoppers into one church door or another. Like companies with competing product lines, churches invariably turn out to be "winners" and "losers." The question is what draws and keeps a loyal consumer? The FACT survey answered that by noting how churches with "identity," "boundaries," and "expectations" do better. "Moral boundaries make a difference," FACT reported. Two of three congregations that accentuate "personal and public morality" reported ample funding and growth. "Congregations that place less emphasis on these standards are more likely to report plateaued or declining membership." Newness helps as well. As any congregation ages its "clarity declines consistently and progressively— suggesting that expectations become more implicit with the institutional aging process."[22]

The FACT survey outlined what is called "the strictness hypothesis" among sociologists of religion, who today also prefer the model of a religious marketplace. The strictness hypothesis has venerable roots. In eighteenth-century Scotland, the father of the free-market theory, Adam Smith, reflected on how established church systems became slow and encumbered. The sectarian groups tended to be centers of energy. The established clergy rested "upon their benefices," Smith said in *The Wealth of Nations* (1776). These clergy neglected to "keep up the fervour of faith." They were finally "incapable of making any vigorous exertion in defense of even their own establishment."[23]

The other part of Smith's observation was that "little religious sects" conveyed the most fervor. In the small and strict religious groups "the morals of the common people have been almost always remarkably regular and orderly." The German sociologist Max Weber, who popularized a similar process of churches going lax and sects breaking away, also noted that "in principle, only relatively small congregations" could keep the strictness and zeal going. As sociologist Benton Johnson summarized the idea: *"A church is a religious group that accepts the social environment in which it exists."* A sect is "in a state of tension with its surroundings"; that is, *"a religious group that rejects the social environment."*[24] This has been expanded further to speak of "inward" looking churches and "outward" looking ones, the first more separatist, the second more willing to mingle with secular civic life. Indeed, among Christian leaders a moral debate would arise. Which is closer to the gospel, the inward or outward thrust?

This church-sect dynamic is widely used to analyze grander forces in organized religion. As large groups become lax and bureaucratic, small intense groups break away. These rival groups grow by their sheer energy. Once they become large, however, they also suffer laxity on membership: "Increasing the size of an organization reduces the level of commitment and conformity." Soon enough the next "upstart sect" will challenge the largest group. By this logic all growth is doomed to failure unless the church obviates the effects of success: tolerance, easy joining, and luxury, things that make members comfortable in "this world." The proposed solution is for growing churches to keep breaking into smaller units. The Mormon Church and Jehovah's Witnesses have done this for decades. More recently, gigantic Sunday schools in Baptist churches discovered the cell system. The small group trend in megachurches—likened to "federalism," with many states in a national unity—is just the latest application. Sometimes called "one church, many congregations," the separate groups can worship at the same location or branch out to new locations.[25]

The American discussion was widened in 1972 by the book *Why Conservative Churches Are Growing*, written by Methodist minister Dean Kelley. He said that sectarian energy is most important for church survival. "If it costs nothing to belong to a community, it can't be worth much," he wrote. Yet he argued as well that while "stringency" among members is healthy, a "stricture" by autocratic or orthodox control causes demise. Sociologists Rodney Stark and Roger Finke tell the success story of stringency in *The Churching of America*, which gives upstart sects credit for stoking the fires of nearly all U.S. church growth. Finally, the new economic theory of "rational choice" was applied to this religious dynamic. The commitment to salvation in one group or another was a cost-benefit analysis.[26]

In addition to group strictness, the other great theory of church growth—and the heart of the movement under that name—was group comfort: Individuals more easily converted to Christianity through their own familial, racial, or occupational group. This theory of church growth was first articulated by Disciples of Christ missionary Donald McGavran, who worked in India before World War II. Faced with the Hindu caste system, McGavran realized that he could not persuade individuals to become Christians across marriage boundaries or social groups. So he proselytized through groups—extended families, tiny tribes, or occupations.

These were the "bridges" to growth cited in his groundbreaking 1955 book *The Bridges of God: a Study in the Strategy of Missions*. "Individualistic Westerners cannot without special effort grasp how peoples become Christian," McGavran said. "In the West Christianization was and is an extremely individualistic process." The alternative, evident in so many other cultures, was to convert by way of social and kin groups. Ten years later McGavran established the Institute of Church Growth at Fuller Theological Seminary. He later used the term "homogeneous unit" to describe evangelism by ethnic, demographic, or age categories. "The homogenous unit might be a tribe or caste, as in the case of Jews in the United States, Brahmans in India, or Uhunduni in the [West New Guinea] highlands."[27]

For church growers it was a gold mine. But for others it seemed a dividing up of Christians by race and class when the Bible seemed to eschew such segregation. When one Protestant leader decried the "suburban captivity" of churches in the 1960s, his protest was against how "religious fellowship became association by likeness." More recent critics call it church growth based on racial, linguistic, and class prejudices. "The greatest danger in the movement may be that it obviously succeeds," writes Ralph H. Elliot of Northshore Baptist Church in Chicago. "The preference is for the suburbs and for each succeeding suburban ring," a targeting strategy that neglects hardship settings. "The biblical concern for the powerless is totally overlooked."[28]

McGavran's successor at Fuller was C. Peter Wagner. A Congregationalist missionary to Bolivia, Wagner expanded the growth principle and defended the Christian ethic of homogeneous evangelism. Citing the debate over "integration or segregation in local churches," Wagner said the ideal was to grow by homogeneity since it worked, and then promote diversity. The "underlying assumption," he argued in his book, *Our Kind of People*, is that when folks become Christian "they will lose their inclinations toward racism and prejudice." It was an age of the "new pluralism," in which not even minorities valued integration that much, but he said nevertheless the urgent question for the church was "how to do both."[29]

A more famous church-growth advocate is Robert Schuller, who wrote the classic 1974 guidebook *Your Church Has Real Possibilities*, for which Wagner wrote a later introduction. The generic ideas—small groups, upbeat sermons, market surveys, homogeneous units, and suburban locations—rapidly trickled down, reaching Southern Baptist missions and inspiring megachurch networks such as Willow Creek and Saddleback. And it all came during a generational shift among clergy. The Schuller Institute, for example, filled "the role for an older generation of church leaders that the Willow Creek Association now fills for the younger," said David S. Leucke, a pastor and growth consultant. Schuller considers Hybels "his leading disciple," Leucke reports. "But Hybels is less excited about the relationship. As he once told Schuller, 'At Willow Creek I preach about sin. I use the *S word*, Bob.'"[30]

The friendly quarrel between them is over Schuller's development of "possibility thinking" and "self-esteem" theology that follows Norman Vincent Peale's sunny view of human nature rather than John Calvin's view of human sinfulness. Schuller has backed his message with a warm, full-service church program. The more Calvinistic Willow Creek did the same. It popularized the "seeker service" for people who did not like churchgoing. The service was designed around a market survey asking people their likes and dislikes about church. With no apologies, the age of marketing had joined the struggle to save souls.

Schuller is candid about the need to mirror modern culture. "I said that the Church of the future must not think of itself as just a worship center, but it must be 'a shopping center' for Jesus Christ," he recalled. "Now I rue the day I used that term because it keeps popping up all over, as if my motivation were commercial." But the point was valid enough—to develop a church that was convenient, had a variety of programs, and spoke to browsing Americans unattached to "traditional" religion. This model espoused strong pastoral leadership, a cheerful autocrat of sorts, and preferably a founding minister. The message was also to be appealing. "As senior pastor," Schuller said, "it is my job to *attract unchurched people into the sanctuary on Sunday mornings* through sermons *that do not sound like sermons*, but which sound like helpful and inspiring messages."[31]

The well-known pollster George Barna, who worked with Willow Creek, wrote his first book on the topic *Marketing the Church* (1988). In the 1990s, after years of working as a consumer researcher for the Disney Corporation, he began gathering strategic information for pastors. As a realist, Barna does not foresee more Americans becoming Christians. His definition of leadership is the ability to turn around institutions so *more* people really are in church. The clergy he meets are nice people and good teachers. But he does not take them to be leaders. "We kill ourselves to give them good information, good research," he said. "And they nod their heads approvingly and then they don't do anything with it." When he gave research to Disney it launched a new program. Barna equated leadership with vision: "Vision is specific, detailed, customized, distinctive and unique to a given church." This may include the "homogeneous unit" approach. Yet Barna now questions the future of megachurches and advocates for more multicultural congregations.[32]

All these proposed revolutions in church growth require some major uprooting. Church-growth expert Lyle E. Schaller argues that the mainline Protestants locked themselves into small sanctuaries and plots of land during the mid-century church-building explosion. His advice? "It's easier to create highly attractive new congregations than to renew the old." Schuller is also happy to give shock treatment to church boards and pastors. "All are prisoners of property they own—or rather, that owns and controls them!" he said. "Ninety percent of all American churches should relocate!" He tells ministers, "You take command. You have the freedom to sell that property! Break loose from the chains that bind you. . . . God cannot be the leader of a church if the creative imagination of human beings is blinded and bound by glass, stone, plaster and dirt."[33]

These sociological and practical theories of growth all lean heavily toward free-market principles, uniform congregations, working in suburban growth areas, and organizing around a founding pastor. Yet there are alternatives, which might be called working with a "religious ecology" in a community. That was the lens through which Ammerman's *Congregation and Community* looked at struggling churches. Faced with changing environments—from dying downtowns and closed factories to racial changes in the neighborhoods—the churches either kept the status quo, resisted change, relocated, or altered the outreach. Some met "severe decline." Others experienced "growth and transformation."[34]

The difference in the ecology model is to accept that a church does not have to show exponential growth, as it might in the Schuller model. Ammerman set the modest goal as this: "simply the congregation's survival as the institution it determines it should be." When it was determined that a church needed to change and grow, the minister was tested in his ability to amicably manage the conflict that ensued, typically when an "old elite" did not want change. "Pastors in the status quo congregations, by contrast, tended not to introduce new ideas and programs." The struggling church did not necessarily lack commitment, but might even have more than the sect or megachurch. "If commitment is measured in terms of regular attendance and giving high percentages of their personal incomes, the members of declining congregations are, on average, the most committed," Ammerman said. "They are giving sacrificially, knowing that with only small numbers everyone's dollars count."[35]

When the Harvard historian Robert D. Putnam proposed his influential "bowling alone" thesis—that Americans have stopped joining all kinds of groups—he said the effect was to rob the nation of "social capital." That capital was made up of the ability and skill for people to work together. At its best the capital improved social peace, progress, and safety. Putnam said religious congregations were unparalleled in social capital production. But he doubted whether even the growth of fundamentalist congregations or megachurches offset the overall national decline in church affiliation. Through the lens of her ecology model, Ammerman was slightly more optimistic. When some groups or affiliations die, she said, others take their place. Fewer Americans may join bowling leagues, but unseen, she said, maybe Sunday school classes are taking over the lanes.

Either way, Ammerman and Putnam would agree that whatever congregation is in question, it creates some form of inward or outward commitment. Putnam has called the inward focus "bonding" social capital, creating close-knit groups. The outward orientation is "bridging" social capital. It helps ameliorate and overcome divisions in society. The growth of conservative churches is providing a pool of the bonding experience. The more liberal churches have lost some of their growing power by building bridges to civil society. Studies confirm a greater degree of civic activism by, for example, mainline Protestant and more liberal Catholic churches. Yet both kinds of social capital are necessary. They are both in shorter supply, if Putnam is correct. The challenge, very much like the church-sect dynamic, is for the conservative churches to build bridges—and see if they still can keep growing.[36]

Americans reportedly give their largest block of charity—a third of the total—to religious organizations. This is frequently emphasized by philanthropic research groups, hoping to keep a rosy outlook on American generosity. A group such as Empty Tomb Inc., which also researches church giving, tries to provide a reality check: It reports that Americans are not giving what they could. On average, Protestant churchgoers in 2000 had twice as much extra cash as churchgoers in 1964 but did not quite double their donations. (The average individual donation for 2000 was $603.) The group's Sylvia Ronsvalle finds it remarkable that Christians feel offended when asked to give money: "Can you imagine belonging to a country club and people not being aware of whether you are up on your dues?"[37]

In all voluntary organizations a few people pay most of the bills and the same is true in churches. According to *Money Matters*, a national study: "A minority of members give the most money." Typically 25 percent of the people give 75 percent (or 20 give 80). Aside from that, the strictness principle seems to be at work: Believers in conservative and inward-looking churches give five times more than those attending liberal churches. The orthodox evangelicals give the most at 3 percent of household income. "Their pastors are more likely to say something like this: 'We are different from the rest of Americans. We have something that they don't have, and we should be thankful.'" Higher rates of giving also show up in Pentecostal traditions. They are more likely to preach that giving ensures material blessings in return. "Church people who believe that God will reciprocate for monetary gifts tend to give more to their churches," *Money Matters* said. Some clergy "preach about how God rewards givers."[38]

Money Matters used Lyle E. Schaller's terminology of "high-expectation churches" for those that are strict and inward, standing in tension with society and therefore drawing more financial devotion from members. The mainline churches and some Catholic parishes operate more like "voluntary associations." Their members' commitments of time and money are diluted by having "more ties and group memberships outside their churches." Their interests and charitable giving are divided. Whether a church looks inward or outward, a "clear identity" always spurs more giving.[39]

The overall giving trend, according to *Money Matters*, focuses more on local than national concerns. Some have argued that Protestants withhold donations because of liberal activism at the headquarters or Catholics hold back in anger at the conservative Vatican. While that may affect their national giving it does not upset the local setting, the study said: "Giving is felt to be a matter between the church member and God or between the member and his or her congregation." Feelings toward denominational leaders "have no noticeable effect on the amount given." People in large and small churches feel an equal amount of "ownership" of the congregation, which somewhat defies the "small group" arguments. Democratic church governance, moreover, is not necessary to stimulate giving: "What *is* crucial is trust in leadership—in whoever actually has the power in the congregation, whether clergy or lay leaders."[40]

As church giving stays more with local congregations, some have warned of a new local selfishness. Yet Schaller has pointed to how it can also promote bridging activity. His key example is the "sister church" phenomenon. A congregation not only sends money to an urban mission or overseas fellowship but goes there to work as well. This may "be the greatest change in 'how we do church in America,'" Schaller said.[41]

More money stays at home, moreover, because of "higher salaries of clergy and lay staff," said *Money Matters*. Local churches also work with fewer volunteers, especially as women have entered the workforce. The estimated median annual budget for a church today ranges from $105,000 to $123,000. Where it goes always puts ministers on the spot. "Clergy receive the lion's share of all the laity's contributions to their churches," said church consultant Loren Mead. While many churches "get a bargain" with outstanding clergy, "the fact remains that this is where the money goes." One historian said that for 250 years "about two-thirds of all congregational expenditures" went to employee salaries. His point, however, was that now clergy salaries are dropping.[42]

Naturally, clergy feel conflicted over the annual stewardship sermon. When the Barna Research Group probed clergy about this in 2002, just 31 percent ranked themselves above average in inspiring giving by members. While 37 percent reported being "average," 23 percent said they were "not too good" or "poor" at that job. Groups such as Empty Tomb have advocated more theological training in the art of promoting stewardship. From a biblical point of view, stewardship advisers say, talking about money is normal. Sixteen of Jesus' thirty-eight parables were on the subject. One in ten Gospel verses takes on mammon. And if the Bible offers a thousand verses on prayer and faith, it has twice that many on money and possessions. Said church finance counselor James D. Berkley: "Stewardship, for most people, arises not from their nature but from a heart turned toward God and God's ways." But the pastor must turn those hearts and also set the example.[43]

At Saddleback church the generous giving reflects the trust in the leadership. Warren's house "is no mansion." He is "generous to a fault, an unpretentious, fun-loving man without boat or beach house," said a *Christianity Today* magazine profile. But for a while he did become known as "the guy who almost messed up pastors' housing allowance."[44] His clash with the Internal Revenue Service nearly touched all ministers in the United States.

Since 1921 federal law has allowed clergy to deduct their cost of housing from their income. The Warrens had bought a $360,000 home in 1992, and three years later deducted $79,999 as their annual housing expense. The IRS rejected the deduction as too high, arguing that the "fair market rental value" of the home was only $59,479. The Warrens protested as a matter of religious freedom, and a federal court backed them. When the IRS appealed to the Ninth Circuit Court of Appeals, however, two of the three judges decided to broaden the case and consider the constitutionality of the 1921 exemption. "Inflating this case to constitutional stature is wholly unnecessary," said the one dissenting judge.[45]

To avert a major legal challenge, the Warrens and the IRS acted swiftly, settling the case to make the complaint moot. In addition, Congress passed a law making clear that clergy had the exemption for the "rental value" only. President Bush signed the bill in 2002. If the exemption had been pulled, American clergy would have paid $2.3 billion more in taxes over the next five-year period. "The purpose of the housing allowance wasn't to make rich clergy richer," said one Texas churchman. "It was to make poor clergy less poor. I'm sure the court said, 'Look at this guy!' And somebody said, 'Well, let's just take the whole thing away.'" One North Dakota lawmaker said, "A clergy's home is not just his shelter, but a central meeting place for all members of the congregation." Though the constitutional challenge was stopped, it nevertheless could be revived again.[46]

When Warren was a young minister, he mirrored the financial strains of most of his clergy peers. He and his wife, Kay, "descended into marriage hell," she said. With no money, they pursued marriage counseling. "MasterCard saved my marriage," said Rick Warren. Many young seminarians today are no less idealistic about starting out on nothing. "My goal is definitely to serve and take what they give me; God will provide," said Vickie Sickles, a student at Gettysburg Lutheran Seminary. "Some churches you serve may not have the money to give back to you. But for me, right now, that's okay. It sounds incredible and maybe naive, but that's what I feel right now."[47]

In ways, a church might feel something is wrong with a minister who can't speak frankly about making a living. "Any preacher who claims that he or she is totally committed to the Lord and cares little about salary is open to suspicion," advised *Money Matters*. Despite the Bible's calls for otherworldly focus and sacrifice, it asks a square deal for ministers. Proverbs 30 says, "Give me neither poverty nor riches." Jesus urged the disciples to move on if a town didn't offer provisions, "for the laborer deserves his wages." And St. Paul was cocksure about this: "The Lord commanded that those who proclaim the gospel should get their living by the gospel." From one point of view, if God commands a person to enter ministry, what real choice does he or she have?[48]

The moral debate rises again: What is an appropriate living? The Pulpit and Pew study of clergy salaries, which is concerned about the fate of the majority, said middle-class status should be the goal. Clergy should earn a salary "sufficient to provide hospitality and a well-lived life." They should be able to rear children, save for education, and plan for retirement. Also at stake is the church's reputation: tightwad or enthusiastic employer. "Clerical salaries have long been used by historians as measures of a church's self-image vis-à-vis the broader culture, whether farmer-preacher Baptists or highly educated and professional Episcopalian priests," writes John R. Stackhouse Jr. Young people deciding what to do with their lives, especially if professionally inclined, also take that measure.[49]

The 1999 median annual income for all full-time American clergy was $40,000, according to the Bureau of Labor Statistics, an average that is rising partly because the number of Catholic priests (who earn less than Protestant clergy) is declining. Either way, the $40,000 includes the cost of housing (provided in the salary or in a church-owned residence). Half of clergy make less than the $40,000 median, of course. But with the cost-of-housing deduction, quite a few clergy save income by dropping into a low tax bracket. Clergy today, in fact, are advised to buy a house (rather than use a free parsonage) to take advantage of the tax break on the mortgage, interest, property tax, and maintenance. "Ministers can exclude those kinds of expenses from incomes and then they can turn around on a Schedule A and deduct them as itemized deductions," said Dan Busby, an expert on clergy taxation. "Anytime you get a double dip with the IRS, that's quite a deal."[50]

When the status of *all* clergy is the question, the polity of churches and the sizes of congregations become crucial issues. Church leaders debate what the gospel asks for: a free-market approach to support clergy or a system that distributes resources more evenly.

The connectional systems of Methodists, Lutherans, Presbyterians, Episcopalians, and Catholics regulate clergy pay. The Baptists, Congregationalists, and most Pentecostal and Bible churches decide about finances at the congregation level. "The polity itself has some effect on salaries offered pastors," the Pulpit and Pew study concluded. Rick Warren notwithstanding, clergy in a regulated system do better. Their median income is $46,000 compared to $39,000 for congregational clergy.[51]

More important than either system, however, is the membership count. "Church size translates directly into market power," Pulpit and Pew said. A big church in a connectional system can certainly pay higher than recommended salaries to draw the top clergy. The large congregational-type churches have no limits, especially with a founding pastor. Having a lot of rich congregants makes no difference, the study found. "The wealth of the laity does not seem to be as important as the number of laity for clergy salaries." And for most churches laity are few and far between. Half the connectional type and two-thirds of the congregation type draw no more than one hundred worshipers a week.[52]

The two systems of clergy compensation are quite at odds. One guarantees a minimum salary. The other rides the free market. The first does not necessarily reward success, but the second creates a remarkable disparity in clergy living standards. The Catholic pay system is the most egalitarian. It also deploys priests evenhandedly. "Centralization is the key factor that insulates the Roman Catholic Church from the free market," said Pulpit and Pew. The free market would have pushed priests' salaries to "possibly unaffordable levels for smaller parishes."[53]

While megachurch pastors are doing fine, and regulated systems guarantee a minimum clergy salary, there are six other concerns worth debating. First is how to compensate clergy who serve the vast number of small churches. The second is to assure new ministry candidates that it is not a road to poverty. A third is how to keep ministry primarily spiritual, since the pursuit of a better salary can be Darwinian indeed, said Pulpit and Pew: "Clergy wishing to maintain a middle-class lifestyle must take on a 'career' as opposed to a 'calling' mentality." In churches where there is an oversupply of clergy, those coming up in the ranks must similarly struggle with the nature of the call, said Matthew Price, who studies clergy financing. These circumstances will create a clergy pool of "young ministers who long to serve the church but do not wish to compete for a few choice appointments."[54]

The fourth concern is that churches not put an "undue emphasis on increasing membership for economic rather than mission-drive reasons," according to Pulpit and Pew. A fifth concern is this: Clergy too dependent on the congregation dole cannot speak "tough love." They cannot be a "prophetic voice." Finally, the "downward pressure on clergy salaries" of small congregations may lower the status of the entire clergy profession. Lay pastors or volunteers may finally squeeze clergy out of their vocations, a final "deprofessionalization" of ministry. How ironic, said church historian James Hudnut-Beumler, that as "national educational attainment is at its highest point ever, the average educational attainment of people serving as pastors of the largest mainstream Protestant denominations should be on the decline."[55]

The heirs of Adam Smith might welcome the end of all church bureaucracy and clericalism. Their radical prescription is akin to union busting. Even tenured members of hierarchical churches warn of the "conflict of interest" in a system where clergy rule over their own benefits. "We have created a power and ownership structure in which the clergy wields most of the power," said Loren Mead, an Episcopal priest. "They are now trapped in that role by history and by arrangements locked in place by customs and laws intended to preserve the institution." The result, he lamented, is an over functioning by clergy and under functioning by the laity. It has become "increasingly impossible for individual clergy to carry out their mandate to be bearers of religious mystery, to have religious rather than institutional authority."[56]

Others would advocate a more regulatory, or "communitarian," model, where a common pot supports clergy work. These advocates, however, have the New Testament record to show how unlikely this could be. It was "first tried two thousand years ago and unraveled due to powerful forces of human nature," said Pulpit and Pew.[57]

In the 1970s, when the problem in the Protestant mainline seemed to be "too many pastors" and shrinking opportunities, one solution of course was for them to leave ministry and pursue other productive careers. It was pointed out, however, how difficult that is. "If a pastor decides to leave the employment of the church and enter a secular profession, people will raise questions as to whether he has lost his faith or has been involved in some type of immoral conduct," wrote two ministers. "Additionally, the concept of the call of God and a belief in an indelible ordination may leave former clergy with an extreme sense of guilt."[58] While clergy today may still opt to pursue other careers, the emphasis in the twenty-first century is how to keep them on board.

In light of the financial strains on ministry, several solutions have been proposed. One is for a minister to simply found a church. If the church succeeds then personal income is assured. Another is to close dying churches and redeploy clergy. Such mercy killings, however, are unlikely. The saying goes that "the hardest thing to do is close a church." The market will itself "create solutions" if the church does not, warned Pulpit and Pew. The study favored "more regulation and cooperation between congregations and among denominations" to sustain small-church pastors. Such approaches have worked already. Some Baptist churches, for example, share the costs of ministers in a group of congregations. And though talk of an institutional unity of mainline Protestant churches has died, sharing of clergy on a bilateral basis is now possible. One example is the case of shared clergy between Episcopal and Lutheran churches.[59]

Another approach is to circumvent salary altogether. Some clergy may be willing to take a vow of poverty, even with families. Second-career clergy with children grown and savings in the bank might also be candidates to work for a minimum. The church "may be better for this" altruism, said Price, the researcher. But he wonders whether such altruism can produce "a large enough group to fill the projected clergy shortages." Also filling the gap could be unmarried clergy. They are more typically ordained women, but also some bachelor or homosexual clergy, who have the flexibility to take hardship assignments without any impact on a spouse or children.[60]

One final adaptation is theologically the most earthshaking: Let the ordained calling, the veritable mark of God on a person, be turned on and off in a lifetime. Lutheran pastor and seminary president Michael L. Cooper-White said that younger generations are being told they may hold five to seven jobs in a lifetime, so rapid are the changes. "People who are twenty today cannot conceive of doing anything for the rest of

their lives," he said. "Then the church, over against that, presents ministry as a lifelong commitment. I wonder if we wouldn't be well served
to change that message somewhat. We could say, 'You'll always be
Christian. But to serve in the ordained pastorate need not be lifelong.'
People can regularly step in and step out for a while. And then come
back a little later." He said that idea is not yet widely discussed. "It's
controversial."[61]

9

Fault Lines

FOR EIGHT SUMMERS IN A ROW the "fidelity and chastity" rule for clergy occupied the annual General Assembly of the Presbyterian Church (USA). The statute, adopted in 1996 to bar active homosexuals from ministry, had survived reversals and national referendum votes. Nerves were frayed, activism was still at a peak, and some alluded to a "constitutional crisis" in this very procedural church. It was time for some humor and a bumper sticker provided it: "Presbyterians do it decently and in order."[1]

By the end of the 1990s, few denominations had not openly debated the sexual behavior of their pastors, priests, and ministers. Every church requires exemplary behavior. Most require clergy to vow compliance at ordination. But in a more permissive culture, secret worlds were being opened and liberalized ethics were being espoused. Some clergy declared a God-given right of "justice-love," which meant consensual sexual relations outside of heterosexual marriage.[2] Few such topics are now off the ecclesiastical table. The ministry fault line over human sexuality has many fractures: ordination of homosexuals, clergy presiding at "same-sex union" ceremonies, sexual abuse and promiscuity. The chaos over sexuality has also produced a male backlash, giving rise to a new search for Christian manhood as well as movements opposing feminism and homosexuality.

The nation's clergy agree that homosexuality is the next great issue in the church. When polled, they say it is not a local issue, but a great national "struggle" with "the possibility of denominational split and membership loss." The televangelist scandals of the 1980s, involving adultery and promiscuity, and the sexual abuse debacle of Catholic priests of 2002, troubled Christian ministry to the core. Yet in a media age of "philandering

clerics and pedophile priests" everything was adding up, reaching beyond clergy "malfeasance" to the symbols of Christian life itself—the created order, the nature of family, the validity of doctrine, biblical authority,
and the trustworthiness of ministers in general.[3]

The debate may run for another decade or generation. Before he retired
from office, Archbishop of Canterbury George Carey urged traditionalists
to stand their ground and stay in church rather than walk away. "We
should 'speak the truth in love' to each other," he said. A Christian editorial framed the clash over sexual identity and behavior as a showdown
between "classical" and "revisionist" Christianity. The classical interpretation said "the created order, as described in Genesis, tells us of God's
purpose for marriage and sexuality," while revisionists claim that "because so many educated people consider Genesis a mere creation myth, it
is irrelevant to the sexuality debate."[4]

The range of practical results can be illustrated by events in the Presbyterian, Episcopal, Catholic, and Methodist churches, augmented by new
studies on clergy misbehavior. And amid this new furor over ministry,
movements such as Promise Keepers—which rejects homosexuality and
urges male sexual integrity—are just one reaction in America's churches.

A half-decade before the Presbyterian Church (USA) was formed in a 1983
merger, the northern and southern denominations that joined to make the
new church had already barred ordination of "self-affirming, practicing
homosexual persons." Such an ordination was a church and societal "contradiction" to Scripture and the will of Christ. Indeed, it was a "sin."[5]

The first open challenge to those rules came in 1991, when the Downtown United Presbyterian Church in Rochester, New York, called Jane
Spahr to be "lesbian evangelist." A native of Pittsburgh, Spahr had been
ordained in 1974, four years before the ban in her denomination, allowing
her to retain her credentials even though her coming out required her to
resign as director of the Oakland (California) Presbyterian Churches.
When New York Presbyterians contested her appointment and filed a
complaint, she won in lower church courts but lost in 1992 before the denomination's top panel, the Permanent Judicial Commission.

At this point, Presbyterians nationally asked for a clear interpretation
of current church resolutions, which still said "the practice of homosexuality is a sin," while acknowledging the difficulty "of rejecting a person's
sexual orientation without rejecting the person." The "authoritative interpretation" came down in 1993: The resolutions stood. In so legislative a
body, however, rules could be rescinded almost yearly. So conservatives
proposed the "fidelity and chastity" amendment in 1996 to give the tenets
more ecclesiastical permanence. The assembly adopted it, and it was affirmed by a majority of the 173 presbyteries (97 to 74). Now, a specific rule

that deacons, elders, or ministers must "live either in fidelity within the covenant of marriage between a man and a woman, or chastity in single-ness" was embedded in the *Book of Order*, the church constitution.[6]

For the next eight years the "fidelity and chastity" rule was embattled. It was sustained by the support of a majority of presbyteries around the country, and its chief advocate was the Presbyterian Lay Committee, an orthodox advocacy group. The effort to rescind the rule came from the More Light churches, which supported homosexual rights, and a liberal alliance of clergy who said the rule was tantamount to a witch-hunt. One counter push had been the attempted passage of an alternative "fidelity and integrity" rule, with the obvious leeway for consenting adults.

Opposition to the chastity rule also came from the heart of the church bureaucracy, the headquarters in Louisville, Kentucky. In 1999, the official Committee on Church Orders and Ministry tried to remove the rule to allow a "more inclusive understanding of leadership." The committee majority (split 24 to 14) believed ordination standards were "a justice issue more than a morality issue."[7] In 2003, the committee went further and urged a rejection of the 1993 constitutional ruling that homosexual practice was sin. That was overwhelmingly defeated at the General Assembly (431 to 92).

During the years of the debate, some clergy came out publicly as being homosexual and resigned in protest. Some were "outed." But Katie Morrison, a "chaste" lesbian who publicly identified her partner, pushed the church debate to a new level of subtlety. Approved by the Redwoods Presbytery, Morrison was ordained in October 2001 at First Presbyterian Church of San Anselmo, California, and installed as a field worker for the More Light Presbyterians. When other California church members filed a complaint, ordaining Pastor Chandler Stokes said: "We don't ask our heterosexual candidates about their fidelity in marriage, or investigate their sexual behavior. I think to do so in this case would clearly have been discriminatory."[8]

Still, the complaint that it was an "irregular" ordination reached the high church court, arguing that Morrison's disclosure of her sexual orientation and partner should have "triggered a duty of further inquiry." On March 4, 2003, the Permanent Judicial Commission rejected that argument. The court ruled, "If a person does not self-acknowledge a practice that the confessions call sin," then an ordination panel should not investigate further—unless there is "direct and specific knowledge" of a behavioral violation. "A hunch, gossip or stereotype is not a sufficient ground to compel further inquiry."

By ruling this way, the commission reversed its own logic used in a 1993 case.[9] At that time it ruled that an ordination review panel was required to ask about sexual activity. But the "fidelity and chastity" law had ironically changed that duty, the Permanent Judicial Commission said in

2003. The "fidelity and chastity" law required only "self-acknowledged practice"—not worries about someone's practice. Thus, the only "reasonable grounds" for asking about behavior were "factual allegations of how, when, where and under what circumstances" the person acknowledged, or engaged in, a sinful behavior.

Turning to the church's rich Calvinist tradition, the commission also declared that it had introduced a serious "theological defect" in the 1993 ruling. It had wrongly assumed "that one category of persons is more prone to sin" than others. "The doctrine of total depravity teaches us that not only do all fall short of the glory of God, but that there is no part of our person that is not in need of the redeeming grace of our Lord Jesus Christ." Sexual orientation was no more grounds to probe than singleness or obesity: "In other words, stereotypical profiling is not a reasonable or valid ground for singling out a candidate for additional questioning."

The Presbyterian drama had focused on conduct of an ordination process. When this topic flared in the Episcopal Church, it focused on an individual bishop, Walter C. Righter, for ordaining a gay man in 1990. Ten other bishops charged him with breaking his ordination vow to "solemnly" uphold the doctrine and discipline of the church. And they included the accusation of heresy for rejecting the doctrine of Christian marriage. When the Righter hearing opened on a balmy morning in May 1996 at the stone gothic Cathedral Church of Saint John in downtown Wilmington, Delaware, it was set to be only the second heresy trial in Episcopal Church history.[10]

By resolution, the House of Bishops in 1977 and the General Convention in 1979 had forbidden ordination of "practicing homosexuals." Yet defiance became more open by 1990. The bishop most willing to confront the situation was liberal John Spong of Newark, New Jersey, who angrily called the House of Bishops hypocritical when it censured him in closed session in 1990 for ordaining a gay man who later criticized monogamy. A few weeks later, Bishop Righter, retired from Iowa but working in Newark, ordained Barry L. Stopfel, an active homosexual, to be a deacon. "I was doing what I thought to be the right thing based on all the screening process for ordination," Righter recalled. "I did not want to confront the church with anything."

The traditional bishops were looking for a test case. They had failed to pass a binding canon requiring clergy "to model in their lives the received teaching of the church that all its members are to abstain from sexual relations outside of holy matrimony." So they chose the actions of Righter, who had also signed a theological manifesto (written by Spong and called the "Koinonia Statement") that equated the morality of homosexual and heterosexual behavior in God's created order. At least seventy bishops had signed the manifesto by the eve of the trial. "This trial is about the doctrine of Christian marriage," said the prosecution advocate. In rebuttal, the defense advocate said the question was not whether "the power of the bishop to ordain is a matter of doctrine or a matter of discipline." More simply, he said, the Episcopal Church had no belief or statute "that puts the word 'doctrine' and homosexual ordination in the same sentence."

The panel of purple-shirted bishops took counsel from the daylong exchange of arguments. As expected, they dismissed both the disciplinary and heresy charges in a 7–1 ruling. "The court finds that there is no core doctrine prohibiting the ordination of a non-celibate homosexual person living in a faithful and committed sexual relationship," they ruled. And "there is no discipline of the church prohibiting" such ordinations. The church's "core doctrine" was limited to Christ's divinity, his resurrection, the presence of the Holy Spirit, and the final judgment. Two bishops concurred with the "technical" ruling but criticized the court for adopting Bishop Righter's argument that where there is "silence" on a matter in Scripture and the church canon, clergy may act even if it harms church unity.

The sole dissenting opinion came from Bishop Andrew Fairfield of North Dakota. He said that sexual relations fell under Bible condemnations of homosexuality and fornication, doctrinal assertions in the Book of Common Prayer, and official church resolutions. Righter's attorney stated the legal precedent this way: "It's not saying it's okay, it's saying it's not illegal." John Howe of Florida, one of the bishops who brought the charge against Righter, said the trial was necessary even if the complaints were dismissed. "We could not resolve it anywhere else," he said. "We felt it would benefit the church to have clarity on the matter."

Whatever had been clarified became irrelevant when, in 2003, the Episcopal Diocese of New Hampshire elected V. Gene Robinson as the first openly gay Episcopal bishop. "I plan to be a good bishop, not a gay bishop," he said to cheering supporters. "I'm so much more than my orientation." Robinson, fifty-six, had left his wife and two daughters over his homosexuality, according to the official account, and later met his partner. When his election was affirmed by the 2003 General Convention, the traditionalists warned of finally breaking away over an "irregular" episcopacy that now openly engaged in homosexual practice. In 1998, a majority of Anglican bishops worldwide had already said it was "incompatible with Scripture," putting a wedge in the episcopacy itself. While Bishop Robinson urged the church to "keep coming together," the *Boston Globe* predicted a "rift likely to widen."[11]

The open lives of a few homosexual clergy, however, were not the whole matter: more fundamental was the redefinition of Christian marriage and relations between men and women. "Ordination is complex, with many kinds of ministry," said New Testament scholar Richard Hays at Duke Divinity School. "But in the debate over same-sex marriages, the issues come into sharper focus for everyone." Weddings for homosexuals are "going to create, ultimately, a great amount of symbolic confusion," he said. "The basis for marriage between man and woman, based on the complementarity of male and female, is deep and profound in Scripture."[12]

The United Church of Christ, which ordains homosexuals, also allows ceremonies for same-sex couples. It is meanwhile considering the next frontier, said Mitzi Eilts, a minister who heads its gay, lesbian, bisexual, and transgender concerns. "We need to be talking about, and not presume, that heterosexual and homosexual are the only forms of family to be sanctified."[13] That is the "slippery slope" many clergy worry about, a worry that includes what to do with fellow pastors who slide in that direction. When the same-sex union debate arose in the United Methodist Church, it revealed that sometimes clergy can make their colleagues pay for breaking rules, and sometimes not. In January 1999, for example, a hall in the Sacramento Convention Center filled with more than a thousand churchgoers, and some clergy, to celebrate the blessed "union" of lesbians Ellie Charlton, sixty-three, and Jeanne Barnett, sixty-eight. They were members of St. Mark's United Methodist Church, where Pastor Don Fado had performed a private "marriage" ceremony and declared the entire event an "act of ecclesiastical disobedience." Fado said that "history is going a certain direction, and that we're on the right side." What made the event significant, however, was that nearly one hundred clergy signed a statement of support. They had openly defied a 1996 policy in the church's Social Principles: "Ceremonies that celebrate homosexual unions shall not be conducted by our ministers."[14]

When complaints arose, the regional bishop, Melvin Talbert, said he backed civil disobedience in support of homosexual rights because as a black minister he used it for civil rights. Despite his support, as bishop he had to act on a legitimate complaint against some sixty-nine clergy. "This is a very painful day," Talbert said. He hoped his "clergy peers will seek justice and act in a way that is consistent with the teachings and compassion of Jesus." While this was not the first "blessing" of a lesbian or homosexual couple by United Methodist clergy—a reported five hundred minister said they would provide them—it made national headlines. "This is our lunch counter, this is our freedom ride," said one participant. In the end no one was punished, diluting some of the moral high ground of civil disobedience. Like so many such violations, it became a "local option"—a local church simply exempted itself from national norms.[15]

Yet two other United Methodist ministers would pay the price. Under the 1996 resolution, Jimmy Creech of Omaha, Nebraska, was tried for presiding at the union ceremony of a lesbian couple. He was acquitted in 1998 because clerics on the tribunal did not believe the rule was a legal statute. The denomination's highest court, the Judicial Council, was called in, and it ruled that his action was a "chargeable offense." Creech resigned his ministerial post and became an independent advocate.[16] In Chicago, meanwhile, urban pastor Gregory Dell of Broadway United Methodist Church had presided over same-sex unions for seventeen years. But after his latest, done for two men a month after the 1996 rule, he was brought to trial in March 1999 and found guilty.

Dell faced thirteen fellow pastors in the tribunal, and the issue for the prosecution was making "a mockery of church law." Said fellow minister and prosecutor Stephen C. Williams: If clergy can't obey the rules "then strike the word 'united' from United Methodist." Pastor Larry Pickens countered for the Dell defense that church founder John Wesley himself violated Anglican statutes. So the issue was "what we do when a pastoral need and a church law conflict." As Dell said before trial, he had to persuade jurors that being a "pastor with integrity means that sometimes you have to intentionally break a rule."[17]

Unable to convince the jurors, Dell was suspended from ministry by a ten-to-three vote until he agreed to comply. "If I can't be a pastor fully to all the people," he said, choking back tears, "you don't want me as a pastor." After his trial Dell said that human sexuality was not an easy topic. While he would be extremely cautious about blessing bisexual or inter-family relations, his dynamic view of the Bible bars him from making any "absolute statement" against them. "I cannot view myself as conducting a wedding for a brother and sister. I would be very reluctant about a three-some." Nevertheless, as a pastor he would feel called to "explore what these relationships meant, and help them understand the challenge of their relationships."[18]

The conflicting approaches in United Methodism blossomed onto a national stage in 2004 when the denomination held its every-four-years assembly, the General Conference. Meeting in Pittsburgh, delegates voted to order their highest court, the Judicial Council, to immediately review the church trial of a lesbian minister in Washington State: In the case, a jury of thirteen pastors acquitted Karen Dammann of charges that her sexual relations with a partner disqualified her from ministry. Two days into the Judicial Council deliberation, a majority of the assembly voted to uphold United Methodism's ban on active homosexual clergy. Hours later, the Judicial Council said it could not reverse the Dammann acquittal. Again, majorities of lay people were backing traditional morality for clergy, while the church courts, made up of fellow clergy, were just as often leaning the opposite way.[19]

Ministerial grappling with the sexual revolution, when in support of more leniency, usually summons the cause of justice and group rights. It had twined itself with the secular gay rights movement of the 1970s, and invariably became part of what sociologist Robert Wuthnow called "the restructuring of American religion." In this restructuring, liberal and conservative "special purpose" or advocacy groups that cross all church lines defined where Christians stood more than denominations themselves.

The growth of government entitlement programs in the 1960s had geared justice-minded clerics to "group rights" more than individual cases, and thus the rights groups proliferated. "Not only were there gay organizations for the religious community in general, but specific organizations emerged for gay Mormons, gay Brethren, gay Lutherans, gay Presbyterians, gay Catholics, gay evangelicals, and gay atheists." The alternative to protest for group rights, Wuthnow said, was the "the tried-and-true method of applying religious values to individual consciences through preaching and teaching."[20]

For clergy, that teaching experience was deepened by study at seminary, where the sexual revolution was apparently launched before it was in the local church or a convention floor. A study of seminary cultures called *Being There* found that the more liberal mainline seminaries challenged students "to confront their own deep prejudices and intolerance." Sexism and racism were primary concerns but so was "homophobia." Some mainline seminaries foster "political activity" among caucuses on campus, producing clergy who do likewise—even excessively—when serving churches in the field. The seminary can also be the first line of attack on dissenters, one mainline professor said in a separate report. To oppose homosexuality, for example, "is tantamount to shooting oneself in the foot in terms of being hired or given tenure," he said. "It is very rare to find a faculty with more than one, two, or three people who support the church's historic stance against homosexual behavior." Professor Hays said that "would be true of some mainline schools, but certainly not all."[21]

The debate on the sources of the homosexual revolution among Christian clergy, however, now focuses most intensely on the Roman Catholic Church. Its problem with clergy and sexual abuse rapidly outlined a broader issue: a homosexual subculture in the Catholic priesthood, particularly in the more recent recruitment system of some Catholic seminaries.

An early expositor of the "orientation crisis" in the modern priesthood was the Cleveland, Ohio, vicar of priests Donald Cozzens. His book *The Changing Face of the Priesthood* (2000) stated: "At issue at the beginning of the twenty-first century is the growing perception—one seldom contested by those who know the priesthood well—that the priesthood is or is becoming a gay profession." Ignoring the issue is easiest, but it "only delays the time when circumstances will demand that it be given attention."[22]

The gay culture in Christianity, which historians have detected in such early disciplinary writings as the *Didache* (A.D. 100 to 120), came into the open in U.S. Catholicism in 1973, with the founding of the lay group Dignity, and four years later "New Ways Ministries," through which priests and nuns affirmed active homosexuals as Christians. The conservative reaction was characterized by the 1982 book *The Homosexual Network*, written by the Rochester, New York, priest Enrique Rueda, who brought his concern unsuccessfully to the Vatican. Yet in 1983 the U.S. bishops were forced to get involved by another event: the case of a priest in Lafayette, Louisiana, who had molested boys since 1974. To investigate, the Vatican had dispatched Thomas Doyle, a Benedictine priest and canon lawyer on the staff of the Vatican's embassy in Washington, D.C. His 1985 report of a brewing crisis was tabled.[23]

The Louisiana case was ferreted out, however, by investigative reporter Jason Berry for the liberal *National Catholic Reporter*. The questions of abuse, pedophilia, and homosexuality were pushed uncomfortably into public attention. The Vatican chose to respond from a different vantage. In 1986 the doctrinal offices in Rome released guidelines "On the Pastoral Care of Homosexual Persons," which famously said same-sex attraction "must be seen as an objective disorder." Soon after, the bishops of the United States barred Dignity groups from meeting in parishes of their dioceses. The candor finally surfaced in several key journals of Catholic opinion. Notre Dame University theologian Richard McBrien raised the curtain in 1987 in *Commonweal* in an article titled "Homosexuality and the Priesthood: Questions We Can't Keep in the Closet." Two years later sociologist Andrew Greeley offered "Bishops Paralyzed Over Heavily Gay Priesthood" in the *National Catholic Reporter*.[24]

More than a decade later, when the sexual abuse scandal broke in the Archdiocese of Boston, the preponderance of gay Catholic priests became the subject of conventional conversation. Cozzens said the situation was aided by "seminary faculties which include a disproportionate number of homosexually oriented persons." Not infrequently, he writes, "The sexual contacts and romantic unions among gay seminarians creates [*sic*] intense and complicated webs of intrigue and jealousy leading to considerable inner conflict." What is more, a significant number of straight heterosexual candidates for ministry were apparently becoming uncomfortable with the setting. As McBrien stated the question: "How many heterosexual seminarians have decided to leave the seminary and abandon their interest in a presbyterial vocation because of the presence of significant numbers of gays in seminaries and among the local clergy?"[25]

One theory is that the departure of twenty thousand priests after the Second Vatican Council—most of them straight young men who wanted to marry—left a much higher "gay/straight ratio" in the priesthood. As a result, more homosexuals saw a kinship with ministry and more dioceses and religious orders became "open to ordaining gay men if they demonstrate a commitment to celibate living." What developed was not only a feeder system but a subculture. Its divisiveness became the next great issue within the priesthood. According to some, much of the priesthood had become a divided world of liberal clerics who wanted to marry, but stayed in the vocation, and young doctrinally conservative "John Paul II priests" who were self-aware homosexuals.[26]

An estimated fourth to a half "of the priests today have a homosexual orientation," said sociologist Dean Hoge. "How many are active? Everyone agrees it is a minority, but no one has exact information." In a study of new priests who had left in their first five years, a fifth said: "More priests are homosexual than the public knows, and the priesthood is becoming homosexual." Half agreed that "the Church needs to deal more openly with gay issues." Another survey of priests across the church, reported in 2002, found that more than half said a homosexual subculture "clearly" or "probably" existed in their diocese or religious order. Four in ten said the same about seminaries they attended.[27]

"We heard numerous negative reports about homosexual subcultures in seminaries," said the researchers. Young priests seemed most aware of the new pressures. While just 3 percent of priests older than sixty-five identified a gay subculture at seminary, 45 percent between the ages of twenty-five and thirty-five did so. "Our conclusion," the study said, "is that homosexual subcultures increased in visibility, and probably also in numbers, in recent decades." Having a homosexual orientation, however, could be just one of many factors drawing men into a celibate and serving vocation like the priesthood. While some Vatican officials openly declared homosexuals should not be recruited, other conservative writers emphasized the importance of the priest's "fidelity" to his vows, whatever his private orientation.[28]

Invariably, the abuse scandal forced a more open discussion of the sexual propensity of men who evoke trust in a caring profession like church ministry. Peter Steinfels, a writer on Catholic affairs, said that since "most priest offenders have targeted male adolescents and not, like true pedophiles, prepubescent children," the attention will eventually turn also to "consensual violations of celibacy, whether heterosexual or homosexual (consensual frequently being an adjective open to dispute)." In the so-called Old World, for example, the priest and his woman—some say "concubine"—was a winked-at part of culture. According to Steinfels, "The scandal may no longer be victimization of minors; it will still be secrecy and hypocrisy."[29]

In the profession of psychological counseling, ethical norms have been debated, printed, and enforced: A counselor cannot have sexual relations with a client. Several states make such relations a crime. In contrast, Christian ministry has been reluctant to establish such written norms and penalties. Since the 1990s, however, such legal statutes—designed to protect churches against lawsuits—are being drafted for clergy compliance.

Psychologists who counsel clergy say "ministry is a very hazardous profession." Stress, temptation, and trusting environments easily combine to produce misbehavior. "The ministry focuses primarily on relationships, and it is only natural that an affectionate bond would develop between minister and parishioner, especially in the counseling setting." The hard-nosed sociologist, however, would call it plain old "clergy malfeasance": the "exploitation and abuse of a religious group's believers by trusted elites and leaders." A survey of 180 schools affiliated with the Association of Theological Schools found that clergy misconduct had become a new and "significant issue." The violation of sexual boundaries, in particular, may become a wider and more subtle issue for ministry in the future.[30]

In the first confidential survey of clergy on the subject, conducted in the mid-1980s with four denominations, "the numbers were astounding." Nearly four in ten (37.15 percent) "acknowledged they had engaged in what they considered to be 'inappropriate sexual behavior for a minister.'" At a time of mass sales of pornography, now unchecked on the Internet, "inappropriate" behavior could be anything to a guilt-sensitive minister. Yet in that same survey of clergy "12 percent admitted to having sexual intercourse with a congregation member other than their spouse." This exceeded even rates at which professional psychologists and psychiatrists erred with clients. The *Journal of Christian Ethics* reported in 2000 that incidents of clergy "sexual misconduct" were "increasing," estimating that a quarter to a third "of clergymen have admitted to sexually inappropriate behavior with parishioners."[31]

The problem is hardly new in ministry. The earliest ethical guidebook for the church, the *Didache*, composed around A.D. 100, said, "Thou shalt not seduce young boys." In colonial America, the first Baptist association oversaw the removal of the Reverend Henry Loveall from a Piscataway, New Jersey, church for bigamy. They said Pastor *Loveall* "seemed to have chosen an appropriate name for himself." After the sexual falls of Assemblies of God (AG) ministers Jim Bakker and Jimmy Swaggart, the church ordered them to "stand aside" and repent. By failing to resign, they were ejected from the clergy rolls and the denomination. "A lot of my colleagues complimented me for the way the AG handled those ministerial lapses," said Assemblies scholar Russell P. Spittler. "They didn't find a different process for famous people."[32]

Denominations have increasingly adopted formal complaint procedures for sexual harassment. But since many incidents are "consensual," or become "he said, she said" disputes, remedies remain difficult. Few would disagree with the assessment of the *Journal of Christian Ethics*. "Ordination and ministerial placement should be limited to persons of the highest spiritual maturity and moral integrity," it said, citing 1 Timothy 3:1–13. "However, clergy sexual abuse is very difficult to predict." Usually a number of factors lead to succumbing to the temptation. One view, presented by Roy Woodruff of the American Association of Pastoral Counselors, is that the minister waiting for this fall is either a prima donna who enjoys power or the "depressed pastor" who bonds with the similar mood in a parishioner of the opposite sex. What is more, "the average parish pastor has no one he reports to or is supervised by," Woodruff said. "He has a lot of needy people coming for help. A pastor who could be needy himself can exploit the needs of others."[33]

Two factors show up most often in advice for counselors: keep clear boundaries and do not confuse how people relate to a ministerial authority figure, a psychological dynamic called "transference." Clergy are not the only people on this emotional frontier. "We all have to deal with boundary problems," said Robert Wicks, who trains pastoral counselors and helps individual clergy. "I don't believe there are people who keep boundaries and people who can't. Everybody has his price, given the different low ebbs in life. No one likes to hear that." He said clergy must discern who in their flock raises a boundary dilemma and try to avoid close relations with them. "I say, 'Pick out people that, when you work with them, you know you *can't* keep boundaries.'" Richard Blackmon, also a clergy counselor, said an "effective prevention strategy" is accountability. With trusted others to talk to, a pastor "can freely discuss ministry relationships, problems that arise, and situations needing outside consultation."[34]

In a kind of anti-puritanical vein, others in church work have acknowledged that all workplaces have normal amounts of "sexual energy and attraction," which can render more productivity, strengthen motivation, soften conflicts, and increase teamwork and personal enrichment. "Some of these benefits might also occur in the church when pastors and parishioners experience sexual interest." Similarly, obsession with sexual sin may make it more dangerous. When some pastoral counselors saw Swaggart preach so vehemently against carnal temptation, they sensed that autobiography was surfacing. Still, the days when humanist psychologists said America's problem was Victorian sexual repression are over. Today, the most common advice is to manage stress, value restraint, and carefully maintain boundaries.[35]

On a second front, Blackmon said, clergy should be trained to "interpret strong emotions toward themselves as transference" and to avoid "counter-transference," taking the hatred or love as a personal attack or overture. People project good or bad feelings on an authority figure, often causing confusion. What minister has not suffered an unexpected outburst of anger from a person who, in fact, was angry at all authority figures, including God himself? Similarly, churchgoers may look on the minister as an intimate or lover never found, or one lost. The minister may take this as "real" sentiments, not just the "transference"—unconscious and thus "unreal"—that everyone seems to launch at authority figures. "The majority of feelings like this arise because of the pastor's role, not because of inherent personal qualities of the minister," Blackmon said.[36]

Another experienced clergy counselor, Lutheran pastor John O. Lundin, advocates "hardiness" training for clergy so they can anticipate the traumas ahead, especially when they constantly hear the troubles of others. "We expect clergy to be many more things than they used to be, which is both good and bad," said Lundin, who counseled scores of broken military families as an Air Force chaplain. "On the bad side, if you have clergy who don't know how to set appropriate boundaries, there are more pitfalls. You have a protective community who will allow things to happen that shouldn't. You have people who reach the point where they no longer make good judgments." A "dark side" can emerge when boundaries are transgressed. He said that both churches and the news media are watching more closely for such transgression. "If somebody in authority is trying to hide the secret, the story is 'they are trying to do something.'"[37]

Lundin believes the Catholic Church began to control its problem by closing seminaries where boys under age eighteen—called minor seminaries—began their celibate isolation, perhaps causing confusion in their early sexual development. The bishops also set down strict rules in 1992 for policing reported abuses. "So in some sense I think it is worse on the Protestant side," he said. There can be less central regulation among Protestants. Also, a new generation of young people may have been overexposed to pornography on the Internet. The excessive arousal might have affected their neurological development, so that "by the time they are adults, they need to have high levels of hyper-stimulation," Lundin said. "Cybersex is a huge issue."

Sociologists are less sympathetic with what makes clergy do wrong: They want to know how widespread the abuse is. That was the agenda of Anson Shupe when, in the first study of its kind, he and collaborators blanketed an entire city—the Dallas-Fort Worth metroplex—for a representative sample. They asked, in effect, "Have you been abused by a religious leader?" In summary, they found that 7.4 percent of a sample (1,067 people) "had intimate knowledge, from friends', coworkers', or relatives' reports or from their own experiences, of some form of clerical abuse." The abuse could be sexual, physical, financial, or authoritarian. When the bad hearsay is subtracted, however, just 3 percent of the Texas respondents experienced something personally.[38]

To counselors such as Wicks and Lundin, a cumulative 7 percent of the public knowing of or experiencing clerical abuse seems high, unless most of it counts for people being offended by clergy comments. "The 7 percent astounds me," said Wicks, suggesting people feeling verbal abuse can exaggerate. "You've got to insult somebody sometime if you challenge them," he said. "People in church, when their brand of religion is challenged, they consider it an insult. The numbers would be more relevant if you pulled out the verbal abuse, which contaminates the data. As a psychologist, I have problems with that." Another aspect of the Shupe report, however, puts those public perceptions of clergy in a rosier context: Accounts of abuse are higher in education (11.4 percent), from public authorities (24 percent), and in corporations (64.8 percent).[39]

The Shupe study, moreover, takes the stance that "clergy malfeasance appears widespread," despite claims that it crops up only in pockets or among bad apples. This debate arose when the scandal in the Boston Archdiocese was at a peak. "I think the case of Boston is unique," said theology professor Stephen Pope in a PBS news segment. "The incidents in Boston are of a different order [and] quantity than what we've seen around the country." In rebuttal, Steve Kruger of the reformist group Voice of the Faithful said Boston was different only because lawyers exposed its secret personnel files. "There is nothing in particular in the drinking water here in the archdiocese that created that [abuse] environment," Kruger said. While Boston was surely an egregious case, the John Jay College of Criminal Justice report in 2004 backed the widespread hypothesis: All fourteen regions of the U.S. Catholic Church experienced a "consistent" percentage of accusations (involving 3 to 6 percent of priests).[40]

What was at issue, Lundin believes, is what he called "a secret world" that can easily develop in a church trying to save face or, with the advice of lawyers, trying to avoid costly lawsuits. His own Evangelical Lutheran Church in America, for example, paid $70 million to settle lawsuits over a single Texas minister who stayed on the job amid complaints from abused boys.[41] Given the doctrine of human sinfulness, "The problem is not that clergy are involved in misconduct," Lundin said. "The problem is how it's been dealt with. And if it's not dealt with, then it blooms into a secret world and all the fears that go with that. If it's something that is dealt with, congregations can move on." The typical lawyer's advice not to say or admit anything "created the secret world," he said. "We don't know how big that secret world is." But he knows from experience that most cases of abuse or betrayal will come out in time.

Compared to secular professions, Lundin gives organized religion better marks for dealing fairly with abuses. "I think the church does a better job, because of the nature of what the church is. Most denominations are very clear about the treatment of problems." Wicks believes that public knowledge of the humanity and struggle of clergy may help take some pressures off the profession. It may also allow truly good people to flourish: "It's a step forward to try to help people realize that there are a lot of wonderful people doing ministry," Wicks said. "They're not perfect. We need to offer them support so we can continue to call people that are wonderful to the ministry."

When forty thousand male clergy met in the Georgia Superdome in 1996—billed the "largest gathering of Christian clergy in the history of the world"—they represented conservative Protestant concern over the failings of the church, the burnout of pastors, and the need for renewal.[42] They were also there in reaction to the sexual confusion in American church life: another major fault line in ministry today.

The gathering was held by Promise Keepers, a Christian men's movement that cheered masculinity, called for more brotherly fellowship, condemned homosexuality, and also challenged men to overcome every kind of promiscuity. The movement swelled from 1990 to 1997 but ran its cycle. The next conference for pastors, in Phoenix, Arizona, in 2003, drew just nine thousand clergy. "The church is in difficulty," said Bill McCartney, the former college football coach who founded the organization. "We want to change the direction of the church." Throughout its history the movement had urged support for local pastors. As it wound down as a mass-gathering event, it added a new point to its vision statement: "equipping [church] leaders to disciple men in the masculine context."[43]

Historical documents suggest that men have never attended church as much as women, though some advocates assume there were better days, a bygone church that was a popular male bastion. Men have always been the official leaders in Christianity, but they often come up short as participating "followers" in the institutional churches. Debate rages today over whether church culture is able to attract enough men—as clergy or as parishioners—to keep a healthy balance. For all churches the male-female ratio for attendance is about 40–60. Black male attendance is as low as 20 or 30 percent. Pollster George Barna has described American males as "one of the massive pagan subcultures on earth." Typically more pessimistic than church leaders, the Barna poll found that just 26 million men (27 percent of adult males) attend church. Some put it as low as 13 million (14 percent).[44]

There are two explanations of this: One falls under the rubric of "culture wars" and the other is a matter of simple demographics. To some, the more immediate culture war is over how feminists and homosexuals have alienated men from going to church. For example, as Promise Keepers stormed America, its most salient church-based opponent was Equal Partners in Faith. The group was coordinated by the Unitarian Universalist Association, the denomination with the highest percentage of female and homosexual clergy. Yet even Promise Keepers combined a kind of hard-soft picture of the male that put off some men. Part of manliness, it said, was to break down in tearful repentance for sin. As a high-flying football coach, McCartney himself had committed adultery but reconciled with his wife. Naturally he preached healing for male "brokenness," harassed as it was by pornography, drink, violence, or anger. "I believe my vulnerability makes me more useful to God," he said in his autobiography, *From Ashes to Glory*.[45]

Yet authors such as Leon J. Podles have argued that Christianity has been "feminized" for centuries. His provocative book *The Church Impotent* traced that to the medieval idea of "bridal" devotion to Christ. That passive love of Christ has neutered males, he said. Men need an aggressive rite of passage that involves struggle and victory, especially over temptation, and then entry into a male brotherhood. Increasing this feminization, or androgyny, in the church, Podles said, are the modern movements "to establish feminism and the toleration of homosexuality as the new orthodoxies." This "can only drive men even further from the Church."[46]

While the theological, psychological, and historical interpretation of Podles has been questioned—even by conservatives—many men identify with the contemporary practical issue of a womanish church. "The 'lamb' side of Jesus is well documented," said Steve Chavis, a spokesman for Promise Keepers. "We are looking for a [Jesus] guy with lines on his face, blisters on his hands and bruises on his knuckles helping me to fight temptation. That's the visceral, energetic Jesus that commanded the respect of Peter the fisherman." Chavis also noted that men, who have a "bottom-line mentality," don't like windy or poetic sermons. "They want to get to the point."[47] But to be fair, men also want their weekends off. Sunday sports have been viewed as an almost epochal rival to the Sabbath, of course, but why they vie with a Sunday *morning* slot is harder to explain.

Since the early 1980s, secular feminists have written widely about an organized "backlash" as women compete with men for professional positions or college admissions. Church feminists have argued likewise. They point to cycles of "backlash" every time women clergy entered clerical turf, usually when economic forces and women's rights movements coincided (such as the 1880s, 1920s, and 1950s). As feminist church writer Paula D. Nesbitt argues, "For women clergy, the *good news* that backlash movements offer is that women have made sufficient cultural and organizational strides in challenging the prevailing norms that they are perceived as a significant force to fend off."[48]

Amid this debate, the sexual dynamic between men and women has also been discussed, and perhaps no more openly than in the black church. "One popular folk explanation of the predominance of female members in black churches is related to the power of sexual attraction between the male pastor and his largely female followers," said historian C. Eric Lincoln, who mostly dismisses it. Said one black woman in ministry about obeisance to male clergy: "Is it because you see that minister up there as your substitute father, lover, husband, and your God?" African-American clergy have said that men may face a jealousy factor: A wife or girlfriend may heed the pastor's message, while the man does not care to. Still, Lincoln said, the one third of churchgoers who are men "are there for religious reasons and the sex of the leader will probably not make a substantial difference." He added, being provocative: "While the power of the patriarchal heritage cannot be summarily dismissed, it would seem just as reasonable to expect that a female pastor would attract a large male following."[49]

The case of the black church also illuminates the power of demographic factors, which is an alternative explanation to fewer males in church. For example, so large a percentage of African-American men are in prison that it cuts into Sunday attendance. Unemployment may also act as a stigma, causing more black males to shy away from the Sunday pews. For white churches, too, a predominance of women is biologically inevitable. Women live longer. According to one survey, women make up 63 percent of churchgoers over sixty-five. Many small churches are made up primarily of aging women. In contrast, large churches with well-funded programs and polished music draw men and families. The difference seems to be size and money, not theology or the pastor. "There are more women than men in the pews in every age category," said one national survey. But the divide is less among youth. For ages fifteen to twenty-four, women exceed men by only 14 percent.[50]

While the churches have begun to discuss how to attract more young men to the clergy calling, the pastors who lead today's congregations have this knotty question: amid the debate on sexual roles, how to keep men active in Christianity. The more conservative voices have heralded a growth in men's groups in churches, both Protestant and Catholic. Male attendance seems to be more intentional than the past, said one evangelical. "Men used to go to church because it was the culturally relevant thing to do," said Phil Downer, a former president of the Christian Businessmen's Committee. "What's happening today is more men are in church because they want to be there. And I believe we've got more men discipling other men than ever before."[51]

Ironically, too, this may account for the boom in second-career men seeking to be ministers, the major trend in clergy recruitment today.

10

Image Makers

IMAGES OF CHRISTIAN MINISTRY and of its practitioners have always made a difference.

At least two young men, moved by images, began their journey to ordination after watching a Hollywood film. The image of Richard Burton playing Thomas à Becket in the 1964 movie *Becket* inspired college freshman Robert K. Johnston to seek ordination in evangelical ministry, and Gregory Elmer to enter the Benedictine order. "My own experience of call to ministry happened in a movie theater," Johnston recalls.

In the movie, King Henry II appointed his "drinking and wenching" pal Thomas to be archbishop of Canterbury to bring the church under his control. "Who rules England?" Henry asked. "The church or me?" Becket is transformed, jettisoning his wealth happily, siding with God, and then stoically facing his assassins on the altar steps. For Johnston, it was Becket's plea to God to make him worthy that kindled his own feelings. "I saw that movie, and I heard God say to me, 'You need not be holy. You only need to be obedient, and I will help to make you holy.'"[1]

Two decades later, Americans viewed another kind of visual drama regarding the clergy. In the late 1980s the fall of so many televangelists began to fill the national media with great fanfare, led by the tearful televised confession to sexual infidelities by Jimmy Swaggart, and followed by Jim and Tammy Bakker, who drew a record late-night audience for a remorseful live interview on ABC's *Nightline.* Soon after, the typically high rating the public gives the clergy profession took a rare dip in the opinion polls, showing again that images do seem to matter.

The two cases—the inspiration of film and the tarnishing power of broadcast media—illustrate how the image of clergy can both expand their calling, on the one hand, and broadcast their faults on the other. It is not a new challenge in the United States. The colonial-era evangelist George Whitefield, considered America's first celebrity figure, had good and bad press during his wide travels. Americans flocked to buy autobiographical tracts with his portrait, while the satirical artist William Hogarth skewered him in an engraving as "St. Money-Trap."[2]

As an image-maker par excellence, Whitefield foreshadowed the Janus-faced fortunes of American clergy down to the present, portrayed as they are in both attractive and repugnant ways. Today, however, the question is this: Can any vocation, including ministry, escape a mass media representation? Some would argue that the media has become the predominant reality, a fact that religious leaders may be slow to realize. Others in ministry dismiss mass media as pure artifice, a false twist on reality. Still, as the public is increasingly bombarded by images, few clergy can ignore the benefits of positive and human portrayals of their work; it authenticates clergy and makes ministry socially relevant.

There is nothing like a good image—in literature, newspapers, cinema, and television—to produce success in the modern mass culture. But even positive images can produce unexpected consequences, such as cynicism and disillusionment, for example, when they become too detached from everyday reality. The media-polished age can raise unrealistic expectations, said Quentin J. Schultze, a researcher on televangelism. When a local church sought its next pastor, "Their concepts of worship and preaching sounded like what one sees and hears on television," he said. "They wanted charisma and flair, a pastor who would also be an entertainer in the pulpit and star in the local community."[3]

Similarly, misdeeds by the few quickly tarnish the many, as vouchsafed by televangelist scandals of the late 1980s and the priest sexual abuse meltdown in 2002. "When one religious leader gets into trouble, the public reports are vivid and unforgiving," said Raymond Chapman, surveying clergy characters in literature. "When thousands are doing their best, working with care and love in the way of life to which they have been called, very few take notice." Even as public trust in all U.S. institutions has declined, trust in clergy remains high—except in 1988 and 2002, when it dipped dramatically.[4]

In many cases, clergy have welcomed a media spotlight on their vocation, believing the sunlight may act as a disinfectant in parts of ministry that need reform. While a few televangelists indeed fell from scandal in the 1980s, most continue to prosper. Ministries that promise the blessing of wealth are still led by wealthy ministers who wish to prove their point. Despite what might seem an embarrassing image to all clergy, television evangelism keeps its large viewing public. And this loyal group continues to blame the news media for any public relations problems faced by the ministry. As a 2003 report said, television preachers "will continue to prosper . . . and journalists will continue to report their excesses. And their supporters . . . will continue to 'chalk it up to a liberal media controlled by Satan.' "[5]

Besides the media images of clergy, their theological images have also been important in determining their roles at any given time in history. In the past, the classic images were of the priest, prophet, shepherd, and servant—all images that endure in varying degrees in ministry today. Yet as times change, many of the classic images have become obsolete, if not offensive to some. The "shepherd" image may have lost its power in a non-agrarian society, said one minister. What is more, "few contemporary congregations care to be characterized as 'sheep,' for that comparison evokes a degree of 'dumbness' and passivity not prized."[6]

Perhaps more rapidly than ever, old images are eclipsed by newer ones—such as "organization man," pastoral professional, or the experienced but vulnerable spiritual guide called a "wounded healer"—and even these are being surpassed. Naturally, some clergy are on the alert for new and relevant ways for culture to see ministry, usually as complex as modern society itself. Obtaining a fixed image of the minister is difficult indeed, and even more liberal theologians argue that the classic portrayals should not be thrown out in the quest for novelty. Long ago, the New Testament proposed ninety-six different images of ministry itself, by one count.[7] So, the clergy will naturally come across in many ways, given the vantage points of the church, the society, and the media.

Within the churches, the work is almost ceaseless in conceiving of ministry for its contemporary context. Many ministers are immersed in the task of developing new theological images of their calling, and how those "mental portraits" come across to the people they serve. In one study of contemporary clergy images, seminary president Donald E. Messer outlines three positive effects of creating the right imagery for the work of the minister: to "inflame the imagination" of society; recover a "sense of urgency" about what ministry does; and adapt to new ways of organizing ministerial work. While the church will hold out traditional images of the minister, that does not rule out efforts to do away with stereotypes, such as the minister as "hired hand," "sexless servant," or "superhuman saint." New images, suggesting the complexity of real ministry, might be the minister as "servant leader," "political mystic," or "practical theologian."[8]

While theologians work on this project, the popular culture moves ahead in shaping the images of all sectors of life, including the clergy. Some of those images may intersect with the theology of the church, but they are far more likely to highlight the human factors of clergy, emphasizing the proverbial Hollywood themes that produce an effective drama. A study of cinema and the Catholic Church, for example, argued that they "co-exist, co-mingle and frequently compete in modern life. Each offers a vision of reality so complete it threatens to preempt the other's existence."

Hollywood's vision of reality has presented a variety of clergy images, both Catholic and Protestant, over the past several decades:[9]

- The Worthy Soul: Clergy virtues are unequivocal in *Boys' Town* (1938), *I'd Climb the Highest Mountain* (1951), *A Man Named Peter* (1955), *One Man's Way* (1963), *The Count of Monte Cristo* (1974), and *Romero* (1989).
- The Young Usurper: Innovators surpass old ways in *Going My Way* (1944) and *The Cardinal* (1963).
- The Tough Priest: Streetwise clergy lead in *San Francisco* (1936), *Fighting Father Dunne* (1947), and *On the Waterfront* (1954).
- The Negligent Husband: Clerics fixate on money and buildings in *The Bishop's Wife* (1947) and *The Preacher's Wife* (1996).
- The Religious Doubter: Ministers move from disbelief to faith in *The Miracle Woman* (1931), *The Exorcist* (1974), *The Third Miracle* (1999), and *Signs* (2002).
- The Frail Human: Clergy try but fail in *Night of the Iguana* (1964), *The Sandpiper* (1965), *Hawaii* (1966), and *The Apostle* (1997).

Whatever the portrayal, it might be better for clergy to risk a showing in popular culture than to be ignored, especially as image-producing technologies become almost godlike in society. Today, Americans live in "a culture that is largely defined by the institutions and practices of the mass media," said one media scholar.[10] For ministry, this has mixed implications. On the one hand, the secular media could arrogate all image-making of clergy. On the other hand, the ministry may outsmart the media moguls, and use their technology to convey the theological and human dimension of ministry, and even its centrality to culture. Most would agree, however, that at this time the moguls are ahead.

A major attraction of the media culture has been its ability to entertain. And when it comes to clergy images, that diversion and amusement have stayed the same from Chaucer's thirteenth-century *Canterbury Tales* down to the present. While the *Tales* feature the laudable Parson, they also introduce such unscrupulous characters as the storytelling Friar, money-seeking Pardoner, and the Nun's Priest. Yet stories and real life often match. Of *Canterbury Tales*, for example, former Catholic priest A. W. Richard Sipe says: "All of these characters are believable, and each has his parallel in modern-day ministry."[11]

Satire has also been a preferred approach to saying something about the clergy. George Eliot's *Scenes of Clerical Life*, Jonathan Swift's Dean Smedley, and Jane Austin's Reverend Collins limn clergy as "vile creatures," reports the *Dictionary of Biblical Tradition in English Literature*. The modern novelists Walker Percy, J. F. Powers, Andrew Greeley, and John Updike have offered "portraits of distorted or unbalanced clergy situations," said a Lutheran writer elsewhere. At least, he said, such fiction shows "the kind of pressures clergy face"—the extremes of activism, daily routine, webs of human relations, and reaching for an elusive God. "That [novelists] pay this kind of attention to ministerial behavior suggests that our clergy may not be as marginal as they think they are."[12]

When the popular press arose in the United States, clergy also received their share of attention, always with mixed feelings. As early as the 1600s, disputes broke out between New England clergy and newspapers. And though Protestant tract societies and reform movements "first dreamed the dream of a genuinely mass medium," the secular penny press overshadowed them during the 1830s; churches lost control of portrayals of ministers. In the Gilded Age, when "princes of the pulpit" regaled from large urban churches, the all-purpose newspaper—with sections on business, sports, ladies, and politics—carved a ghetto for clergy as well. The job of "religion page" editor first materialized in 1915 (at the *Hartford Courant*). Yet the deference peaked after World War II: "Long gone are the days when any articulate preacher could capture the local paper's front page week after week, merely for delivering a sermon on a timely topic."[13]

Since 1923, the cover of *Time* has been a touchstone of clergy image-making, featuring roughly 160 religious figures on the covers of some four thousand issues. The first clerics to appear were Episcopal and Catholic bishops, but also the young Harry Emerson Fosdick in 1925, portrayed in a cherubic-looking sketch as the modernist Baptist pastor of the Rockefeller-built Riverside Church in New York City. Theologians made up the clergy images of the forties and fifties. The sixties began to showcase dissenters. Thereafter, no clerics appeared—save the many papal covers and two with Billy Graham—while trends and controversies prevailed: from the Death of God and Jesus movement to televangelist scandals, missionaries, and the historical Jesus.[14]

Despite the occasional flattering imagery, ministers today feel that news coverage of religion is "unfairly negative, and too sensational." Too much ink is given to "publicity seeking" ministers, they say. But attitudes are different across the church traditions. Mainline clergy take less offense at the news than evangelical or Catholic pastors. Six in ten mainliners agree that society has "benefited greatly" by coverage of the worst scandals and abuse, while six in ten evangelicals feel the opposite. Catholic priests are evenly divided on this issue. While 58 percent of mainline clergy agree that news "is biased against ministers and organized religion," an overwhelming 91 percent of conservative evangelicals and 70 percent of Catholic priests concur.[15]

The dissatisfaction of Catholics and evangelicals is a characteristic feature of modern clergy commentary on the news media. Evangelicals have been on the wrong side of the secular media since at least the 1925 Scopes "Monkey Trial," when an open season was declared on conservative Protestants. Into the 1990s, the trend may have endured because journalists remained alienated from the human side of conservative church life, said *Time* political reporter Laurence I. Barrett. "Those of us who do attend religious services go to mainstream institutions," he said. Barrett cited a study of religious practice in professions: "Among the 'media elite,' the study found zero practitioners professing to be fundamentalist, born–again, or evangelical."[16] It has also been argued that evangelicals, by being judgmental and legalistic on morality, set themselves up for juicy "hypocrisy" stories when newspapers learn of their own peccadillos.

While many American Catholics are writers, editors, and commentators in the secular media, the press has been notoriously unsympathetic with the agenda of Rome, except for the liberal reforms of the Second Vatican Council that began in 1962. Due to its hierarchical nature, and the ease of citing authoritative statements by the papacy, Catholicism still receives the lion's share of U.S. news coverage on religion. Media coverage of the 2002 sexual abuse scandal in the American church was nothing short of devastating to the image of priests. Striking a conciliatory theme with the press, Bishop Wilton Gregory, president of the Catholic bishops, would often say, "The media didn't create the story." Yet he just as quickly complained that for all the abuse cases in society the Catholic clergy have been beaten up more than anyone else, given the firestorm of news coverage.[17]

Historians of religion such as Philip Jenkins and newsmen such as *Newsweek's* former religion editor Kenneth Woodward argue that anti-Catholicism in American news, television, and film can never be underestimated. They call it "the last acceptable prejudice." And it has gotten worse, Jenkins argues: "In marked contrast to the situation fifty years ago, stridently anti-Catholic themes today are widely present in popular culture and the popular media."[18] While the media treatment has grown worse for well-known cultural reasons—secular aversion to the Holy See's conservative moral decrees—the negtive shift in film and television has had a direct political cause: the rise and fall of the Hollywood Production Code that prevailed from 1930 to 1966.

During that period both Catholic and Protestant clergy were treated respectfully. Between the 1940s and the 1960s in particular, "traditional religion received very favorable treatment in Hollywood and, in exchange, studio moguls were often rewarded with large box office returns." Clergy in the movies were generally protected from abuse by the Code's declaration that "ministers of religion in their character as ministers of religion should not be used as comic characters or villains."[19]

The film industry was only the start of a mass culture that would inundate the clergy. According to some, movies became "for the masses 'what theology is for the elite.' " If organized Christianity had once been steward of the primary "image and narrative" for society, the pictures and stories were now "more and more in the media's control."[20] Film viewings drew astounding crowds: Weekly film attendance by 1930 was up to 90 million people in a population of 120 million. It is no wonder that culture mavens called cinema a new religion. The largest theater in the world, the Roxy in New York City, became known as "the cathedral of the motion picture" after it opened with six thousand seats in 1927. The Chinese Theater opened that same year on Hollywood Boulevard with a film about the minister of *all* ministers—Cecil B. De Mille's *King of Kings*.

The active lobbying effort by Catholics and Protestants in Washington, D.C., and Hollywood has been vividly told already, but the net effect was a collection of popular and positive portrayals of clergy in both traditions.[21] For Protestants, such upbeat films as *One Foot in Heaven* (1941) and *The Bishop's Wife* (1947) appeared. In 1951, *I'd Climb the Highest Mountain*, the story of a country preacher filmed in the hills of Georgia, was a big hit in the South, and *A Man Called Peter* (1955) had a national audience with its story of Peter Marshall, the Scotsman who became a Presbyterian pastor in Washington, D.C., and then chaplain to the U.S. Senate. The popular Norman Vincent Peale even had a hand in the Hollywood portrayal of his life in *One Man's Way* (1963).

While mainline Protestants had been the early arbiters of decency in Hollywood, it was lay Catholic activists who drafted the Production Code—called the Ten Commandments of moviemaking when it began in the 1930s—and persuaded studios to follow it. American Catholicism was thus instrumental in the rating system still used on today's Hollywood fare. On the heels of such success, Catholics even exceeded Protestants in promoting positive cinema, from the attractive role of Spencer Tracy as a "priest among men" in 1936, and then Bing Crosby as Father O'Malley in *Going My Way*, which won the Oscar for best picture in 1944. "For Catholics over age fifty, it is difficult to exaggerate Father O'Malley's hold on the Catholic imagination's image of the ideal priest," said one vicar of priests.[22] Some Catholics today wince at such unreal portrayals, but there was plenty of Catholic realism in films such as *Keys of the Kingdom* (1944) and *Nun's Story* (1959).

In general, clergy frequently appeared in traditional roles that were not at all unattractive, such as director John Ford's use of them in the epic Westerns *High Noon* (1952) and *The Searchers* (1956). While some have called these "marrying and burying" roles of clergy irrelevant, others call them a valid realism in film. "When you think of clergy in the forties and fifties, you are thinking of the clergy in a professional role; doing the overt things that clergy do: funerals, occasional baptisms, and weddings," said James Wall, a longtime minister and film critic. He said he "put no stock" in the criticism of such portrayals. "Because that is what clergy do. Those are the roles they perform to the general public's attention."[23]

Some clergy portrayals have been more endearing than others, and the case of the Los Angeles minister at the wedding scene in *The Graduate* (1967) illustrates the more humiliating side; the minister is reduced to ridiculous impotence as Benjamin Braddock (Dustin Hoffman) storms the suburban church to claim his sweetheart Elaine (Katharine Ross), swinging a steel cross like a sword to escape—amid a Simon and Garfunkel soundtrack. Between *Going My Way* and *The Graduate*, of course, the Production Code had been abandoned. It was replaced in 1968 by guidelines urging "artistic expression by expanding creative freedom" that were "responsible and sensitive to the standards of larger society."[24]

The 1960s changed Hollywood, as it did much of the nation. The transitional film for Protestant portrayals was *The Sandpiper* (1965), staring Richard Burton as Reverend Doctor Hewitt, a married Episcopal priest. After committing adultery with Laura, a single mother and artist (Elizabeth Taylor) who lives in an avant-garde beach house, his repentance is ambivalent. To resolve the conflict, he leaves the parish, his wife, and his lover behind, packs his car and heads south down California's dramatic coastal highway for an uncertain future. While many took the movie as just another vehicle for a cinematic romance between Burton and Taylor, clergy aside, it did mark a new era of imagery. "The film's mixed portrayal of the minister forecast a shift away from reverential treatment of religious characters toward a more 'normal' status" compared to non-religious characters.[25]

The Code's legacy still inspires debate, even among clergy. "Most of the best films ever produced were made during that thirty-five-year time period, since creativity and imagination had to replace the cheap lures of sex and violence to attract an audience into the theaters," said Ted Baehr, founder of the Christian Film Commission. Others say the Code was to blame for the backlash seen after 1966. While the Hollywood film office could not use the Code to shut down anyone, fines and control of theaters was enough to sink anti-preacher screenplays such as *The Soul Merchant*, *The Revival*, and *The Money Changer*, as well as alter religious dialogue in those that went to market. Such cases as these "go a long way toward explaining the backlash against Christianity in films since the 1960s," said Mark Hulsether, a writer on the topic.[26]

Yet even the Code could not stop one movie that created a lasting impression of hell-fire evangelists and faith-healing preachers in America, the 1960 Hollywood-success *Elmer Gantry*. Based on Sinclair Lewis's satire on religion as big business, actor Burt Lancaster circumvented the Code by setting up his own company to produce the movie, which won him an Oscar for best actor. "Elmer Gantry is just an all American guy interested in money, sex, and fun," he told *Variety*. "Just because he is a minister doesn't make him un-American."[27]

Whatever the anti-Christian backlash engendered by the Code, the movie industry was free of the requirement of only positive portrayals, and it followed the secular drift of society as well, in which ministers lost some ground. From the 1970s onward, three decades of top-grossing Hollywood films reflect this secular trend, according to a study by movie expert Stanley Rothman. While clergy prominence might be expected to decline as movies became more secular, the drop was still more dramatic for this reason: Until 1966 the clergy portrayals had to be 100 percent positive under the Production Code.

Since then, Rothman said, religious figures have virtually disappeared from movie plots, dropping from 19 percent of all characters at mid-century to 4 percent by the 1990s. Positive portrayals also took a nosedive—though it perhaps made clergy look more normal on the whole. Even after 1976, half of all clergy portraits were positive, a third were negative, and the rest mixed. Religious characters today show about the same "success" rate in movie plots as the Code era, but they more often suffer "defeat" in their stories—a third of the time now compared to 15 percent in the past. Hollywood began to prefer "satiric or radical" images of clergy to traditional ones, and the backdrop for their work was less the monotheistic cosmos of Judeo-Christianity and more a world of supernatural and paranormal forces, a science-fiction ambiance of evil entities and benevolent extraterrestrials.[28]

When Hollywood's laudatory image of the clergy prevailed in the mid-1950s, television came on the scene to challenge the studios' monopoly over entertainment. Television reached half of all homes by 1954, and scholars of mass communication today say that it is surely the "dominant medium," despite Hollywood blockbusters. Billy Graham said "television is the most powerful tool of communication ever devised by man," and theologians stood in awe, ranking the medium as co-equal with religion as "the two most powerful storytellers in our culture." Some would even put aside the religious stories and say television has no peers.[29]

In its early influence, however, television was in sync with the movie code, treating religion and clergy well enough. One network produced *Crossroads*, a dramatic weekly anthology that aired from 1955 to 1957, depicting the lives of ministers. Problem plots were resolved by characters changing for the better. The clergy were "sensitive, caring, and very human." Ministers showed up in dramatic series such as *Combat!* and *Gunsmoke*, but increasingly as institutional men. "They questioned neither their own faith nor their church superiors," said media scholar S. Robert Lichter. When the 1960s introduced the "idiot sitcoms"—with Martians, talking horses, witches, and genies—the religious version was *The Flying Nun*. Though gimmicky, the series was "commended by real-life religious orders for humanizing the work of nuns." In general, the television portrayal of clergy was no worse than *M*A*S*H*'s Korean War chaplain Father Mulcahy—"ineffectual but endearing."[30]

Still, the role of clergy was taking on a distinctly new cast, according to Lichter. Amid the anti-establishment theme of television begun in the 1970s, clergy fared better than business executives, politicians, and military brass. Yet fewer religious figures appeared in serials and dramas as time passed, especially after 1975, according to Lichter's four-decade study. "Of the various establishment groups, only the clergy have always commanded television's respect," he said. "They have always been one of television's good-guy professions." To remain in that favored light, however, clergy had to become more social activists than priests, more progressive do-gooders than theologians. Lionel Chetwynd, a Hollywood writer, director, and producer, agrees with that finding: "On the rare occasion that a religious person is depicted (positively), they are less clergymen or women than they are social workers in clerical collars."[31]

In the modern mass media, with its nonlinear communication and emotional ambiguity, the role of the clerical collar is playing a larger role than many ministers may imagine. The reason is simple: Image-makers have little else besides the collar to designate the clergy character in, say, a television series or even a movie.

While in reality the collar may represent a Lutheran, Episcopalian, or even Pentecostal minister, it typically brings to mind Roman Catholic clergy, according to media critics. Stewart Hoover, a scholar of mass media, focused on one episode of the popular series *Northern Exposure* to illustrate the sartorial point. The cleric, who did not come off so attractively, at first looked like a Catholic priest, but then his father's life as a minister was also cited. Whichever tradition he represented, his role was more as a prop than a look at reality; in the end the cleric was confessing to a medical doctor, not the other way around. Thus, a television episode "redefines the priesthood and does so through a not-so-subtle visual language," Hoover said.[32]

Hoover argues that while movies, television, and news reports don't bend backwards to besmirch clergy, their treatment is certainly not ennobling. "While the clergy are not negatively shown, they are not shown as being particularly effective or important either," he said. "So the overall impression you get is that they are a kind of ineffectual force in the social universe."[33]

To the surprise of many, this bland direction seemed to reverse for a brief sparkling moment in the late 1990s, particularly on television, but in movie fare as well. Even critics such as Baehr laud the years 1995 and 1996 as rich with cinema that "presented the gospel, extolled Jesus Christ, commended the Bible, and commended church." With so many films produced in the 1980s and 1990s, the segment with religion themes also expanded. Close to 90 religion-flavored films appeared in the eighties; more than 130 were made in the nineties. Media scholar Joyce Smith, mean-while, has found that the mid-1990s was in fact the very peak of the twentieth century when it came to the percentage of annual films that included at least some kind of religious character.[34]

Television also took a turn in 1997, marked by the rarity of a *TV Guide* special report on religion—or "caring for prime time's soul." As might be expected, it was as much about "spirituality" as about organized religion with ministers. Still, the last such attention given to religion was in 1983, when *The Thorn Birds*, a ten-hour miniseries, aired, telling the story of Australian priest Father Ralph de Briscassart and his love affair. Priest-sociologist Greeley put the best face on the celibate priesthood, despite the "sins" of Father Briscassart. "Celibate priests are fascinating men precisely because they are men of mystery," he wrote in *TV Guide*. "They live different lives from anyone else because they are committed to a reality beyond this world."[35]

But as a benchmark of where the clergy might stand in the television age, 1997 was a season in which four networks rolled out six religious serials or sitcoms. As television writers tell the story, the networks sought to imitate the great success of CBS's *Touched by an Angel*, which of course was about those benevolent beings, not about ministers. Still, clergy characters appeared in half of the religion plots that swept the 1997 calendar: *Promised Land* on CBS, *Seventh Heaven* on WB, *Nothing Sacred* and *Soul Man* on ABC, *Good News* on UPN, and *Teen Angel* on ABC.

While the trend lasted, some critics were refreshed by the possibilities. All the series portrayed "the difficulties of the ministry compassionately," reported the *Christian Science Monitor*. These were not TV's typical "hypocrites and fools," but ministers "taxed to the extremes, sending the message that the selfless life of a pastor is nothing to sneer at." The networks should be credited for discovering "that clergy can be interesting characters," said *Christian Century*. Rabbi Gerald Zelizer, writing in the *Los Angeles Times*, worried over an assault on "private lives" of ministers. "On any given night, on one channel or the other, a priest, minister or rabbi will be doubting his faith in God, his calling or his sexual fidelity." Yet Zelizer also conceded a "healthy side" to the humanizing of clergy. Finally, weak ratings ended the cavalcade of clergy shows and only *Seventh Heaven*, which is plotted around a minister and his family, survived.[36]

When religion was treated positively on television in the 1990s, it was usually the faith of an individual, according to the Media Research Center (MRC). Prime-time shows did not do the same for traditional fixtures, however. Clergy, doctrine, and organized churches received twice as many negative as positive portrayals, according to the MRC's "Faith in a Box" reports from 1993 to 1995. The next year, prime-time television made amends with "slightly more positive than negative depictions of the clergy." Still, the MRC said, "The growth in the number of 'religious shows' may obscure the fact that some of them seldom deal explicitly with religion." While television's treatment of religion clearly fluctuates, no rule of thumb for clergy portrayals has emerged.[37]

At a time when everyone knows that people should watch less television—and read books or become active in groups or sports—many clergy might care less about that unreal TV world. The media mavens, however, say they will do so at their own peril.

Under modern media pressures, Americans are less likely to accept religious traditions as a package of beliefs and rituals safeguarded by clergy. Instead, the media urges the public to pick and choose in life, producing as much "cafeteria" religion today as traditional faith. What is more, Hoover said, Americans are "increasingly visually oriented in our ways of learning and talking about contemporary cultural experience." While many sectors of society have taken this visual power seriously—business, politics, and education in particular—"the world of religious believers has been slower to catch on." Catching on will be particularly important for clergy who want to present an entire tradition to the public. Despite all the signals, Hoover said, "It has been difficult for religious authorities to grasp the nature and extent of the challenge posed by the modern mass media."[38]

This mass media reality has presented two hurdles for the ministry. The first challenge is for many clergy to overcome their natural distrust of the artificial media world. After dedicating their lives to such notions as truth, spiritual insight, and human authenticity, many ministers see the media as the opposite, a facade and a falsehood. The second hurdle is the risk that many ministers feel about giving up traditions, or presenting their work in seemingly faddish ways to suit the voracious appetite of visual technology. There is no easy solution to the problem of media superficiality. But on the second point, some theologians have presented the case that clergy roles have always been flexible, so perhaps bending them for modern tastes is not a complete loss of tradition. In his *Models of the Church*, the Catholic theologian Avery Dulles said that even the New Testament images of the minister "cannot be decisive for our terminology today, if only because the structure of ministry seems to have been different in different communities."[39]

United Methodist minister and seminary president Donald Messer, argued in his *Contemporary Images of Christian Ministry* that there is ample room for imagination in presenting the clergy to the modern world. With a little creativity, he said, new and powerful images of clergy could be found. This could in turn improve five areas of ministry: the power to remind people; interpret for people; protest the wrong; advocate the right; and provide a vision for the future.[40] Theologians such as Dulles and

Messer are speaking to people within the churches, though there is always the hope that secular media will come to appreciate these spiritual descriptions of the minister.

The entertainment industry, if it wants to treat the clergy respectfully, faces its own hurdles too. To portray them too realistically would perhaps scandalize the ideals, morals, and beliefs at the heart of their Christian tradition. Yet to sanitize the clergy would make them unbelievable and, where entertainment is concerned, an incredibly dull lot. In a word, it is difficult to create theatrical intensity with a pious or virtuous character. Depicting religious practice "is not very interesting or dramatic to an audience," said television producer Bob Gales. "If Fred went to his pastor for help, got questionable advice, took it, and got himself into deeper trouble, that would be dramatic; but it would be perceived by many viewers as an anti-religious story."[41]

Yet there must be a way to meld authentic clergy with cinematic drama, some ministers believe. "Why not create a '911 format' about ministers, priests, and rabbis?" said Joan Brown Campbell, former National Council of Churches general secretary. "Along with police, fire fighters, and medical personnel, who is called on more frequently in times of emergency than the clergy? It might be a real draw for the public to see how the leaders of churches respond to the thousands of emergencies that pull them into action day after day." In the weeks after the emergency of the September 11 terrorist attacks, in fact, the nation's newspapers gave an "unusually high" amount of coverage to religious leaders, a study found.[42]

Film imagery in *Becket* ignited the faith of Robert Johnston back in the 1960s, and for most of his life as a minister, James Wall found the marks of God in many films that were insightful and beautiful. They both tend to agree, however, that literal and sunny images do not provide fair winds for ministry. "The moment you get to religious images, you get to somewhat insipid images," Wall said. "It softens too much, and kids are not drawn to that." What is more, the secular media are ultimately "afraid to touch overt religious feelings"—which may be too volatile for a mass-market movie. "The image of the minister is not shown in popular films in a way that would be a very good recruiting tool," Wall concludes. "If anything, they're going to be recruited to join the army, the CIA, or be a doctor."

It might be enough in an age of so much imagery for openhearted Americans to see images about the depth of life, human aspiration, and a mysterious and transcendental universe. That may get people thinking new thoughts, Wall believes. "And then the young person will say, 'I'm touched by that film's ability to see depth in human existence. How can I know more about that?' The next step is to say, 'Well, there is a profession known as the clergy.'"

Johnston, who teaches Christianity and culture at Fuller Theological Seminary, said *The Third Miracle* illustrates an important point for today. "It's a story about his recovery of faith and his taking seriously his vocation," he said. "A sort of human priest who yet is faithful." That is an image that people today can relate to. "A holier-than-thou clergy person does not connect. If you're not able to show how your life is connected to God's in a believable way, you don't have credibility."

To Johnston's surprise as well, the culture has taken an "upturn" on some religious image-making fronts, a rising tide that could loft clergy upward as well. "You have the full range [of good and bad], which would be understandable given that the clergy are human, and given all the news today"—from televangelism to sexual abuse. "It's not film, or newspaper or television news, or sitcoms or the Internet that's done the most damage," he said. "It's the clergy themselves. It's Jimmy Swaggart, Jim Bakker, and Cardinal Law—their images have hurt the clergy profession more than Homer Simpson."

The context for this age of Christian ministry, Johnston believes, comes across in the advertising imagery seen at the typical Super Bowl extravaganza. "They're all paradox and cynical stories with a little twist," he said. "There's an attempt to rag on reality. And if it can make you smile, you are apt to go get the product." Whether clergy can indeed win over contemporary culture, either by good images, theological profundity, human sincerity, or jokes on themselves, it will take place in the current atmosphere of ministry. Some argue that the mood is one of "crisis," and that is the debate on which most everything else will hang.

11

The Soul of Ministry

THE CLERGY OF AMERICA certainly do live in interesting times. To live in "interesting times," according to the old Chinese curse, is to live in uncertainty. For ministry in America, that ambiguity may end up a virtue when trying to decide whether modern ministry faces a "crisis." The positive and negative trends are complex, as this survey of ministry hoped to show. Yet behind the surface activity, ministry continues to premise itself on supernatural ideas, grounding its hope in unseen factors, where it finds its surest footing amid the shifting ground of American culture. Ministry goes on the promises of the Bible. And the themes of Isaiah and Revelation, where "new things" are foretold and God makes "all things new," are still taken seriously enough.[1]

With that in mind, however, the intimations of an earthly crisis for the American clergy may also be taken seriously. From that perspective, the most debilitating threats to the future of ministry have both cultural and institutional sources. In American culture, authority figures in general may lose ground in the future. Ministers are part of that celebrated company. And they are also stewards of belief systems—"big stories" about reality—and such systems are reportedly facing hard times. These are the predictions of Eddie Gibbs, an Anglican priest ordained in the 1950s, when he wore his collar making pastoral visits to working-class homes. Wearing clergy garb no longer impresses people in England, and he predicts the same kind of secularization for America. "Today, you're not a pastor to the community, but you are a mission outpost within the community." In his generation, skeptics simply denied God's existence. Now, young Americans don't deny God but are "very suspicious of any kind of metanarrative—that is, a big story," said Gibbs, who wrote *Church Next*.

"The gospel is a big story. So how do you speak of the big story in a pluralistic and segmented society?"[2]

Ministers today say that their toughest challenge—professed by 74 percent—is teaching the gospel to a modern society, with its privatized faith and thirst for experience rather than doctrine. Weak denominational loyalty further complicates a minister's work: Catholic priests perform a third of their marriages between Catholics and non-Catholics, and a third of Protestants in the pews have "switched" from the tradition of their upbringing. According to some, a "consumer mentality" has eclipsed both denominational loyalty and the need for clergy as its mediators. Church attendance may tell that story: While four in ten Americans say they attend on a given weekend, other studies push that down to just two in ten. Not surprisingly, Christian literacy has declined, making it harder to tell the "big story."[3]

The generation of Eddie Gibbs is now being succeeded by people such as Nathan Hieb, an evangelical from Minnesota. Hieb was ordained in the early years of the twenty-first century. "I'm not very concerned about preserving the traditions of the church," he said. "I'm very interested in translating Christianity, the message of Jesus, into the new cultural climate."[4] His generation's challenge is to keep the church in the cultural picture. It must persuade people to seek meaning not only through immediate experiences and marketplace choices but also ancient texts, traditions, and memories. Many clergy still pledge in their ordination vows to preserve such ecclesiastical legacies.

The youthful enthusiasm of Hieb points to probably the single most bewildering challenge of American ministry—the recruitment of young people to make it a lifelong calling. With the present low recruitment levels, the day might come when most American churches have no ordained ministers in their pulpits. At present, the number of clergy under age thirty is remarkably small. Ordinations today average in the mid-thirties. "The dearth of young clergy sounds a wake-up call to the already called," said one younger minister. "Pastors have a crucial role to play in stimulating the vocational imagination of the youth in their congregations." He cited an estimate that if just 10 percent of pastors raised up a young apprentice, "the tide would turn."[5]

Clergy who offer an inspiring example are still a major force in persuading others to enter ministry. Yet the modern ministry may send out just as many negative signals. In every clergy life cycle there is plenty of room for a grim realism, all too visible to young recruits. The Pulpit and Pew surveys in 2000, for instance, discovered that two-thirds of parish-serving clergy had experienced conflict in their congregation in the past two years. Two in ten said the internal church conflict was "significant" or "major." Major conflicts prompted members to leave the church.[6]

A tenth of the clergy also said they suffered depression much of the time. About one in four felt "at times depressed or worn out." Their health may contribute to the emotional drag as well, since 30 percent of clergy are obese by medical standards, and another 37 percent are overweight—a total (67 percent) that exceeds national averages. Men in ministry have the problem more than women. Given such physical and emotional strains, it is not surprising that four in ten ministers have "doubted their call" and nearly a third have "considered leaving." The onus seems to fall on ministers with fewer years in the profession; perhaps longevity produces the optimum of joys, adjustments, and benefits. That seems to be the case with priests, according to one Catholic survey. Among the oldest priests, 93 percent say they *never* "seriously considered" leaving the priesthood. The youngest group, however, can only say that at a rate of 69 percent.[7]

Keeping the sense of call is no minor task. Pastoral counselor Robert Wicks knows the stories of clergy burnout and low morale all too well. They are plotted around the zeal of the calling as it confronts trials, change, and years gone by. A minister's sense of the call, mission, and link to God is never fixed in stone. "Developmental psychology teaches us that at different points in our life there are different tasks, challenges, and questions," Wicks said. "So the call has to be revisited. In the beginning, it's a motivational thing. If you get excited about the task, you find the task is wonderful. Rather than faithfulness to God, which is a ministerial goal, you are into success."

No one, it turns out, can be utterly successful in ministry—because success can never be truly defined. "In burnout, you get further and further from your original passion," explained Wicks. "It's not activity that burns people out. It's their perception about what they are doing. Some people have a zillion things in the air. But they are not burning out because they love what they do. There's a real joy in it. There's a real faithfulness in it, and it's irrelevant whether they succeed or not." Faithfulness, not success, is the key for ministry: "Faithfulness involves availability to God."[8]

The balancing of faithfulness and success is usually lived out in a minister's workweek, and it is here that he faces yet another challenge to morale. Researchers call it the problem of "role ambiguity," which in any profession leads to demoralization. Both the Protestant minister and the Catholic priest are at risk of a blurring line between their role and the new activism of the laity. Fortunately, one study of Protestant ministry found that lay involvement allows a minister to focus on fewer priorities, which helps to clarify the clergy role. But the "ambiguity" is never erased permanently. Ministers in hierarchical traditions, for example, can be buffeted by so many tasks sent down from headquarters that job ambiguity is almost inevitable.[9]

The corollary, of course, is whether congregations and regional supervisors of clergy have the lifetime development of individual clergy in mind. Do they allow clergy to take stock, go for a next stage of training, or enjoy the occasional retreat or sabbatical for the long haul? More likely, it seems, congregations worry that clergy are slacking off. According to Pulpit and Pew, "Pastors express concern that their members seem mystified over how they spend their time." With no factory timecard in ministry to view, outspoken members of a church invariably question the minister's productivity. And whole congregations tend to resist "the idea that the pastor should have a set day off or time away from ministry for renewal."[10]

Bill Hybels, one of the most successful pastors in modern American history, once felt the need for a break, at least long enough to refresh himself after years of relentless activity at Willow Creek Community Church outside Chicago. So he went to an ordinary pastoral counselor, looking for insights, wondering about his own stages of development. Not surprisingly, the gossip mill of church folks came into play, and it was not just about taking time off for a counseling appointment. "Sure enough, . . . my office started receiving calls from across the country and around the world," said an amused Hybels. " 'Is it true that Bill Hybels is having an emotional breakdown?' . . . They'd say, 'we heard he'd cracked up' Or, 'We heard that his marriage is going down.' " In sum, Hybels tells pastors to not be reluctant to work on themselves; seek a personal change and damn the rumors.[11]

Meanwhile, the perceived clergy "crisis" has major institutional contributions as well. For a start, ministers soon may have to bite the bullet and close down thousands of small, dying churches. Roughly 20 percent of U.S. congregations, and perhaps more, have no future. Most will peter out; they will go on until retirements, departures, deaths, or mergers close them down. "We cannot afford to keep eighty tiny churches propped up," said one regional executive. "Let's identify fifteen mission sites where we have to be, come hell or high water, and let's put all our money into those."[12]

As the flux in small congregations affects the lives of many ministers and the prospects of new recruits, the majority of Americans have shifted to larger churches: 10 percent of congregations in the United States host 50 percent of the churchgoing public. New pressures are being put on a minority of congregational leaders, therefore, and their ability to accumulate experience before taking leadership is becoming critical. Large congregations "are complex ministerial environments that need pastors with a decade or so of experience by early mid-career," said Daniel Aleshire, head of the Association of Theological Schools. In other words, the church needs clergy who started out young enough to "come to these congregations with experience and high career energy."[13] What the churches often have, however, are clergy starting out late in life.

A final institutional crisis hinges on the aging clergy corps. Some call it the "actuarial crisis." A major segment of American clergy will retire soon, and live longer than any previous generation. The cost to denominational pension systems will be staggering. Some retirement packages are better than a working minister's salary. Many retired pastors are helping beyond the call of duty. Yet time marches on. The passing of a generation is most visible as great ministers of the age—like John Paul II, Billy Graham, or Robert Schuller—move into their twilight. "How chastening to know that God does number our days," said Elizabeth Eisenstadt-Evans, an Episcopal priest impressed by Schuller's dramatic story: from farm boy to Crystal Cathedral. "And how encouraging for all of us to know that somewhere, out there in another farming community or an inner-city row house, God continues to call new visionaries to dream his dreams."[14]

In addition to the cultural and institutional pitfalls ahead, ministry is facing up to one other contemporary reality: the impact of the marketplace. The "religious economy," as it is called, produces winners and losers, just as with any franchise or product line. And everyone wants a bargain. Some have hailed the market for improving ministry, rewarding excellence and sloughing off mediocrity. Others say just the opposite: The market has increased hucksterism and religious gimmicks. One Methodist bishop lamented that this "consumerist culture" and "market idolatry" has been widely adopted even by Christians. The market flux has also been described as a shift from a church-affiliated "spirituality of dwelling" in America to a footloose "spirituality of seeking," the latter being less promising for organized religion.[15]

An increase in America of spiritual transience is clearly changing the nature of ordained ministry. But the market forces have even entered the life of established congregations, and this may have an even greater impact on the role of the minister. In the full-blown market, consumers shop for inexpensive ministers or pleasing ministers, and clergy may be forced to tailor much of their calling to changing tastes—to simply stay employed. At worst, the time may come when it is extremely difficult to match clergy to congregations.

After graduating from Gettysburg Theological Seminary, Chad Rimmer went into the field serving Lutheran churches, well aware of the market forces but filled with youthful idealism. He thinks the local church should do what is right, not only what is pleasing or gotten at a bargain. "People think that ministry is good sermons and fun worship," said Rimmer. But sometimes, "the pastor acknowledges that 'pastoral care' can be a swift kick in the pants, telling the congregations, 'You are about the wrong business.'" Yet in the marketplace, the swift kick is not as accepted as it used to be, according to one provost of a rabbinic theological school, who credits a "society-wide assault on authority" as the fate of clergy today. Only in recent years has a warning about "clergy killer" congregations come into vogue.[16]

Extending the marketplace metaphor, Jackson Carroll, a retired Methodist pastor, said the rejection of ministry may be due to what Harvard business-school thinkers call "misalignment" of an industry with a marketplace. In misalignment, consumers do *not* want a product, worthy as it may be. In the case of ministry, the public is standoffish about the gospel's demands. In another respect, pastors are becoming misaligned with congregations because of a new factor that has intruded into local church life—"special purpose groups." A growing number of these groups, either on the ideological right or left, "bombard clergy and laity alike with advocacy for various social or doctrinal positions," according to Carroll. It makes direct communication between the pastor and congregation dicier than ever.[17]

Fortunately, most clergy report finding greatest job satisfaction in a good match with a congregation. As one lay leader said, "Even if we don't like the minister we will come here and continue to work." Yet congregational expectations of clergy remain high. One Pulpit and Pew survey found that congregations, when looking for a new pastor, expect the extraordinary: competence, religious authenticity, good preaching and worship, strong spiritual leadership, and parish commitment. The minister should also keep boundaries with people, be warm and approachable, have "people skills," be young but experienced, and excel as an evangelist, entrepreneur, and consensus builder who is responsive to laity. This survey did not even mention affordability.[18]

Quite naturally, such high expectations have produced a good amount of cathartic humor for stressed ministers. They speak of the southern congregation, for example, that insists on a clergyman with a Scottish brogue and a Confederate general in his ancestry. And every synagogue, of course, wants a rabbi "who is twenty-eight years old but has preached for thirty years."[19]

Faced with this grim survey of the clergy challenge, which might reach the threshold of a clergy "crisis," churches and seminaries are trying to gain the high ground. They are urging support for clergy and vivifying ministry as a player in society. They have also embarked on a lively debate about recruitment of new blood for ministry and begun to emphasize leadership as a ministerial skill.

Technology and the marketplace are helping in some of this. Since 1993 a Clergy Appreciation Day has set its eyes on gaining the status of a Mother's or Father's Day; the effort has been bolstered by grassroots promotion and a commercial push in greeting cards by Hallmark and one of its new subsidiaries. The day comes on the second Sunday of October and has been extended by some ministries into a Clergy Appreciation Month.[20]

At the same time, the power of electronic communications continues to change traditional ministry, and in some sectors it has revolutionized the thinking of pastors. The Roman Catholic Church is transmitting more Masses over television in the absence of priests. When Lloyd John Ogilvie retired as U.S. Senate chaplain, he hoped to again raise the stature of the pulpit in America, both in churches and on the airwaves. "There has been a de-emphasis on preaching," he said. "We're not calling into the preaching role the most articulate, committed, compassionate communicators."[21] Ogilvie was known as one of the very good guys of religious broadcasting, sending his weekly sermons in a Los Angeles sanctuary onto the national airwaves with dignified presentations and transparent financial accountability.

The world of television evangelism has its well-known abuses, and yet for better or worse, ministry can only ignore such electronic media at its peril. Successful educational projects such as the ten-part Alpha Course on basic Christianity have spread by way of videos shown to small groups in someone's home. Alpha also aired on national television in England and Canada. The next step, according to a young Wesleyan pastor in Texas, is to take what television began to new horizons, and those horizons are flashy video imagery and the powers of the Internet. Writing in the Internet magazine *New Wave*, Texas youth pastor David Hopkins said: "Image is not everything. It's the only thing." MTV knows its audience intimately and that has a lesson for ministry, he added. "How many churches know their own communities at this intimate level?"[22]

Listings of church services and locations, posting of weekly sermons, and forums for theological discussion have all grown with the Internet revolution. The number of consumers of the Internet's religious materials, called "religion surfers," has risen from 20 million to 82 million in the four years since 2000, according to one set of studies. Predictions that teenagers would choose Internet religion over church attendance have not yet proved true, however. Televangelism did not cut into church attendance, and the Internet has shown to be just as innocuous. Churchgoers, in fact, are the most active consumers of Internet religion; it "supplements their ties to traditional institutions" rather than offers an alternative. Meanwhile, clergy who do Internet ministry full time are extremely rare, for it takes continual funding. Yet the attempts can be innovative: The Methodist Church in England operates a "virtual church" website. Visitors take on an animated body, enter the sanctuary, and participate in worship.[23]

With the rise of new technologies, moreover, the debate over "why conservative churches are growing" is taking on a new dimension. With the new century, some of that touted conservative growth has in fact stopped, raising a new puzzle for church dynamics. The cases in point have been the no-growth years of the Southern Baptists, over-reporting by Pentecostals, and the precipitous loss of clergy in the conservative Lutheran Church-Missouri Synod, which saw 1,305 ministers leave in the decade before 1997. What is more, another question about growth has been raised. Some had believed that conservative churches were growing because of the "southernization" of American religion, the spread of a strict but enthusiastic evangelical faith. The counterargument is now made that evangelical growth outside the South was driven by the "Californication" of religion, a "catering to the culturally hip" with trendiness and music, but fewer moral demands.[24]

In any case, sociologist Roger Finke has tried to give an explanation of growth and decline that occupies the middle ground. The requirement for growth, he proposed, is not only conservation of a core supernatural belief or purpose—the "conservative" element—but twinning that with an effective cultural adaptation, or "innovative accommodation." In other words, being liberal outside and conservative inside may be the new requirement for growth. The accommodation, which may include music, dress, leadership styles, terminology, or uses of the Internet and audiovisual effects, becomes a liberalizing mantle over a conservative body of doctrine. According to this theory of innovation and accommodation, only *some* conservative churches are truly growing.[25]

The need to recruit younger candidates for ministry has meanwhile stirred another perennial debate in America: Shall we have a trained or untrained clergy? While graduate school seminaries are offering one alternative, the apprentice-style training of megachurches or Pentecostal correspondence courses is proposing the other. As both sides watch each other, hoping to learn from the best success, the powerful group of entrepreneurial clergy groomed in the megachurch field seem to have the leading edge. "Questions about the relevance of theological education drift through the hallways at megachurch conferences," said Aleshire, an expert on traditional seminaries. The megachurch puts the very existence of seminary education into question.[26]

Still, graduate school seminaries are rolling out their best efforts at recruiting high-quality candidates and showcasing the best training programs. On this more elite end, there are recommendations to design an "honors track" for high-achieving students in seminaries that might have otherwise lowered standards to ensure full classes and obtain necessary revenues. One group backing a seminary revival is the Fund for Theological Education, Inc., the latest in a tradition of funding young seminarians for a trial year of study. At the fund's summer conferences young people are inspired "to hear someone articulate" what they inchoately feel about serving God. "We must offer this kind of external call," said Melissa Wiginton, a fund official.[27]

These programs look for "the best and brightest," trolling for students with backgrounds in religion and liberal arts in particular, but also with "marks of resistance" to the secular culture; in other words, capable young people who nevertheless question "the ethic of accomplishment." The marks of resistance include: having an interior life; experiencing "modest economic practices"; sensing wonder in arts or cultures; a "significant wounding" in life to instill human empathy; and interest in ritual and worship. Many of the Fund's recruits are children of pastors. But the net is cast in a range of upscale waters, seeking youth with two seemingly opposite qualities, what Wiginton called "distinctive intellectual and leadership skills and humble engagement with the radically equalizing gospel."[28]

As in most generations, church leaders today are balancing the three factors of recruitment: letting God work, getting enough clergy, and screening for quality. Recruiters are finding that young seminarians, reared in the 1980s and 1990s, were distinctly shaped by their era, which was more secular and less denominational than in the past. According to Aleshire, a Baptist clergyman, this new crop is "less religiously formed than previous generations." They also came of age in a very psychiatric time. The *Diagnostic and Statistical Manual of Psychological Disorders* (DSM) has cast an even greater shadow over the process called "clergy assessment." Many denominations now use a psychologist to interview candidates before ordination.[29]

John Esau, a retired minister in Kansas, thinks this winnowing out of potentially destructive personalities is a must in ministry. After years of church work, the meeting of other pastors, and hearing many stories, he makes an emphatic argument. "Persons with significant personality disorders ought not to be in ministry," he said. "This has been one of the most important learnings for me, but also one of the saddest." Clergy with bad tempers are one thing, but sexual abuse by ministers is the new arena of concern. Priests and pastors who abuse this power are few. But with the open admission by Catholic authorities that "many dysfunctional and psychosexually immature men were admitted into seminaries and ordained in the priesthood," screening is getting tougher everywhere. Still, openness about homosexual clergy in some church sectors is likely to grow. But if the flaunting of homosexual behavior grows among the clergy, churchgoers will simply vote with their feet, leaving behind small islands of sexually liberal ministry, cut off from the church mainland.[30]

The personalities of ministers can be as much a concern as their sexual lives, and on this front recruiters are always caught between external judgments and the mystery of who God is calling. Some very odd people, for example, have turned out to be impressive ministers, said James E. Dittes, a teacher of pastoral psychology at Yale Divinity School. He points to the personality deficits of Moses, a timid shepherd with a stutter, and the fact that society rejected Jesus, *the* role model of ministry. "The tendency is to suppose that the 'effective clergy' is one who shows characteristics of being 'healthy' or 'normal' or someone who is a good 'student' or an effective 'leader,'" Dittes said of "scientific" assessment. "God's call to ministry may well be a call out of the 'world' and away from the standards the world uses—a call to those who are 'different' and a call to be 'different.'"[31]

Once a minister has entered the vocation, the challenge is to provide leadership. "Until recently, many seminaries and lay ministry training programs did not rank leadership potential as a critical factor in their admissions," said Donald Cozzens, a former vicar of Catholic priests. "Today we know leadership is at the heart of parish ministry."[32]

Research on clergy leadership dates to the 1950s, when the Ministerial Activity Scale (MAS) came into being. Other indexes have followed, but the equations are about the same. Typically, the research provides a list of the many "functions," or jobs, of the minister in a local church and follows that with the human "leadership skills" that help carry out those tasks. "Although parish clergy are 'generalists' and churches expect them to function in each of these [MAS] roles," two clergy psychologists said, "it is a very rare minister who can perform equally well in all of them."[33]

Since the 1960s, according to some, the emphasis had been on training ministers to be "enablers" of laity, helping churchgoers to carry out their own ideas and interests. The tide is shifting, however. The new emphasis is on the minister taking a higher leadership profile in order to revive the churches and evangelize the unchurched. If the earlier non-directive approach had the image of a shepherd, the new assertive one has the colorful image of a "rancher," an overseer who takes in the big picture to direct overall growth of a congregation. For the times, more ranchers than shepherds may be required. "Training and use of a directive leadership style probably bears careful consideration by seminaries and clergy," writes Allen Nauss, a Lutheran researcher who has updated the MAS scheme.[34]

As the leadership theme gains prominence in modern ministry, a lot of different images and proposals have cascaded forth. Management guru Peter Drucker has hailed "pastoral" churches serving human needs as centers of the American "community." Nevertheless, he rejects fancy theories about leadership styles, traits, or personalities, and that goes for church leadership as well. The best leaders he has met "had little or no 'charisma,'" he said. "The only definition of a *leader* is someone who has *followers*." The fruits of leadership are results. "Leaders are highly visible. They therefore set *examples*." Rather than mounting up titles or privileges, leaders take responsibility.[35]

Hybels, the pastor of the Willow Creek Community Church, is now urging "courageous leadership" that is caring but bold, and also takes the vulnerability of the pastor into account. Hybels identifies leadership as a "spiritual gift" to be recognized and cultivated, not a technique to be learned. For Father Cozzens, the spiritual leader is one who has achieved a calmness of soul. "Effective pastoral ministers ring true," he said. Parishioners can sense when the minister "not only knows *about* God but knows God." From a mainline Protestant perspective, clergyman Anthony B. Robinson of Seattle argues that churches must now take leadership skills as seriously as do education, industry, and politics. In his diagnosis local church leadership comes down to two priorities: to "maintain a clear focus amid competing agendas, and bring about needed change when people are resistant or at best ambivalent about change."[36]

Pulpit and Pew surveys found that American clergy widely agree on some aspects of leadership, but differ vastly on others. The preferred "style" of leadership (72.1 percent) is to encourage members to make decisions—with ministers taking "action alone" only when needed. Only a fifth of clergy made most decisions themselves. A tenth let members make "most of the decisions." Black pastors were most likely to decide themselves; ministers in small churches tended toward lay dominance. When it comes to change in a congregation, with its prospects of conflict, mainline clergy and younger clergy most prefer to keep "things stirred up." Seven in ten ministers, however, seek gradual change by trying to "keep things functioning smoothly." Young clergy are most open to innovation, while ministers in small churches or who are orthodox try to keep everyone "focused on the inherited traditions and practices of the church."[37]

While the calls for a more directive leadership to revive and grow churches seem to be loudest today, most clergy still are inclined to be servants of the laity. The directive and servant approaches are not mutually exclusive, of course. But as the call for ranchers, rather than shepherds, gains currency, it is worth remembering that ministry has always been done under two different theological views and guided by two different temperaments. Theologically, some ministers have been more exclusive in their ministry and others have been more open, or inclusive. In addition, some ministers have focused on the big picture and growth, while others have focused on providing stability and guidance for individuals. This fourfold aspect is congenital to ministry, and it seems proper not only to recognize it but encourage it.

The two theological approaches to ministry were highlighted by the terrorist attacks on the World Trade Center and the Pentagon in September 2001. Twelve days afterward, interfaith leaders, celebrities, and government officials gathered on the windy field of Yankee Stadium for "A Prayer for America," a show of national unity that was widely televised. One of the participants was David H. Benke, a pastor and district president for the conservative Lutheran Church-Missouri Synod around New York City. When Benke's turn came, he said, "Take the hand of the one next to you now and join me in prayer on this field of dreams turned into

God's house of prayer." He closed his prayer with "in the name of Jesus."[38]

What happened next illustrated how exclusive and inclusive ministries think, and it was the talk of American ministers for the next year. Eighteen clergy in Benke's national church charged him with the heresy of praying with people who believed in different gods, especially in the Asian or Islamic traditions. As the pastor of St. Peter's Lutheran Church in Cypress Hills, Brooklyn, Benke was quite used to working amid such cosmopolitan diversity, yet felt he had always testified to Jesus as the Lord. His accusers were not mollified. They said, "To participate with pagans in an interfaith service and, additionally, to give the impression that there might be more than one God, is an extremely serious offense."

Benke's suspension, and then his clearance on the complaint, was a dramatic example of the essential choice to be made even in American ministry today: to preach an exclusive gospel of salvation, and to organize ministry accordingly, or to find some broader door to society but at the risk of diluting the theological claims that gives ministry rationale and identity. For Benke's part, a balance must be struck. "We can be concerned about the truth of strong doctrine, but if we do so . . . without an eye toward the rest of the world, we will become a sect," said the pastor of thirty-one years. "Well, thirty years, plus one year off for bad behavior."

The disagreement characterized by the Benke case runs through American ministry as a whole and may stake out the basic split, both psychologically and theologically, in how clergy perceive their calling. Some perceive that their call is to proclaim a definitive and unambiguous truth. Others allow for a great amount of openness, which they attribute to an implicit mystery, even in a revealed religion of propositional truths and explicit creeds such as Christianity. To use the classic terminology, some clergy are more orthodox and others more modernist; some lean liberal and others conservative.

It would go too far to always call the first approach fundamentalist. But the exclusive-type claim is always cast as accepting or rejecting certain propositions to be right with God. Examples abound. When the Congregation for the Doctrine of the Faith in Rome issued its document "Dominus Jesus" in 2000, it claimed that salvation comes only through the Catholic Church. That raised hackles among Protestants and Orthodox in dialogue with Catholics. To many of them it seemed more a slap at the "separated brethren" than, as the Vatican explained it, an attack on religious and secular relativism. Similarly, when leaders of evangelical organizations were polled in 2002 about how Christians should relate to Muslims, 89 percent said it was "very important" to "insist" on the truth of the gospel.[39]

For the other approach—the less exclusive view of ministry—one is reminded of the *Christian Century* editorial during the Benke affair. "For

Christians, interfaith worship can be an act of humility," it said. "At best we can witness to the truth as we know it and have experienced it." Indeed, half of all churchgoers in America take a "relativist stance" that is positive to all religions, according to one survey. Edward Wimberly, a United Methodist who works in clergy training, believes the more inclusive approach has the future, according to the arrow of history. In the past, clergy had been trained as "master" of ancient sources, later as master of "discrete disciplines," and more recently as "professional manager and therapist." In the future, Wimberly foresees "the role of the minister as a bearer of faith," not a dispenser of absolute truths. The pastor would be more a storyteller who provides "healing, identity, meaning, and direction" for the lives of Christians.[40]

For American ministry, there seems to be plenty of room for both strict and open approaches. The "strictness hypothesis" tends to favor more exclusive ministry, for by exclusive claims a church can focus more on inward loyalty and resources: Growth and vitality may be the reward. But some ministers do not hear an exclusivist message from God, and are less enamored of exponential growth. This two-sided view of ministry perpetuates standard themes heard so much today: a culture war, orthodox versus modernist, and conservative Catholics and evangelicals on one side of the aisle and liberal Catholics and mainline Protestants on the other. Yet the bifurcation will not go away. At the least, Americans are constantly shifting back and forth across this boundary, as are the clergy.

One way to appreciate the complementarity of the strict and the open is to return to Robert Putnam's distinction in *Bowling Alone* between two kinds of social capital that improve the human condition. One is the "bonding" social capital, found in inward-looking groups, such as sectarian faiths. The other is "bridging" social capital, which is produced by groups that seek ties with other segments in a society.[41] This dynamic represents how ministries operate at the far ends of the conservative-to-liberal spectrum. At their extremes, these ministries provide what the other does not. They also remind each other of a part of the gospel that might be neglected. By all the evidence, moreover, there are excellent, authentic, and faithful clergy doing their work on either side of this aisle.

After this difference of theological approach to ministry, the fourfold view of American ministers next considers their leadership temperaments, and here also one finds two different pathways, often determined by the individual character of the minister. One approach takes a big view and goes for growth, while the other focuses on the needs of individuals. If one is more charismatic, the other is more stoical, and the two temperaments can appear in both orthodox and modernist ministry.

There may be a parallel to this in the two kinds of leadership styles noted by James MacGregor Burns in his 1978 study of presidential characters, *Leadership*. He speaks of transactional and transformational styles of leadership. "The relations of most leaders and followers," he said, "are transactional—leaders approach followers with an eye to exchanging one thing for another: jobs for votes, subsidies for campaign contributions." Transformational leadership tries to do more, he said. "The transformational leader recognizes and exploits an existing need or demand of a potential follower," Burns said. "The transformational leader looks for potential motives in followers, seeks to satisfy higher needs, and engages the fuller person of the follower"; here is the "elevating power of leadership."[42]

While this has a secular and political ring to it, the transactional and transformational leaders are very much like the shepherds and ranchers in ministry jargon; one cares for the soul, the other builds the institution. The strength of the first, or transactional, approach is its service and nurturing relationship, though it could well come under the rubric of the "status quo." In times of a struggling church, this approach naturally has its critics. "That's what I call a 'maintenance leader,'" said Greg Ogden, who was ordained in the Presbyterian mainline but now works with evangelical and independent churches.[43]

Having been a pastor since the early 1970s, and serving churches in Pittsburgh, the San Francisco Bay area, and Los Angeles, Ogden said the days of maintenance clergy are over. "There's an urgency to recruit a different kind of clergy than we've had in generations past," he said. The "teacher-caregiver" was workable when society was predominantly Christian. "If you could teach fairly effectively, especially your denominational doctrine, give care to the congregation and help in times of crisis, and be a passable administrator, then you did what was needed," Ogden said. "So you got a lot of [ordained] people with mercy gifts or people gifts, but not people who were visionaries or entrepreneurial or missional leaders. Now we need equipping leaders who create a ministry culture, making our churches more missional and evangelically focused." In other words, transformational.

The megachurch boom gives the impression that "transformational" or "visionary" leadership of institutions is the strongest hand to play for the future of ministry. But clearly, not all clergy can build megachurches. Not all Americans want to attend them. The pastoral role—call it a transactional or maintenance approach—will find a home in a large sector of the churches. All church leadership can't be institution building, said Marshall Shelley, editor of *Leadership*, a journal for ministers. "Once pastoring meant shepherding," he said, "knowing your people by name, being able to inquire as to their spiritual condition." He doubts that the church, "amazingly resilient" in history, will die for lack of transformational leadership: "Spiritual vitality is not going to become extinct just because we don't have a certain kind of leader."[44]

Some have argued that the maintenance approach may simply need some correcting, especially after taking on so much modern psychology. That is one theme of E. Brooks Holifield's *A History of Pastoral Care in America*, the shift "from salvation to self-realization." According to Holifield, the need for church growth has not eclipsed the idea of the minister as "doctor of the soul," as still resonates for many churchgoers. He suggests that pastoral work of a more traditional sort has unfortunately lost its way in the jungle of modern psychology. It mingled too deeply with Freudian theories and humanist presumptions, captured so well by the slogan "I'm Okay, You're Okay." Holifield says that the classic art of soul doctoring, with its resources in various traditions—Puritan, Anglican, Catholic, and holiness—retains its relevance. But there is always a trade-off it seems: Ministry with this focus will miss the bandwagon of church growth, institution building, and evangelizing the masses.[45]

The doctor of the soul has been described in other ways and is often found in the non-demonstrative pastor. Father Cozzens said, "Often the pastor's leadership style will be more quiet than dramatic, more subtle than direct." Lutheran minister and family counselor John O. Lundin points to "the competent man of faith" as a type of minister he sees regularly. As some women in ministry argue, this non-hierarchical type of religious work—"more relational," "more cooperative," or "partnership-based"—might be a strength they bring to ministry, typically dominated by the pulpit-style leadership. Yet that old-fashioned profile of a minister commanding from the mountaintop, awed and prophet-like, is relevant as well. This is the charismatic, transformational, equipping leader found in the church landscape. Such leaders are acutely necessary at a time of great institutional change. These, of course, would be the megachurch founders and the launchers of national ministries.[46]

For all its challenges and particular areas of "crisis," ministry is likely to endure with these four chief characteristics in all their combinations. There will be ministers who lean to exclusive claims to generate the spiritual energy of the gospel, and then clergy who will lean toward more open visions of God's salvation work. Among both of these ranks will also be found two kinds of clergy temperaments. One is the more pastoral leader, serving the needs of loyal congregants who turn to the pastor through the joys and crises of life. From the clergy ranks will also spring the more charismatic minister, a second temperament. These more demonstrative clergy are founders, national entrepreneurs, major prophetic voices for social change, and those credited with large-scale transformational leadership.

Yet for all ministers, just as ministry begins with the call, it must keep some semblance of that divine connection, search, or faith throughout. Without this, clergy agree, ministry itself loses its integrity, and ministers lose the power to be examples. Spiritual integrity is a normal requirement of ministers of God, but not easy to achieve, said the Kansas preacher John

Esau, who listed ten things "I didn't learn in seminary," things that can only come by experience. "Ministry is good," he said. "It is a daunting task that requires the highest level of competence and character. The margins of error have been greatly narrowed in ministry as in many other vocations." Then he quoted the apostle Paul: "Since it is by God's mercy that we are engaged in this ministry, we do not lose heart."[47]

Notes

Abbreviations for the Notes

AP   *Associated Press*

BCA   Eric Lincoln and Lawrence H. Mamiya, *The Black Church in African-American Experience* (Durham: Duke University Press, 1990).

Census 2000   Census 2000 "Special EEO Tabulation" for occupations at http://www.census.gov/eeo2000/index.html.

CACD   Richard A. Hunt, John E. Hinkle Jr., and H. Newton Malony, eds., *Clergy Assessment and Career Development* (Nashville: Abingdon Press, 1990).

CC   *Christian Century*

CCAP   Sue E. S. Crawford and Laura R. Olson, eds., *Christian Clergy in American Politics* (Baltimore: Johns Hopkins Press, 2001).

CFP   Donald B. Cozzens, *The Changing Face of the Priesthood: A Reflection on the Priest's Crisis of Soul* (Collegeville, Minn.: Liturgical Press, 2000).

CT   *Christianity Today*

FACT   Carl S. Dudley and David A. Roozen, "Faith Communities Today: A Report on Religion in the United States Today." Hartford Institute for Religion Research, March 2001, at http://fact/hartsem.edu.

FGC   Cynthia Woolever and Deborah Bruce, *A Field Guide to U.S. Congregations: Who's Going Where and Why* (Louisville, Ky.: Westminster John Knox, 2002).

GSC   Jeffrey K. Hadden, *The Gathering Storm in the Churches* (Garden City, N.Y.: Doubleday, 1969).

HM   Becky R. McMillan and Matthew J. Price, "How Much Should We Pay the Pastor?: A Fresh Look at Clergy Salaries in the 21st Century," Pulpit and Pew report, Duke Divinity School, 2003, at http://www.pulpitandpew.duke.edu/salary.html.

JSSR   *Journal for the Scientific Study of Religion*

KAR   Ho-Youn Kwon, Kwang Chung Kim, and R. Stephen Warner, eds., *Korean Americans and Their Religions: Pilgrims and Missionaries from a Different Shore* (University Park: Pennsylvania State University Press, 2001).

MHP   H. Richard Niebuhr and Daniel D. Williams, eds., *The Ministry in Historical Perspective* (New York: Harper and Brothers, 1956).

NYT   *New York Times*

QHG   Robert Wuthnow and John H. Evans, eds., *The Quiet Hand of God: Faith-Based Activism and the Public Role of Mainline Protestantism* (Berkeley: University of California Press, 2002).

RAL   Jon Butler, Grant Wacker, and Randall Balmer, *Religion in American Life: A Short History* (New York: Oxford University Press, 2003).

RRS   *Review of Religious Research*

SBU   "State of the Black Union: The Black Church" Conference, Corby Hall, Detroit, February 2, 2003 (author's tape recording).

SFP   *The Study of the Impact of Fewer Priests on the Pastoral Ministry* (Washington, D.C.: National Conference of Catholic Bishops, 2000).

USCCB   United States Conference of Catholic Bishops

WDL   Adair T. Lummis, "What Do Lay People Want in Pastors? Answers from Lay Search Committee Chairs and Regional Judicatory Leaders," Pulpit and Pew report, Duke Divinity School, 2003, at http://www.pulpitandpew.duke.edu/pastorsearch.html.

WR1   Rosemary Radford Ruether and Rosemary Skinner Keller, eds., *Women and Religion in America: The Nineteenth Century, A Documentary History,* vol. 1 (San Francisco: Harper and Row, 1981).

WR3   Rosemary Radford Ruether and Rosemary Skinner Keller, eds., *Women and Religion in America: 1900–1968, A Documentary History,* vol. 3, (San Francisco: Harper and Row, 1986).

WT   *Washington Times*

Yearbook 2003 Eileen Lindner, ed., *Yearbook of American and Canadian Churches 2003* (Nashville: Abingdon Press, 2003).

Acknowledgments

1. Osmund Schreuder, "A Review of Ministry Studies," *Social Compass* 17 (1970): 588; Martin E. Marty, "The Clergy," in *The Professions in American History,* ed. Nathan O. Hatch (Notre Dame, Ind.: University of Notre Dame Press, 1988),

76n.5; Donald E. Messer, *Contemporary Images of Christian Ministry* (Nashville: Abingdon Press, 1989), 22.

Introduction

1. John Bartlett, *Bartlett's Familiar Quotations*, 15th ed. (Boston: Little, Brown and Company, 1980), 137n.9; William Shakespeare, *Henry VI*, part 2, act 4, scene 2, line 86.
2. Census 2000. In 2000, there were 3.3 lawyers and judges and 1.37 clergy for each 1,000 Americans; from 1970 to 2000 the clergy "occupation" has varied from 1.1 to 1.3 ministers per 1,000 Americans.
3. Robert Wuthnow, "Beyond Quiet Influence," in *QHG*, 385.
4. Matthew Price, "Fear of Falling," *CC*, August 15–22, 2001, 18.
5. Peter J. Thuesen, "The Logic of Mainline Churchliness," in *QHG*, 45; Andrew Abbott, *The System of Professions* (Chicago: University of Chicago Press, 1988), 308; S. Robert Lichter et al., *Prime Time* (Washington, D.C.: Regnery Publishing, 1994), 389; Stephen Powers, Stanley Rothman, and David Rothman, *Hollywood's America* (Boulder, Colo.: Westview Press, 1996), 127; E. Brooks Holifield, "Theology as Entertainment," *Church History* 67 (September 1998): 499–520.
6. *CFP*, 130; George Barna, *Today's Pastors* (Ventura, Calif.: Regal Books, 1993), 59; Jackson W. Carroll, "Protestant Pastoral Ministry at the Beginning of the New Millennium" (paper presented at the Society for the Scientific Study of Religion and Religious Research Association, Houston, Texas, October 18, 2000), 1.
7. Quoted in Laura R. Olson, "Mainline Protestant Washington Offices and the Political Lives of Clergy," in *QHG*, 59.
8. Richard J. Foster, *Money, Sex, and Power* (San Francisco: Harper and Row, 1985); interview with Russell P. Spittler, February 26, 2001, Pasadena, Calif.
9. Quoted in Dean Hoge, Benton Johnson, and Donald A. Luidens, *Vanishing Boundaries* (Louisville, Ky.: Westminster John Knox Press, 1994), 2.
10. Martin E. Marty, "The Clergy," in *The Professions in American History*, ed. Nathan O. Hatch (Notre Dame, Ind.: University of Notre Dame Press, 1988), 87.
11. Barna, *Today's Pastors*, 59; quoted in HM, 30; quoted in David Goetz, "Why Pastor Steve Loves His Job," *CT*, April 7, 1997, 19; WDL, 20.
12. Quoted in James D. Glasse, *Profession: Minister* (Nashville: Abingdon Press, 1968), 34; E. Brooks Holifield, "The Clergy," in *Encyclopedia of American Social History*, vol. 3, eds. Mary K. Cayton, Elliott J. Gorn, and Peter W. Williams (New York: Charles Scribner's, 1993), 2466.
13. Quoted in Sidney E. Mead, "The Rise of the Evangelical Conception of the Ministry in America," in *MHP*, 233; quoted in Francis L. Hawks, *Narrative of Events Connected with the Rise of the Protestant Episcopal Church in Virginia* (New York: Harper, 1836), 65; quoted in *RAL*, 94, 177.
14. Quoted in Mead, "The Rise," 218n.29, 217n.28. The other French chronicler was J. Hector St. John de Crevecouer, who lived in America several years and published his *Letters of an American Farmer*.
15. Donald M. Scott, *From Office to Profession: the New England Ministry, 1750–1850* (Philadelphia: University of Pennsylvania Press, 1978), 113; quoted in Mead, "The Rise," 144n.109.

16. Quoted in Lawrence N. Jones, "The Organized Church," in *Directory of African-American Religious Bodies*, ed. Wardell J. Payne (Washington, D.C.: Howard University Press, 1991), 7; Holifield, "The Clergy," 2470; quoted in Mead, "The Rise," 132; quoted in Marty, "The Clergy," 86.
17. Quoted in Holifield, "The Clergy," 2471; Glasse, *Profession: Minister*, 13; Austin P. Flannery, ed., *Documents of Vatican II* (Grand Rapids, Mich.: Eerdmans Publishing Company, 1975), 832; *GSC*, 240.
18. Marty, "The Clergy," 87; *GSC*, 266.
19. Thomas G. Long, "Preaching," in *Encyclopedia of Religion in the South,* ed. Samuel S. Hill (Macon, Ga.: Mercer University Press, 1984), 593.
20. Nesbitt, *Feminization of the Clergy*, 148–49. The new lay titles include: "ecclesial lay minister" and "Eucharistic minister" for Catholics; "certified lay speaker" and "limited population pastor" for United Methodists; "nonstipendiary priests" in the Episcopal Church; "certified ministers" for the Assemblies of God; "commissioned deacons" in the Lutheran Church-Missouri Synod; and "preaching elders" in the Reformed Church in America. See WDL, 33–34.
21. *Baptism, Eucharist and Ministry*, Faith and Order Paper No. 111 (Geneva: World Council of Churches, 1982), 9.
22. Loren B. Mead, "Definitions of Congregational Growth," in *Church and Synagogue Affiliation*, ed. Amy L. Sales and Gary A. Tobin (Westport, Conn.: Greenwood Press, 1995), 33.
23. James M. Gustafson, "The Clergy in the United States," *Daedalus* 92 (Fall 1963): 730.
24. Pastor quoted in Nancy Ammerman, "Connecting Mainline Protestant Churches with Public Life," in *QHG*, 146.
25. William Shakespeare, *Hamlet*, act 1, scene 2, line 47; Geoffrey Chaucer, *Canterbury Tales* (Harmondsword, England: Penguin, 1951), 39.
26. Raymond Chapman, ed., *Godly and Righteous, Peevish and Perverse* (Grand Rapids, Mich.: Eerdmans Publishing Company, 2002), x.

Chapter 1

1. Brewster quoted in Larry Witham, "The Graying of Black Collars," *WT*, July 5, 2001, A1; interview with Melissa Keeble, February 26, 2001, Pasadena, Calif.
2. John M. Mulder, "Call," in *Concise Encyclopedia of Preaching*, ed. William H. Willimon and Richard Lischer (Louisville, Ky.: Westminister John Knox, 1995), 58; Isaiah 6:8; see fishermen at Mark 1:16–20, Matthew 4:18–22, Luke 5:1–11, and John 1:40–42.
3. Austin P. Flannery, ed., *Documents of Vatican II* (Grand Rapids, Mich.: Eerdmans Publishing Company, 1975), 884; *The Book of Common Prayer* (New York: Seabury, 1979), 531 (emphasis added).
4. Interview with Robert Wicks, December 3, 2002, Columbia, Md.
5. Interview with John O. Lundin, November 22, 2002, Alexandria, Va.; Barbara Wheeler, "Fit for Ministry," *CC*, April 11, 2001, 16; "Priests in the United States: Satisfaction, Work Load, and Support Structures," *CARA Working Paper No. 5*, September 2002, 17. The study found that 72 percent of older priests (born before 1943) completed parochial high school compared to only 43 percent of younger priests (born after 1960).

6. Based on Census Bureau, "Detailed Occupation of the Economically Active Population" for 1900 to 1970, 1970 to 1980, 1990, and 2000. From 1910 to 2000 there averaged from 1.1 to 1.2 clergy per thousand population, with a downturn during the Depression (1.06 clergy) and upturn in recent years (1.3 clergy).

7. Census 2000; The 60 percent to 40 percent comparison is based on "serving" and "total" clergy in the *Yearbook 2003*, 377; for Catholic clergy see "Active and Retired Priests in 1999," *SFP*, v, 29, which reports 27,015 of 46,709 priests (58 percent) are active in parishes.

8. Percentages based on clergy counts in *Yearbook 2003*, 365–377. The "23 percent" includes the Church of Jesus Christ of Latter-day Saints (LDS), which reported 36,418 ministers (6 percent of *all* U.S. clergy). All worthy males are in the LDS "priesthood," but become "clergy" on leadership assignment. The Community of Christ (formerly the "Reorganized" wing of the LDS in 1860) has 19,319 clergy. Less than 1 percent of all clergy are Eastern Orthodox, a total of 2,100 for the Greek, Russian, Antiochian, Serbian, and Romanian branches in America.

9. Based on Census regions and Census 2000; demographics in FACT, 8.

10. See states in Census 2000.

11. Telephone interview with Robert K. Johnston, January 29, 2003; see also Robert K. Johnston, *Reel Spirituality* (Grand Rapids, Mich.: Baker Academic, 2000), 29–30.

12. Bruce Chilton, *Rabbi Jesus* (New York: Doubleday, 2000), xvii–xviii.

13. "Truett," in *The Wycliffe Biographical Dictionary of the Church*, ed. Elgin S. Moyer (Chicago: Moody Press, 1982), 406; interview with K. Randel Everett, February 11, 2003, Arlington, Va.

14. Interview with Jane Holmes Dixon, January 21, 2003, Washington, D.C.

15. Interview with Lloyd John Ogilvie, February 12, 2003, Washington, D.C.

16. Interview with John Odean, January 17, 2003, Millersville, Md.

17. Milton quoted in Winthrop S. Hudson, "The Ministry in the Puritan Age," in *MHP*, 205; Cartwright quoted in Sidney E. Mead, "The Rise of the Evangelical Conception of the Ministry in America: 1607–1850," in *MHP*, 239.

18. Robinson quoted in Larry Witham, "Searching for Shepherds," *WT*, July 2, 2001, A11; Jacquelyn Grant comments at SBU.

19. Donald M. Scott, *From Office to Profession* (Philadelphia: University of Pennsylvania Press, 1978), 118.

20. E-mail interview with Jackson W. Carroll, October 15, 2003. The Pulpit and Pew project, which began in 1999 with $3.5 million and thirty researchers, was completed over four years. See http://www.pulpitandpew.duke.edu.

21. Quoted in Witham, "Searching for Shepherds," A10.

22. Jackson W. Carroll, "First- and Second-Career Clergy," Pulpit and Pew report, Duke Divinity School, 2003, tables 1, 3, at http://www.pulpitandpew.duke.edu/careercomparison.html; with thirty as the average ordination age for new Catholic priests, fewer had time to develop first careers.

23. Carroll, "First- and Second-Career Clergy," tables 3, 4, and quote from table 5.

24. Ibid., tables 6, 7.

25. Becky R. McMillan, "The View from Pulpit and Pew: Provocative Findings of Pastoral Leadership in the 21st Century," February 21, 2003, 2, at http://

www.pulpitandpew.duke.edu/SACEM%20Keynote%20Talk1.pdf; "Age Distribution of Diocesan and Religious Priests," *SFP*, 27. The average age for diocesan priests is fifty-seven and for religious priests sixty-three. Only 298 priests are under age thirty; David J. Wood, "Where Are the Younger Clergy?" *CC*, April 11, 2001, 18.

26. See growth rates at Census 2000.
27. See Paula D. Nesbitt, *Feminization of the Clergy in America* (New York: Oxford University Press, 1997), 26; and Patricia Chang and Viviana Bompadre, "Crowded Pulpits," *JSSR* 38 (September 1999): 408–9.
28. Percentages in Witham, "Searching for Shepherds," A10; Barbara Wheeler, "Fit for Ministry?" *CC*, April 11, 2001, 18, 22.
29. These median salaries include housing. See HM, 6; Matthew J. Price, "Fear of Falling," *CC*, August 15–22, 2001, 18.
30. Jackson W. Carroll and Robert L. Wilson, *Too Many Pastors?* (New York: Pilgrim Press, 1980), 130, 36; Becky R. McMillan, "What Do Clergy Do All Week?" Pulpit and Pew report, Duke Divinity School, 2002, table 3, at http://www.pulpitandpew.duke.edu/clergyweek.html.
31. *FGC*, 22; Lyle E. Schaller, *What Have We Learned* (Nashville: Abingdon Press, 2001), 98.
32. FACT, 64, figure 6.8; "Selected Findings From the National Clergy Survey," Pulpit and Pew report, Duke Divinity School, February 2002, 1, 2, at http://www.pulpitandpew.duke.edu/clergy_letter_1.pdf
33. John Knox, "The Ministry in the Primitive Church," in *MHP*, 2.
34. Raymond E. Brown, *An Introduction to the New Testament* (New York: Doubleday, 1997), 648.
35. See 1 Thessalonians 5:12; I Corinthians 12:4, 28; and Ephesians 4: 11.
36. Knox, "The Ministry," 22.
37. Ibid., 24.
38. Acts 5:2–4; papacy quoted in Flannery, *Documents of Vatican II*, 384.
39. George Williams, "The Ministry of the Ante-Nicene Church," in *MHP*, 28.
40. Wilhelm Pauck, "The Ministry in the Time of the Continental Reformation," in *MHP*, 139; Paul spoke of priestly roles in Romans 15:16 and I Peter 2:5, 9.
41. Harry S. Stout, *The New England Soul* (New York: Oxford University Press, 1986), 5; interview with Eddie Gibbs, February 26, 2001, Pasadena, Calif.
42. Scott, *From Office to Profession*, 52.
43. Nathan O. Hatch, "The Democratization of Christianity and the Character of American Politics," in *Religion and American Politics: From the Colonial Period to the 1980s*, ed. Mark A. Noll (New York: Oxford University Press, 1990), 104. For an overview of the democratic religious movements see Nathan O. Hatch, *The Democratization of American Christianity* (New Haven: Yale University Press, 1989).
44. Scott, *From Office to Profession*, 53, 52, 74.
45. Ibid., 131, 153, 122.
46. *Baptism, Eucharist and Ministry*, Faith and Order Paper No. 111 (Geneva: World Council of Churches, 1982), 25, 22.
47. Catholic and Orthodox responses quoted in John N. Collins, *Diakonia* (New York: Oxford University Press, 1990), 257; World Evangelical Fellowship, "An

Evangelical Response to Baptism, Eucharist and Ministry," *Evangelical Review of Theology* 13 (October 1989): 307.

Chapter 2

1. Interview with Chuck Smith, February 25, 2001, Santa Ana, Calif.
2. "In Jesus' Name?" *CC*, September 25–October 8, 2002, 5.
3. Erling and Byars quoted in Larry Witham, "Searching for Shepherds," *WT*, July 2, 2001, A11.
4. Greenhaw quoted in Ibid.
5. FACT, 67.
6. William R. Hutchinson, "Past Imperfect," in *Liberal Protestantism*, ed. Robert S. Michaelsen and Wade Clark Roof (New York: Pilgrim Press, 1986), 71; "Twelve Great American Preachers," *Time*, April 6, 1953, 126–312.
7. Dean R. Hoge, Benton Johnson, and Donald A. Luidens, *Vanishing Boundaries* (Louisville, Ky.: Westminster John Knox, 1994), vii, 2.
8. "Introduction," *QHG*, 17; "Evangelicals and Catholics Together," *First Things* 43 (May 1994): 15–22.
9. *Yearbook 2003*, 365–77; the ratio of mainline clergy serving parishes and those not is 50/50, while it is 60/40 for all U.S. ministers.
10. Wade Clark Roof and William McKinney, *American Mainline Religion* (New Brunswick, N.J.: Rutgers University Press, 1987), 82–84. An eighth but smaller "sister" is the Reformed Church in America, a denomination categorized as moderate. Roof and McKinney said moderate denominations account for 24.2 percent of Americans, liberals 8.7 percent, and conservative evangelical denominations 15.8 percent.
11. "Introduction," *QHG*, 18, 8–9.
12. Ibid., 8–11.
13. Jennifer McKinney and Roger Finke, "Reviving the Mainline," *JSSR* 41 (December 2002): 772, 776.
14. Ibid., 776.
15. "Introduction," *QHG*, 19; quoted in John Dart, "Proud of the UMC Label," *CC*, September 12–19, 2001, 12.
16. Becky R. McMillan, "What Do Clergy Do All Week?" Pulpit and Pew report, Duke Divinity School, 2002, at http://www.pulpitandpew.duke.edu/clergy week.html.
17. Ibid.
18. Sandi Brunnette-Hill and Roger Finke, "A Time for Every Purpose Under Heaven," *RRS* 41 (Fall 1999): 58; quoted in Witham, "Searching for Shepherds," A10.
19. Brunnette-Hill and Finke, "A Time for Every Purpose," 54–55, 58.
20. The figure of two hundred members was cited by Jackson W. Carroll and Robert L. Wilson, *Too Many Pastors?* (New York: Pilgrim Press, 1980), 36; Lutheran percentages are from interview with Michael L. Cooper-White, February 8, 2001, Gettysburg, Pa.; Presbyterian Research Services, *Comparative Statistics 2003* (Louisville, Ky.: Presbyterian Church USA, 2003), table 15; quoted in Witham, "Searching for Shepherds," A10.

21. Interview with Cooper-White.
22. *Yearbook 2003*, 370; interview with Cooper-White.
23. Kohler quoted in Witham, "Searching for Shepherds," A10.
24. David J. Wood, "Where Are the Younger Clergy?" *CC*, April 11, 2001, 18. The portion of ministers thirty-five or younger is 4 percent in the UCC; 3.7 percent in the Disciples; 3.9 percent in the Episcopal Church; 5.8 percent for American Baptists; 6.1 percent in the ELCA; 6.7 percent for United Methodists; and 7 percent in the Presbyterian Church (USA).
25. The "return to normalcy" argument was made in Hutchinson, "Past Imperfect," in *Liberal Protestantism*; "Introduction," *QHG*, 11.
26. Peter Berger, *The Sacred Canopy* (Garden City, N.Y.: Doubleday, 1967). For his rethinking see "Epistemological Modesty: An Interview with Peter Berger," *CC*, October 29, 1997, 974.
27. Hoge et al., *Vanishing Boundaries*, 112–15, 184–85, 6.
28. Dean Kelley, *Why Conservative Churches Are Growing* (New York: Harper and Row, 1972), 89
29. Peter J. Thuesen, "The Logic of Mainline Churchliness," in *QHG*, 27.
30. Ibid., 28, 42.
31. Ibid., 41; Harry Emerson Fosdick, "Shall the Fundamentalists Win?" in *American Sermons*, ed. Michael Warner (New York: Library of America, 1999), 776, 778.
32. *RAL*, 352; see Robert T. Handy, "The American Religious Depression, 1925–35," *Church History* 29 (1960): 3–16; see *The Education of Ministers in America*, 4 vols. (New York: Institute of Social and Religious Research, 1934).
33. Joel A. Carpenter, *Revive Us Again* (New York: Oxford University Press, 1997), 15, 31.
34. Robert S. Michaelsen, "The Protestant Ministry in America: 1850 to the Present," in *MHP*, 255, 256.
35. Carpenter, *Revive Us Again*, 69, 48.
36. "History of the NAE," at http://www.nae.net/index.cfm?FUSEACTION= nae.history; see the cover story "Born Again," *Newsweek*, October 25, 1976.
37. The "third force" was recognized in Henry P. Van Dusen, "Force's Lesson for Others," *Life*, June 9, 1958, 122–24.
38. R. Albert Mohler Jr., "Against an Immoral Tide," *NYT*, June 19, 2000, A19.
39. For clergy "serving parishes" and "total" clergy, see *Yearbook 2003*, 365–77.
40. While some estimate hundreds of Pentecostal groups, twenty-four reported clergy data in *Yearbook 2003*. Clergy figures are rounded.
41. McKinney and Finke, "Reviving the Mainline," 781; FACT, 64. FACT said that 12 percent of clergy had less than a Bible college education or no formal ministerial training at all.
42. Nathan O. Hatch, *The Democratization of American Christianity* (New Haven: Yale University Press, 1989), 14. For "seven sister" seminaries see Association of Theological Schools at http://www.ats.edu; Robert Patterson, "Why Evangelicals Have the Biggest Seminaries, and Why They Are in Crisis," *CT*, January 12, 1998, 50.
43. Patterson, "Why Evangelicals," 50; recruitment at evangelical seminaries was described by Greg Ogden of Fuller Theological Seminary in an interview, February 26, 2001, Pasadena, Calif.

44. Jackson W. Carroll et al., *Being There* (New York: Oxford University Press, 1997), 11, 205, 208–9.
45. Ibid., 205, 220, 225, 213 (emphasis in original).
46. Barbara Wheeler, "Fit for Ministry?" *CC*, April 11, 2001, 18, 22, 23. The 1998 survey was sent to 10,000 students and received a 25-percent response.
47. Jack Wertheimer, "The Rabbi Crisis," *Commentary* 115 (May 2003): 37, 35, 36, 38.
48. Samuel Haber, "The Professions," in *Encyclopedia of American Social History*, vol. 2, eds. Mary K. Cayton, Elliott J. Gorn, and Peter W. Williams (New York: Scribner's, 1993), 1586; the 1933 study was A. M. Carr-Saunders and P. A. Wilson, *The Professions* (New York: Oxford University Press, 1933); Edward Wimberly, "Spiritual Formation in Theological Education and Psychological Assessment," in *CACD*, 27.
49. H. Richard Niebuhr, *The Purpose of the Church and Its Ministry* (New York: Harper, 1956), 48, 57.
50. Samuel W. Blizzard, "The Minister's Dilemma," *CC*, April 25, 1956, 508, 509.
51. James M. Gustafson, "The Clergy in the United States," *Daedalus* 92 (Fall 1963): 732, 737; Gibson Winter, *The Suburban Captivity of the Churches* (Garden City, N.Y.: Doubleday, 1961); quoted in Matthew J. Price, "After the Revolution," *Theology Today* 59 (October 2002): 434n.28.
52. John A. T. Robinson, *Honest to God* (Philadelphia: Westminster, 1963), 17; Harvey Cox, *The Secular City* (New York: Macmillan, 1965), 3; *GSC*, 190.
53. *GSC*, 250, 233, 251, 234.
54. Ibid., 233.
55. Ibid., 240, 261, 258–59.
56. Gustafson, "The Clergy," 735; Haber, "The Professions," 1586; James D. Glasse, *Profession: Minister* (Nashville: Abingdon Press, 1968), 146.
57. Glasse, *Profession*, 41.
58. Ibid., 18–19.
59. Gilbert R. Rendle, "Reclaiming Professional Jurisdiction," *Theology Today* 59 (October 2002): 409, 418.
60. "Remarks by the Reverend Billy Graham at the Memorial Service for the Victims of the Terrorist Attacks of September 11th," *Federal News Service*, Washington, D.C., September 14, 2001.

Chapter 3

1. Quoted in David O'Reilly, "Female Episcopal Priests Started Here 25 Years Ago," *Philadelphia Inquirer*, July 28, 1999, A1.
2. 14 percent is the highest available figure and comes from the 2000 Census. Other estimates range from 10 to 13 percent female ministers; *RAL*, 288; Rosemary Radford Ruether, *Women-Church* (San Francisco: Harper and Row, 1985); for the Re-Imagining controversy see Stewart M. Hoover and Lynn Schofield Clark, "Event and Publicity as Social Drama," *Review of Religious Research* 39 (December 1997): 153–171.
3. Quote in *ELCA New Service*, "ELCA Celebrates 30th Anniversary of Women's Ordination," June 16, 2000. Of *all* ELCA clergy, active and retired, women made up 13.4 percent in 2000.

4. "Number of Women Leaders in Church Compares Favorably to U.S. Work Force," June 25, 2004 press release, USCCB, Washington, D.C. The report, "Women in Diocesan Leadership Positions: Progress Report, 2003," said that while women made up 51 percent the nation's executive, administrative, managerial, and professional workforce, women also made up 48.9 percent of diocesan administrators.

5. Mark Chaves, *Ordaining Women* (Cambridge: Harvard University Press, 1997), 16.

6. Cited in Barbara Brown Zikmund, "The Protestant Women's Ordination Movement," *Union Seminary Quarterly Review* 57 (2003): 133.

7. Barbara Brown Zikmund, Adair T. Lummis, and Patricia M.Y. Chang, "Women, Men and Styles of Clergy Leadership," *CC*, May 6, 1998, 485; Paula D. Nesbitt, *Feminization of the Clergy in America* (New York: Oxford University Press, 1997), 3.

8. Nesbitt, *Feminization of the Clergy*, 164, 165.

9. Quoted in ibid., 4.

10. Interview with Barbara Brown Zikmund, January 25, 2001, Rockville, Md.

11. Barbara Brown Zikmund, Adair T. Lummis, and Patricia Mei Yin Chang, *Clergy Women* (Louisville, Ky.: Westminster John Knox, 1998), 97.

12. Joy Charlton, "Women and Clergywomen," *Sociology of Religion* 61 (2000): 422, 423.

13. Brock quoted in Julia Duin, "Feminization of Clergy Rebuffed," *WT*, July 4, 2001, A1; interview with Melissa Keeble, February 26, 2001, Pasadena, Calif.

14. *RAL*, 133; quoted in Letha Dawson Scanzoni and Susan Setta, "Women in Evangelical, Holiness, and Pentecostal Traditions," in *WR3*, 234.

15. Mary Ellen Konieczny and Mark Chaves, "Resources, Race, and Female-Headed Congregations in the United States," *JSSR* 39 (September 2000): 262, 265.

16. Ibid., 263, 268. On Catholic women, see Philip J. Murnion and David De-Lambo, *Parishes and Parish Ministers* (New York: National Parish Life Center, 1999), 26. This study found that women were 82 percent of "non-priest" ministers in parishes.

17. Konieczny and Chaves, "Resources," 268; Patricia Chang and Viviana Bompadre, "Crowded Pulpits," *JSSR* 38 (September 1999): 408–9.

18. Konieczny and Chaves, "Resources," 264, 268.

19. *HM*, 14; Paul Perl and Patricia M.Y. Chang, "Credentialism Across Creeds," *JSSR* 39 (June 2000): 174. Zikmund, *Clergy Women*, 73, estimates women earn 91 percent of what male clergy earned.

20. Becky R. McMillan and Matthew Price, "At Cross Purposes? Clergy Salaries," Pulpit and Pew working paper, 2001, 18, at http://www.pulpitandpew.duke.edu/atcrosspurposes.pdf; Matthew Price, "Fear of Falling," *CC*, August 15–22, 2001, 19.

21. *Statistical Abstract of the United States: 2003* (Washington, D.C.: U.S. Census Bureau, 2003), 9, 65. See Table 74 on "Family Households With Own Children Under Age 18." From this table, I calculate that married men under age 40 with children and a homemaker wife make up no more than 5 percent of the U.S. population, and perhaps far less.

22. Quoted in Duin, "Feminization of Clergy," A8.

23. Quoted in Zikmund, *Clergy Women*, 56; on megachurch leaders see Scott Thumma, "Exploring the Megachurch Phenomena," Hartford Institute for Religious Research, at http://hirr.hartsem.edu/bookshelf/thumma_article2 .html.

24. Interview with Zikmund.

25. Zikmund, *Clergy Women*, 56, 7–15; Zikmund, "Women, Men," 478, 483, 479 (emphasis in original).

26. Zikmund, *Clergy Women*, 121, 19, 107–8.

27. Barbara Brown Zikmund, "Winning Ordination for Women in Mainstream Protestant Churches," in *WR3*, 347.

28. Chaves, *Ordaining Women*, 5. Chaves lists the "external" pressures as the state, the women's movement, social gender equality, other denominations and church networks (38); see Zikmund, "Winning Ordination," 347.

29. Barbara Brown Zikmund, "The Struggle for the Right to Preach," in *WR1*, 194.

30. *BCA*, 307, 294; quoted in Zikmund, "Winning Ordination," 242, 301.

31. Quoted in Zikmund, "The Struggle," 204; quoted in Zikmund, "Winning Ordination," 231.

32. I borrow this twofold concept from Chaves, *Ordaining Women*, 83.

33. Interview with Jane Holmes Dixon, January 21, 2003, Washington, D.C.

34. For one account of the "conscience clause," see Joseph H. Fichter, *The Pastoral Provisions* (Kansas City, Mo.: Sheed and Ward, 1989), 87; quoted in Larry Witham, "D.C. Gets 1st Female Episcopal Bishop," *WT*, November 20, 1992, A3.

35. Bishop Jack Iker quoted in Larry Witham, "Bishop–elect Faces Wrath of PC Dioceses," *WT*, December 21, 1992, A6; and in Duin, "Feminization of Clergy," A9.

36. Barfoot quoted in Duin, "Feminization of Clergy," A9.

37. *United Methodist News Service*, "Backgrounder on Clergy Women," October 2001, at http://www.umns.umc.org/backgrounders/clergywomen.html [cited November 2003].

38. William V. D'Antonio et al., *American Catholics* (Walnut Creek, Calif.: Alta Mira, 2001), 11, 12; John Paul II, "Collaborative Ministry Must be Faithful to Sacramental Doctrine," *L'Obsservatore Romano*, English ed., July 7, 1993, 3.

39. Raymond E. Brown, *An Introduction to the New Testament* (New York: Doubleday, 1997): 574; Phyllis Zagano, "Catholic Women Deacons," *America*, February 17, 2003, 9, 11. Zagano notes that a study of deacons commissioned by Pope Paul VI and "suppressed" found that "ordination of women deacons in the early church was sacramental."

40. Barbara Brown Zikmund, "UCC Celebrates an Anniversary: 150 Years of Women Clergy," *UCC News*, September 2003, at http://www.ucc.org/ucnews/sep03/past.htm.

41. Dilday quoted in Julia Duin and Larry Witham, "Baptist Pastors Lead From the Right," *WT*, July 3, 2001, A1; see 1 Corinthians 14: 33–35 and 1 Timothy 2:11–12.

42. Robert A. Baker, *The Southern Baptist Convention and Its People* (Nashville, Tenn.: Broadman, 1974), 398–99, 416–17.

43. Quoted in "Southern Baptist Convention Passes Resolution Opposing Women as Pastors," *AP* in *NYT*, June 15, 2000, A22.

44. R. Albert Mohler, Jr., "Against an Immoral Tide," *NYT*, June 19, 2000, A19.
45. The comments from Southwestern Seminary reported in Duin and Witham, "Baptist Pastors," A9.
46. Gustav Niebuhr, "Daughter of Graham to Address Evangelists," *NYT*, July 31, 2000, A12.
47. Grant Wacker, *Heaven Below* (Cambridge: Harvard University Press, 2001), 162.
48. Deborah Menken Gill, "Ripe for Decision: Women-in-Ministry Issues of Century Twenty-One," *Enrichment* 6 (Spring 2001): 41–43. The data is from the "A/G Ministers Report, 1999," at http://discipleship.ag.org/cod/articles/ripefordecision.cfm.
49. Zikmund, *Clergy Women*, 13–14; *BCA*, 307; Konieczny and Chaves, "Resources," 270.
50. John Knox, "The Ministry in the Primitive Church," in *MHP*, 16–17; Raymond E. Brown, *An Introduction to the New Testament* (New York, Doubleday, 1997), 574n.37; see 1 Corinthians 14:34, Romans 16:1, and 1 Corinthians 15:6.
51. Ben Witherington, *Women in the Earliest Churches* (Cambridge, England: Cambridge University Press, 1988), 1, 219, 220.
52. Ibid., 219, 209.
53. Interview with David Scholer, February 26, 2001, Pasadena, Calif. Bible quotes supporting women in ministry typically include: Galatians 3:28; 1 Corinthians 11:4–5; and Acts 2: 16–18.
54. Dryer cited in Scanzoni and Setta, "Women in Evangelical, Holiness, and Pentecostal Traditions," 227.
55. Vern S. Poythress and Mark Strauss, "The TNIV Debate: Is This New Translation Faithful in its Treatment of Gender?" *CT*, October 7, 2002, 37–45; quotes from Genesis 1:27 and Luke 17:3 (emphasis mine).
56. Quoted in Lauren F. Winner, "The Man Behind the Megachurch," *CT*, November 13, 2000, 58; Randall Balmer and Jesse T. Todd, Jr., "Calvary Chapel, Costa Mesa, California," in *American Congregations*, vol. 1, ed. James P. Wind and James W. Lewis (Chicago: University of Chicago Press), 690.
57. Interview with Lisa Huber, February 26, 2001, Pasadena, Calif.
58. Charlton, "Women and Clergywomen," 420.
59. *RAL*, 61; Marcia Louise Dyson comments at SBU.
60. *RAL*, 287–88; Zikmund, "Struggle for the Right," 194.
61. Robert Booth Fowler, Allen D. Hertzke, and Laura R. Olson, *Religion and Politics in America*, 2nd ed. (Boulder, Colo.: Westview, 1999), 188, 191; Iker quoted in Duin, "Feminization of Clergy," A9; see survey in Sue E.S. Crawford, Melissa M. Deckman, and Christi J. Braun, "Gender and the Political Choices of Women Clergy," in *CCAP*, 53.

Chapter 4

1. John Paul II, *I Will Give You Shepherds (Pastores Dabo Vobis)* (Washington, D.C.: United States Catholic Conference, 1992), 94 (emphasis in original).
2. Burns quoted in Larry Witham, "The Graying of Black Collars," *WT*, July 5, 2001, A11; Austin P. Flannery, ed., *Documents of Vatican II* (Grand Rapids, Mich.: Eerdmans Publishing Company, 1975), 712.
3. Pamphlet in author's file; quoted in Witham, "The Graying," A1.

4. Flannery, *Documents of Vatican II*, 864, 110.

5. "700 Priests Removed Since January 2002," February 27, 2004, press release, USCCB, Washington, D.C.; John Jay College of Criminal Justice, *The Nature and Scope of Sexual Abuse of Minors by Catholic Priests and Deacons in the United States, 1950–2002* (Washington, D.C.: USCCB, 2004), 4; Diocesan priests (4.3 percent) had more allegations than religious order priests (2.4 percent).

6. Investigative Staff of the *Boston Globe, Betrayal: The Crisis in the Catholic Church* (Boston: Little, Brown and Company, 2002); quoted in Sacha Pfeiffer, "More Abuse, Secrecy Cases," *Boston Globe*, December 4, 2002, A1.

7. Fox Butterfield, "789 Children Abused by Priests Since 1940, Massachusetts Says," *NYT*, July 24, 2003, A1; Robert O'Neill, "Pedophile Ex-Priest is Killed in Prison," *AP*, August 23, 2003; Kevin Cullen and Stephen Kurkjian, "Archdiocese Settlement Seeking to Close the Cases," *Boston Globe*, September 10, 2003, A1.

8. Quoted in Aviva L. Brandt, "Portland Archdiocese Filing Chapter 11," *AP*, July 6, 2004.

9. Langsfield quoted in Witham, "The Graying," A10.

10. Hans Kung, *Why Priests?* (Garden City, N.Y.: Doubleday, 1972), 17, 58.

11. Avery Dulles, "Vatican II: the Myth and the Reality," paper presented at Georgetown University, Washington, D.C., October 30, 2002, 2, 5.

12. Schuth quoted in Witham, "The Graying," A10.

13. William V. D'Antonio et al., *American Catholics* (Walnut Creek, Calif.: Alta Mira, 2001), 52, 12; Daniel Pilarczyk, "The Changing Image of the Priest," *Origins* 16 (July 3, 1986): 141.

14. Philip Murnion comments at the "Priestly Identity in a Time of Crisis: New Research on Catholic Clergy" conference, Catholic University of America, Washington, D.C., September 9, 2002, author's tape.

15. Dean Hoge et al. "Religious Beliefs and Practices of American Young Adult Catholics" (paper presented at the Religious Research Association, Montreal, November 7, 1998, 13, 19); D'Antonio, *American Catholics*, 110.

16. D'Antonio, *American Catholics*, 146, 147; James Davidson comments at the "Decline and Fall? Catholicism since 1950" conference, Catholic University of America, March 22, 2003. See his survey findings in James D. Davidson et al., *The Search for Common Ground* (Huntington, Ind.: Our Sunday Visitor, 1997).

17. D'Antonio, *American Catholics*, 12; the 8,400 departures is calculated by the author; see resignation data in Dean R. Hoge, *Future of Catholic Leadership* (Kansas City, Mo.: Sheed and Ward, 1987), 10; Donald Cozzens uses 20,000 in *CFP*, 100.

18. D'Antonio, *American Catholics*, 11; Dean Hoge comments at "Priestly Identity" conference; *SFP*, vii.

19. *SFP*, vi, 23, 18. See D'Antonio, *American Catholics*, 12, which reports a 1999 ratio of priests to *all* U.S. Catholics at 1 to 1,330. Yet accurate ratios are elusive; just 70 percent of *all* Catholics register with a parish.

20. *SFP*, 72.

21. Ibid., 29.

22. Resignation rates estimated by sociologist Katarina Schuth. These, and ordination decline rates, cited by Hoge at "Priestly Identity" conference; *SFP*, vi, 22.

23. Hoge comments at "Priestly Identity" conference; Dean R. Hoge, *The First Five Years of the Priesthood* (Collegeville, Minn.: Liturgical Press, 2002), 2, 3.

24. Hoge, *The First Five Years*, 63–64; Hoge comments at "Priestly Identity" conference.

25. Teresa Watanabe, "Young Priests Hold Old Values," *Los Angeles Times*, October 21, 2002, A1. The survey asked priests in eighty dioceses whether they were "satisfied or dissatisfied with the way your life as a priest is going these days?" 70 percent were "very" and 21 percent were "somewhat" satisfied.

26. Bryan Froehle comments at "Priestly Identity" conference. His survey found that 93 percent of the older priests had not considered leaving, while the same was true for 78 percent of priests born after 1960 and 69 percent of priests born in the late 1960s and the 1970s. See his findings in "Priests in the United States: Satisfaction, Work Load, and Support Structures," *CARA Working Paper No. 5*, September 2002.

27. Hoge, *The First Five Years*, 42, 49; Thomas Kunkel, *Enormous Prayers* (Boulder, Colo.: Westview, 1998); Michael S. Rose, *Priests* (Manchester, N.H.: Sophia Institute Press, 2003).

28. James M. Gustafson, "The Clergy in the United States," in *Daedalus* 92 (Fall 1963): 734; quoted in Witham, "The Graying," A10–11; see canon 517.2.

29. National Conference of Catholic Bishops, *Program of Priestly Formation*, 4th ed. (Washington, D.C.: United States Catholic Conference, Inc., 1993), iii, 3, 9; "Instruction on Certain Questions Regarding the Collaboration of the Non-Ordained Faithful in the Sacred Ministry of Priests" quoted in *CFP*, 8.

30. Hoge comments at "Priestly Identity" conference; Dean R. Hoge, "New Research on the Priesthood," paper presented at the "Priestly Identity" conference, Washington, D.C., September 9, 2002, 5.

31. Murnion comments at "Priestly Identity" conference.

32. Baima and O'Malley quoted in Witham, "The Graying," A10.

33. Minnesota prelate's comments made at "Priestly Identity" conference (author's tape recording); older priest interviewed by author; McCloskey quoted in Larry Witham, "Priests' Group to Take up Peer Reviews for Accountability," *WT*, July 18, 2002, A3.

34. Froehle comments at "Priestly Identity" conference; Hoge comments at "Priestly Identity" conference; Hoge, "New Research on the Priesthood," 7.

35. Silva quoted in Witham, "Priests' Group," A3.

36. The Iowa priest in this July 2002 telephone interview wished to remain anonymous; John Jay College, *The Nature and Scope of Sexual Abuse*, 26–27, 5. See 208–20 for national rates of sexual abuse and abuse related to religious groups, Boy Scouts, Big Brother, the YMCA, athletics, babysitters, and child care.

37. Interview with Russell Shaw, September 25, 2003, Washington, D.C.; Sister Sharon Euart comments at "Priestly Identity" conference.

38. Silva quoted in *AP*, "Federation Leader Says More Needs to be Done to Protect Priests," May 7, 2003.

39. Bishop quoted in Larry Witham, "Theology Possibly an Impediment," *WT*, June 14, 2002, A14; Clohessy quoted in Larry Stammer, "Group Official Pans Abuse Policy," *Boston Globe*, May 7, 2002, A7.

40. Silva quoted in *AP*, "Federation Leader Says"; Larry B. Stammer, "Most Priests Say Bishops Mishandled Abuse Issue," *Los Angeles Times*, October 20, 2002, A1.

41. *CFP*, 112; Doyle quoted in David Gibson, *The Coming Catholic Church* (San Francisco: HarperSanFrancisco, 2003), 112.
42. *CFP*, 121; A. W. Richard Sipe, *Sex, Priests, and Power* (New York: Brunner Mazel, 1995), 4.
43. Bennett quoted in Amanda Mantone, "Review Board Probes 'Causes and Contexts' of Abuse," *Religion News Service*, February 27, 2004; John Jay College, *The Nature and Scope of Sexual Abuse*, 6. The 1985 internal church report, which warned bishops of the scope of the abuse problem, included a psychiatric assessment that pedophile behavior could be curbed or healed. See Peter Steinfels, *A People Adrift* (New York: Simon and Schuster, 2003), 55
44. Peter Steinfels, "The Church's Sex-Abuse Crisis," *Commonweal*, April 19, 2002, 15, 14; John Jay College, *The Nature and the Scope of Sexual Abuse*, 5.
45. Baima quoted in Larry Witham, "U.S. Cardinals Face Decision in June," *WT*, April 26, 2002, A6; Cathleen Falsani, "Number of Priests on the Rise Despite Scandal," *Chicago Sun-Times*, August 4, 2002, 8.
46. National Conference of Catholic Bishops, *Program of Priestly Formation*, 20, 4.
47. Richard P. McBrien, "Homosexuality and the Priesthood," *Commonweal*, June 19, 1987, 380–83; Andrew Greeley, "Bishops Paralyzed Over Heavily Gay Priesthood," *National Catholic Reporter*, November 10, 1989, 13; Russell Shaw, "Clergy Sex Abuse," *2003 Catholic Almanac* (Huntington, Ind.: Our Sunday Visitor, 2003), 79; Silva quoted in Witham, "Priests' Group," A3.
48. John Paul II, *I Will Give You Shepherds*, 76; Schleupner quoted in Witham, "The Graying," A11.
49. Quoted in Witham, "The Graying," A11.
50. Andrew Greeley, "The Times and Sexual Abuse by Priests," *America*, February 10, 2003, 17.
51. Quoted in Witham, "The Graying," A11.
52. *SFP*, 76.
53. Ibid., vi, iv, vii.
54. Germain Grisez and Russell Shaw, *Personal Vocation* (Huntington, Ind.: Our Sunday Visitor, 2003).
55. Quoted in Witham, "The Graying," A11.
56. For a full account, see Joseph H. Fichter, *The Pastoral Provisions* (Kansas City, Mo.: Sheed and Ward, 1989), 31–33, 56, 41.
57. Interview with Shaw; D'Antonio, *American Catholics*, 109.
58. Hoge, "New Research on the Priesthood," 6, 7; for the second survey see Richard Ostling, "Many U.S. Priests see a Gay 'Subculture' Among Clergy," *AP*, August 16, 2002.
59. *SFP*, v, 33. The largest blocs among all 3,583 foreign-born priests are Ireland (827), India (342), Philippines (327), Poland (256), Vietnam (231), Mexico (224), Columbia (143), and Nigeria (101); see 32 percent in Hoge comments at "Priestly Identity" conference.
60. *SFP*, vii; Hoge comments at "Priestly Identity" conference.
61. Flannery, *Documents of Vatican II*, 387; *SFP*, 66.
62. *SFP*, iv, vii, 53, 66; quoted in D'Antonio, *American Catholics*, 105.
63. *SFP*, iv; James Davidson comments at "Decline and Fall? Catholicism Since 1950" conference, Washington, D.C., March 21, 2003; interview with Shaw. For

lay "clericalism" see Russell Shaw, *To Hunt, To Shoot, To Entertain: Clericalism and the Catholic Laity* (San Francisco: Ignatius, 1993).

64. *SFP*, vi, 59; Davidson comments at "Decline and Fall" conference; pope quoted in *Vatican Information Service*, "Preserving a Balanced Relationship Between Pastors and Laity," January 10, 2004.

65. On women as parish leaders see Philip J. Murnion and David DeLambo, *Parishes and Parish Ministers* (New York: National Parish Life Center, 1999), 26; Hoge comments at "Priestly Identity" conference; *SFP*, 79.

66. Larry Witham, "Priests Find Laity Growth a Blessing," *WT*, May 5, 2000, A7; Froehle comments at "Priestly Identity" conference; *CFP*, 18.

67. Quoted in Witham, "The Graying," A11.

Chapter 5

1. James C. Hefley, *The Truth In Crisis*, vol. 5 (Hannibal, Mo.: Hannibal Books, 1990), 65.

2. Ibid.

3. Ibid., 71.

4. "Southern Baptist Convention," in *Yearbook 2003*, 376; in 2000 the SBC's six historic seminaries had 9,851 students (total head count), or 13.5 percent of total U.S. students in seminary (72,728) according to *Fact Book of Theological Education, 2000–2001* (Pittsburgh: Association of Theological Schools, 2001), 23, 50–62; Dale E. Jones et al., eds., *Religious Congregations and Membership in the United States, 2000* (Nashville, Tenn.: Glenmary Research Center, 2002), 520; Roger Finke, "The Quiet Transformation," *RRS* 36 (September 1994): 15; James Dotson, "Part-Time Salary, Full-Time Harvest," *SBC Life* (February–March 2003): 18.

5. Oran P. Smith, *The Rise of Baptist Republicanism* (New York: New York University Press, 1997), 177.

6. James L. Guth et al., *The Bully Pulpit* (Lawrence, Kan.: University Press of Kansas, 1997), 107, 183; Falwell quoted in Hefley, *Truth in Crisis*, vol. 5, 68.

7. Earl Black and Merle Black, *Politics and Society in the South* (Cambridge: Harvard University Press, 1987), 267–68; Smith, *Baptist Republicanism*, 2.

8. Finke, "Quiet Transformation," 16.

9. Samuel S. Hill, "The Story Before the Story," in *Southern Baptists Observed*, ed. Nancy T. Ammerman (Knoxville: University of Tennessee Press, 1993), 38.

10. Smith, *Baptist Republicanism*, 97.

11. Taylor Branch, *Parting the Waters* (New York: Simon and Schuster, 1988), 488; W. A. Criswell quoted in Walker L. Knight, "Race Relations," in Ammerman, *Southern Baptists Observed*, 167–68, 177; W. A. Criswell, *Standing on Promises* (Dallas: Word Publishing, 1990), 204.

12. Nancy T. Ammerman, *Baptist Battles* (New Brunswick, N.J.: Rutgers University Press, 1990), 104, 143.

13. Hill, "The Story," 42, 43; Ralph Reed, *Politically Incorrect* (Dallas: Word Publishers, 1994), 18. Harvard sociologist Nathan Glazier coined the term "offensive-defensive."

14. Guth et al., *Bully Pulpit*, 5; Smith, *Baptist Republicanism*, 153, 163.

15. W. A. Criswell quoted in Ellen M. Rosenberg, *The Southern Baptists* (Knoxville: University of Tennessee Press, 1989), 103; Arthur Emery Farnsley, *Southern Baptist Politics* (University Park: Pennsylvania State University Press, 1994), 83; Hebrews 13:17.
16. Farnsley, *Southern Baptist Politics*, 80, 79, 77n.5.
17. Interview with K. Randel Everett, February 11, 2003, Arlington, Va.
18. Drennan quoted in Julia Duin and Larry Witham, "Baptist Pastors Lead From the Right," *WT*, July 3, 2001, A1, 8.
19. Robert A. Baker, *The Southern Baptist Convention and Its People* (Nashville: Broadman, 1974), 331, 332.
20. Finke, "Quiet Transformation," 13–14, 15.
21. Quoted in Dotson, "Part-Time Salary," 18. Their churches are Council Valley Baptist Church in Oklahoma and Gladeville Baptist Church in Tennessee.
22. Charles Willis, "Forced Terminations of Pastors, Staff Leveling Off," August 2001 news release, LifeWay Ministry, at http://www.lifeway.com/about_pro8011.asp [cited November 2003].
23. Willis, "Forced Terminations"; Rosenberg, *The Southern Baptists*, 103; LifeWay's Neil Knierim quoted in Willis, "Forced Terminations."
24. David Goetz, "Forced Out," *Leadership* 17 (Winter 1996): 42.
25. G. Lloyd Rediger, *Clergy Killers* (Louisville, Ky.: Westminster John Knox, 1997); Leicht quoted in Gerald L. Zelizer, "Revolving Clergy Harms Religion," *USA Today*, February 21, 2002, A17.
26. Smith, *Baptist Republicanism*, 13; Oakes quoted in Steve DeVane, "Control Main Issue When Pastors Fired," *Biblical Recorder*, April 19, 2003, 9.
27. Interview with Doug Wead, September 1988, Crystal City, Va.
28. Telephone interview with Doug Wead, April 2001.
29. Robert Wuthnow, "Beyond Quiet Influence," in *QHG*, 385; Ted G. Jelen, "Protestant Clergy as Political Leaders," *RRS* 36 (September 1994): 23.
30. Sue E. S. Crawford and Laura R. Olson, "Choices and Consequences in Context," in *CCAP*, 230.
31. Larry Witham, "Politics From Pulpit Proliferating," *WT*, June 25, 1996, A1, 18. See survey by Pew Research Center for the People and the Press, Washington, D.C., June 24, 1996.
32. The "Religion and Politics Survey" is reported in Wuthnow, "Beyond Quiet Influence," 387. See also Larry Witham, "Protestants Make Their Presence Felt," *WT*, March 17, 2001, A2.
33. James M. Penning and Corwin E. Smidt, "Reformed Preachers in Politics," in *CCAP*, 162, 168, 170.
34. The key studies of liberal clergy from that period are: *GSC*; Harold E. Quinley, *The Prophetic Clergy* (New York: John Wiley and Sons, 1974); and Rodney Stark et al., *Wayward Shepherds* (New York: Harper and Row, 1971).
35. "Challenge-oriented" and "comfort-oriented" clergy were first contrasted in *GSC*; Ted. G. Jelen, "Notes for a Theory of Clergy as Political Leaders," in *CCAP*, 22; Penning and Smidt, "Reformed Preachers," 170.
36. Jelen, "Notes," 23; Crawford and Olson, "Choices and Consequences," 229; James L. Guth, "Reflections on the Status of Research on Clergy in Politics," in *CCAP*, 39.

37. Wuthnow, "Beyond Quiet Influence," 398, 397.
38. James L. Guth, "The Mobilization of a Religious Elite," in *CCAP*, 140.
39. Guth, "The Mobilization," 146, 154.
40. James L. Guth, "Southern Baptist Clergy, the New Christian Right, and Political Activism in the South," in *Politics and White Religion in the South* (Lexington: University of Kentucky Press, 2005 [forthcoming]); Nancy T. Ammerman, "Southern Baptists and the New Christian Right," *RRS* 32 (March 1991): 221; Guth, "Reflections," 40; Guth, "The Mobilization," 152, 156.
41. Guth et al., *The Bully Pulpit*, 135.
42. Ibid., 184.
43. Ibid., 137, 122, 184; Guth, "Southern Baptist Clergy." Some find the "two party" explanation of clergy politics "unsatisfying" because it looks only at liberal-conservative extremes in election years. See Paul A. Djupe and Christopher P. Gilbert, *The Prophetic Pulpit* (Lanham, Md.: Rowman and Littlefield Publishers, 2003), 213–15. This study found high degrees of non-electoral political and civic activity by Episcopal and Evangelical Lutheran Church in America clergy.
44. Baker, *The Southern Baptist Convention*, 355–57; Larry Witham, "Immigration Changes Face of U.S. Religion," *WT*, April 14, 2000, A14.
45. Eric Reed, "Southern Baptists Take Aim at Urban America," *CT*, July 12, 1999, 24; quoted in Richard N. Ostling, "Southern Baptists Warn of Stagnation," *AP*, June 17, 2004.
46. Reed, "Southern Baptists Take Aim," 24; quoted in Gayle White, "SBC Leader Will Push New Baptisms at Home, Abroad," *Atlanta Journal Constitution*, May 30, 1998, C4.
47. Interview with W. Robert Spinks, March 1, 2001, Richmond, Va.
48. E-mail interview with Nancy Ammerman, March 2001.
49. Richard N. Ostling, "Southern Baptists Quit World Alliance," *AP*, June 15, 2004.
50. Quoted in Dan Martin, "Jesse Fletcher: Calvinism is Longstanding Baptist Dispute," *Baptist Press*, November 12, 1997; Russell H. Dilday, "A Serious Look at the *Baptist Faith and Message* Revisions," in *Stand With Christ*, ed. Robert O'Brien (Macon, Ga.: Smyth and Helwys, 2002), 44. See also Keith Hinson, "Calvinism Resurging Among SBC's Young Elite," *CT*, October 6, 1997, 86–87.
51. Dilday, "A Serious Look," 45; "Do Good Fences Make Good Baptists?" *CT*, August 7, 2000, 36; e-mail interview with James Guth, October 7, 2003.
52. Reed, "Southern Baptists Take Aim," 24.
53. Ibid.

Chapter 6

1. The sermon was delivered on March 31, 1968. See *The Congressional Record*, April 9, 1968.
2. See covers of *Time* magazine for February 18, 1957 and September 17, 2001.
3. Counts of black clergy vary widely. The 2000 census reports 8.3 percent of all "occupational" clergy and the 1990 census reports 6.6 percent; blacks were reported as congregation leaders in a range from 11.9 to 19.7 percent nationally

in the National Congregations Study of 1998. See Mark Chaves, *Congregation in America* (Cambridge: Harvard University Press, 2004), 223; and the Pulpit and Pew survey of clergy found 16 percent were black. Hispanics typically are reported as half the number of black clergy. While Koreans are a prominent Christian group, they are the fourth largest Asian group in the United States after Chinese, Filipinos, and Asian Indians. See Jessica S. Barnes and Claudette E. Bennet, "The Asian Population: 2000," *Census 2000 Brief*, U.S. Census Bureau, issued February 2002, 5, 9.

4. *Fact Book on Theological Education, 2002–2003* (Pittsburgh, Pa.: The Association of Theological Schools, 2002), 8, 10, 11. See also "ATS Data Tables, 2002–2003," tables 2.12 and 3.1, at http://www.ats.edu/download/factbook/facttoc.html.

5. U.S. Census Bureau, Current Population Reports, Series P23-205, *Population Profile of the United States: 1999* (Washington, D.C.: U.S. Government Printing Office, 2001), 65, 66; Jesse McKinnon and Karen Humes, "The Black Population in the United States," *Current Population Reports*, U.S. Census Bureau, September 2000, 2, 5; Melissa Therrien and Roberto R. Ramirez, "The Hispanic Population in the United States," *Current Population Reports*, U.S. Census Bureau, March 2001, 2, 6.

6. Won Moo Hurh and Kwang Chung Kim, "Religious Participation of Korean Immigrants in the United States," *JSSR* 29 (1990): 24; Kwang Chung Kim and Shin Kim, "The Ethnic Roles of Korean Immigrant Churches in the United States," in *KAR*, 73, 75.

7. Quoted in Larry Witham, "Neo–Pentecostalism Re–energizes the Spiritual Life for Many Blacks, *WT*, April 13, 2000, A13; Therrien and Ramirez, "The Hispanic Population," 3; Won Moo Hurh, *The Korean Americans* (Westport, Conn.: Greenwood Press, 1998), 53.

8. See Philip Jenkins, *The Next Christendom* (New York: Oxford University Press, 2002), 79–81, 83–94.

9. See the Baptist election in Taylor Branch, *Parting the Waters* (New York: Simon and Schuster, 1988), 500–507; Lawrence N. Jones, "The Organized Church," in *Directory of African-American Religious Bodies*, ed. Wardell J. Payne (Washington, D.C.: Howard University Press, 1991), 14; *BCA*, 177, 182.

10. *BCA*, 364.

11. Jeremiah A. Wright and James Cone comments at SBU. As to the diversity of black clergy, see Peter Paris, *Black Religious Leaders: Conflict in Unity* (Louisville, Ky.: Westminster John Knox Press, 1991), 17–26. He gives biographical examples of four "types" of black clergy leadership: priestly, prophetic, political, and nationalist.

12. Gardner Taylor and Marvin Winans comments at SBU.

13. Eugene Rivers comments at SBU; see the *Newsweek* cover "God vs. Gangs," January 12, 2000.

14. Jones, "The Organized Church," 1; Mary R. Sawyer, "Theocratic, Prophetic, and Ecumenical," in *CCAP*, 70–71.

15. W. E. B. Du Bois, *The Souls of Black Folk* (New York: Modern Library, 2003), 191, 81; R. Drew Smith, ed., *New Day Begun* (Durham: Duke University Press, 2003), 59.

16. The church's declining role in preparing leadership is noted in Jones, "The Organized Church," 14; Walters quoted in Witham, "Neo-Pentecostalism," A13.

17. Smith, *New Day Begun*, 60.
18. Payne quoted in *BCA*, 354; Southern Baptist leader Paige Patterson quoted in David Van Biema, "Spirit Raiser," *Time*, September 17, 2001, 52.
19. *BCA*, 22, 47–48.
20. Ibid., 118, 96.
21. Ibid., 123.
22. Ibid., 273. Lincoln and Mamiya began their five-year survey in 1978, conducting personal interviews with 1,895 black clergy.
23. Ibid., 97, 105, 111.
24. Ibid., 120, 137, 158.
25. Ibid., 136, 130, 175–77.
26. Allison Calhoun-Brown, "The Image of God," *RRS* 40 (March 1999): 207; *BCA*, 177.
27. Katie Day, "The Construction of Political Strategies among African-American Clergy," in *CCAP*, 86–87, 102.
28. HM, 14; *BCA*, 98, 131, 331.
29. Ibid., 273; HM, 14.
30. *BCA*, 129; HM, 14; Jackson W. Carroll, "First– and Second–Career Clergy," Pulpit and Pew report, Duke Divinity School, 2003, at http://www.pulpit andpew.duke.edu/careercomparison.html.
31. Jeremiah A. Wright and Marvin Winans comments at SBU.
32. Lawrence H. Mamiya, "A Social History of the Bethel African Methodist Episcopal Church in Baltimore," in *American Congregations*, vol. 1, ed. James P. Wind and James W. Lewis (Chicago: University of Chicago Press, 1994), 264, 265.
33. Quoted in Witham, "Neo-Pentecostalism," A13.
34. Mamiya reports 40 percent in "A Social History of Bethel," 280; Lincoln and Tilgham quoted in Witham, "Neo-Pentecostalism," A13.
35. Quoted in Witham, "Neo-Pentocostalism," A13; Larry Witham, "Methodists Back Off Merger," *WT*, November 28, 2002, A9.
36. Telephone interview with Miguel Solorzano, January 22, 2003; Therrien and Ramirez, "The Hispanic Population," 1; Gaston Espinosa, Virgilio Elizondo, and Jesse Miranda, "Hispanic Churches in American Life: Summary Findings," *Interim Reports* (Institute for Latino Studies, University of Notre Dame) 2 (January 2003): 14.
37. "Hispanic Affairs: Demographics," USCCB, at http://www.usccb.org/hispanic affairs/demo.shtml#1. See also *SFP*, 68–69.
38. Quoted in Larry Witham, "Immigration Changes Face of U.S. Religion," *WT*, April 14, 2000, A14. See also Ana-Maria Diaz-Stevens and Anthony M. Stevens-Arroyo, *Recognizing the Latin Resurgence in U.S. Religion* (Boulder, Colo.: Westview, 1998). For the Mexican impact on U.S. Catholicism see Jay P. Dolan and Gilberto M. Hinojosa, eds., *Mexican Americans and the Catholic Church, 1900–1965* (Notre Dame, Ind.: University of Notre Dame Press, 1994).
39. Pope quoted in J. A. DiNoia, "The Neocatechumenal Way," in *New Catholic Encyclopedia*, vol. 19, supplement, 1989–1995 (Washington, D.C.: Catholic University of America, 1996), 280.
40. Espinosa, "Hispanic Churches," 15; Mateo Perez, "Spirituality in the Ministry to Hispanics," in *Handbook of Spirituality for Ministers*, vol. 1, ed. Robert J. Wicks (Mahwah, N.J.: Paulist, 1995), 518–19.

41. Telephone interview with Esdras Betancourt, January 22, 2003; on church attendance, Christopher Ellison quoted in Witham, "Immigration," A14.
42. Espinosa, "Hispanic Churches," 16; quoted in Witham, "Immigration," A14; on machismo see Elizabeth E. Brusco, *The Reformation of Machismo* (Austin: University of Texas Press, 1995).
43. Interview with Betancourt.
44. Telephone interview with Edwin Hernandez, January 23, 2003; see "ATS Data Tables, 2002–2003" for Hispanic students (table 2.12) and faculty (table 3.1) at http://www.ats.edu/download/factbook/.
45. Espinosa, "Hispanic Churches," 17, 22.
46. Perez, "Spirituality in the Ministry to Hispanics," 515, 516; Therrien, "The Hispanic Population," 1, 3.
47. FACT, 16; Therrien, "The Hispanic Population," 1; interview with Hernandez.
48. Peter T. Cha, "Ethnic Identity Formation and Participation in Immigrant Churches," in *KAR*, 140.
49. Kwang Chung Kim, R. Stephen Warner, and Ho-Youn Kwon, "Korean-American Religion in International Perspective," in *KAR*, 11.
50. "Centennial Sunday Will Celebrate Korean-American Ministries," *United Methodist News Service* press release, December 17, 2002.
51. Hurh, "Religious Participation," 24. For a survey that found slightly fewer Presbyterians (40 percent) and Catholics (13.6 percent) and more non-denominational affiliates (13.4 percent), see Kwan Chung Kim and Shin Kim, "Korean Immigrant Churches in the U.S." in *Yearbook of American and Canadian Church 1995*, ed. Kenneth Bedell (Nashville: Abingdon Press, 1995), 7.
52. R. Stephen Warner, "The Korean Immigrant Church," in *KAR*, 25, 33; Hurh, *The Korean Americans*, 107, 109.
53. Interview with Louis Weeks, March 1, 2001, Richmond, Va.
54. Kim, "The Ethnic Roles," 75, 83; Hurh, "Religious Participation," 25.
55. Kim, "The Ethnic Roles," 84; *Yearbook 2003*, 372.
56. Clergy figures in "Centennial Sunday," *United Methodist New Service* press release; Warner, "The Korean Immigrant Church," 28.
57. Quoted in "PCUSA Koreans," *CC*, November 10, 1999, 1080.
58. Kim, "The Ethnic Roles," 90, 81, 89.
59. Jin S. Kim, "A Proposal for New Church Development," Korean Presbyterian Church of Minnesota, English Ministry, at http://www.kpcmem.org/main/staff.asp.
60. Robert D. Goette, "Transformation of a First-Generation Church into a Bilingual Second-Generation Church," in *KAR*, 135; Warner, "The Korean Immigrant Church," 48; Cha, "Ethnic Identity Formation," 139.
61. Allen D. Clark, *A History of the Church in Korea* (Seoul: The Christian Literature Society of Korea, 1971), 41; Andrew E. Kim, "Korean Religious Culture and its Affinity to Christianity," *Sociology of Religion* 61 (Summer 2000): 119.
62. Kim, "Korean Religious Culture," 120. Chung quoted, 119.
63. Cho quoted in John N. Vaughan, *The World's 20 Largest Churches* (Grand Rapids, Mich.: Baker Books, 1984), 19; Kim, "Korean Religious Culture," 120; Kim et al., "Korean-American Religion in International Perspective," 8.
64. On immigrant religion see Oscar Handlin, *The Uprooted* (Boston: Little, Brown and Company, 1951) and Will Herberg, *Protestant, Catholic, Jew*, rev. ed. (Gar-

den City, N.Y.: Anchor, 1960); Karen J. Chai, "Beyond 'Strictness' to Distinctiveness," in *KAR*, 159; quoted in "PCUSA Koreans," 1080; quoted in Anthony W. Alumkal, "Being Korean, Being Christian," in *KAR*, 183.

65. Quoted in *BCA*, 125.
66. Ibid.; Alumkal, "Being Korean, Being Christian," 191.

Chapter 7

1. Interview with John Odean, January 17, 2003, Millersville, Md.
2. Richard Quebedeaux, *The New Charismatics* (Garden City, N.Y.: Doubleday, 1976), 106.
3. Donald E. Miller, *Reinventing American Protestantism* (Berkeley: University of California Press, 1997), 2, 5, 13.
4. Smith quoted in Ibid., 32.
5. Interview with Chuck Smith, February 25, 2001, Santa Ana, Calif.
6. Miller, *Reinventing American Protestantism*, 188.
7. "The New Rebel Cry: Jesus is Coming," *Time*, June 21, 1971, 61.
8. Quoted in Grant Wacker, *Heaven Below* (Cambridge: Harvard University Press, 2001), 33.
9. Steve Turner, *Amazing Grace* (New York: HarperCollins, 2002), 213.
10. Ibid., 153.
11. *BCA*, 359.
12. Turner, *Amazing Grace*, 158.
13. Quoted in Steve Rabey, "Maranatha! Music Comes of Age," *CT*, April 29, 1991, 45.
14. C. Peter Wagner, *The Third Wave of the Holy Spirit* (Ann Arbor, Mich.: Servant Publications, 1988), 25, 15–18; Miller, *Reinventing American Protestantism*, 45.
15. See Margaret Poloma, "The 'Toronto Blessing,'" *JSSR* 36 (June 1997): 257–71; and Steve Rabey, "Pensacola Outpouring Keeps Gushing," *CT*, March 3, 1997, 54–57.
16. Quoted in Larry Witham, "Americans Worship in Songs, Laughter," *WT*, January 2, 2000, C3; Lyle E. Schaller, *What Have We Learned?* (Nashville: Abingdon Press, 2001), 136; Michael S. Hamilton, "The Triumph of the Praise Songs," *CT*, July 12, 1999, 30, 34.
17. Barna Research Group, "Focus on 'Worship Wars' Hides the Real Issues Regarding Connection to God," press release, November 19, 2002, at http://www.barna.org/FlexPage.aspx?Page=BarnaUpdate&BarnaUpdateID=126; Mark Chaves, *How Do We Worship?* (Bethesda, Md.: Alban Institute, 1999), 2; FACT, 25.
18. Chaves, *How Do We Worship?*, 39, 32, 37.
19. FACT, 34, 40.
20. *FGC*, 31; FACT, 29, 31, 33; David S. Leucke, "Is Willow Creek the Way of the Future?" *CC*, May 1, 1997, 483.
21. Gilbert R. Rendle, "Reclaiming Professional Jurisdiction," *Theology Today* 59 (October 2002): 414.
22. Quoted in "Focus on 'Worship Wars.'"
23. See Bruce Barron, *The Health and Wealth Gospel* (Downers Grove, Ill.: InterVarsity, 1987) and D. R. McConnell, *A Different Gospel*, updated ed. (Peabody,

Mass.: Hendrickson, 1995). McConnell argues for the Christian Science roots of Hagin's Word of Faith theology.

24. David Edwin Harrell Jr., *Oral Roberts: An American Life* (Bloomington: Indiana University Press, 1985), 423.

25. Price quoted in Barron, *The Health and Wealth Gospel*, 160; Copeland quoted in Bill Sherman, "Tulsa Made a Big Impact on Copelands," *Tulsa World*, July 3, 2004, A10; Jim Bakker, *I Was Wrong* (Nashville: Thomas Nelson, 1996), 532–33.

26. McConnell, *A Different Gospel*, 25; Roberts quoted in Barron, *The Health and Wealth Gospel*, 63.

27. Harrell, *Oral Roberts*, 425; Vinson Synan, "Faith-Formula Fuels Charismatic Controversy," *CT*, December 12, 1980, 66; Barron, *The Health and Wealth Gospel*, 176n.2, quoting Richard N. Ostling, "Power, Glory—and Politics," *Time*, February 17, 1986, 69.

28. John Dart, "Pastor Frederick Price's 'Faith Dome'," *Los Angeles Times*, Sept. 9, 1989, A1; Pete Evans and Todd Bates, "They're Leavin' on a Jet Plane," *The Wittenberg Door*, May/June 2004, 38.

29. J. Lee Grady, "Fair Warning," *Charisma*, August 2003, 8; Rusty Leonard of Wall Watchers quoted in Bill Smith and Carolyn Tuft, "TV Evangelists Call Signals From Same Playbook," *St. Louis Post Dispatch*, November 19, 2003, A12.

30. Joel A. Carpenter, *Revive Us Again* (New York: Oxford University Press, 1997), 237.

31. Quebedeaux, *The New Charismatics*, 53.

32. Ibid., 10, 59.

33. John N. Vaughan, *Megachurches and America's Cities* (Grand Rapids, Mich.: Baker Books, 1993), 26, 51.

34. Scott Thumma, "Exploring the Megachurch Phenomena," at http://hirr .hartsem.edu/bookshelf/thumma_article2.html. See also Scott Thumma, "The Kingdom, the Power, and the Glory: Megachurches in Modern American Society," Ph.D. diss., Emory University, 1996, and John Dart, "Close-knit Megachurches," *CC*, September 12–19, 2001, 11. The survey found 14 percent were charismatic and 11 percent Pentecostal; Michael S. Hamilton, "Willow Creek's Place in History," *CT*, November 13, 2000, 65.

35. Hamilton, "Willow Creek's Place," 64–65, 68.

36. Thumma, "Exploring the Megachurch," 2, 6–9.

37. Ibid., 9, 3.

38. Ibid., 9, 6; Leucke, "Is Willow Creek the Way of the Future?" 481.

39. Interview with Russell P. Spittler, February 26, 2001, Pasadena, Calif.

40. Leucke, "Is Willow Creek the Way of the Future?" 483.

41. Telephone interview with Eileen W. Lindner, March 12, 2003.

42. Synan quoted in Sandra K. Chambers, "Regent University Celebrates 25 Years of Spirit-Filled Education," *Charisma*, May 2003, 32.

Chapter 8

1. Nancy Ammerman, *Congregation and Community* (New Brunswick, N.J.: Rutgers University Press, 1997), 346.

2. Quoted in Tim Stafford, "A Regular Purpose-Driven Guy," *CT*, November 18,

2002, 42, 48. The five purposes of the "Purpose-Driven" approach are: 1) knowing Christ; 2) growing in Christ; 3) serving Christ; 4) sharing Christ; and 5) worship.

3. James D. Berkley, *The Dynamics of Church Finance* (Grand Rapids, Mich.: Baker Books, 2000), 55; HM, 19.

4. HM, 4.

5. FACT, 20; Ammerman, *Congregation and Community*, 334.

6. FACT, 20.

7. Jon N. Vaughan, *Megachurches and America's Cities* (Grand Rapids, Mich.: Baker, 1993), 22, 26; quoted in Stafford, "A Regular Purpose-Driven Guy," 42; Dean R. Hoge et. al., *Money Matters* (Louisville, Ky.: Westminster John Knox, 1996), 174.

8. FGC, 22; quote from Congregational Life Survey press release, in Larry Witham, "The State of Grace," WT, May 8, 2002, A1; Zikmund quoted in Larry Witham, "Searching for Shepherds," WT, July 2, 2001, A11.

9. Peter Steinfels, *A People Adrift* (New York: Simon and Schuster, 2003), 106; Bryan T. Froehle and Mary L. Gautier, "National Parish Inventory Project Report," Center for Applied Research in the Apostolate, Georgetown University, Washington, D.C, October 1999, 6, 7.

10. Quoted from Congregational Life Survey press release in Witham, "The State of Grace," A1, 10. For data see FGC, 52, 46–47. For the rise in non-belief see the American Religious Identification Survey 2001 (which found that Americans with "no religion" doubled to 14 percent over a decade) at www.gc.cuny.edu/studies/studies/_index.htm#aris_1.

11. FGC, 12, 35, 38 (emphasis added).

12. Lyle E. Schaller, *What Have We Learned?* (Nashville: Abingdon Press, 2001) 27; Robert Wuthnow, *The Restructuring of American Religion* (Princeton: Princeton University Press, 1988); quoted in Stafford, "A Regular Purpose-Driven Guy," 47.

13. Steinfels, *A People Adrift*, 11.

14. Data and quote in Sam Dillon and Leslie Wayned, "Scandals in the Church: The Money," NYT, June 13, 2002, A36.

15. Froehle and Gautier, "National Parish Inventory," 18; Avery Dulles, "Vatican II: the Myth and the Reality," paper presented at Georgetown University, Washington, D.C., October 30, 2002, 2,5; Avery Dulles, "Orthodoxy and Social Change," *America*, June 20, 1998, 14, 16.

16. Ellison Research, "Study Shows Many Pastors Are Not Upbeat About the Future of Christianity in America," press release, October 29, 2002, at http://www.ellisonresearch.com/ERPS%20II/Release%204%20Future.htm.

17. "Introduction," QHG, 7–8.

18. Quoted in Larry Witham, "Anglicans Spread Faith With Novel New Course," WT, October 21, 1995, C4.

19. Quoted in Ibid.; Tom Verde, "Crash Course in Christianity Is Winning Over Churches and the Wayward," NYT, December 27, 1998, A24.

20. See at http://www.alphausa.org/; for a critic see Tom Harpur, "Alpha's a Giant Leap Backward," *Toronto Star*, November 30, 2003, F7; quoted in "The Church of England: Alpha Plus," *Economist*, U.S. edition, November 7, 1998, 61.

21. Kenneth L. Carder, "Market and Mission," a lecture presented at Duke Divinity School, October 16, 2001, at http://www.pulpitandpew.duke.edu.kencarderlecture.pdf.

22. FACT, 22.

23. Adam Smith, *An Inquiry into the Nature and Causes of the Wealth of Nations*, 2 vols. (Indianapolis, Ind.: Liberty Fund, 1981), 789.

24. Ibid., 317; Weber quoted in Rodney Stark and Roger Finke, *Acts of Faith* (Berkeley: University of California Press, 2000), 155; Benton Johnson, "On Church and Sect," *American Sociological Review* 28 (1963): 242, 244 (emphasis in original).

25. Roger Finke, "The Quiet Transformation," *RRS* 36 (September 1994): 7; on Sunday school cells see Vaughan, *Megachurches and America's Cities*, 20, 36–37; on federalism see Schaller, *What Have We Learned?*, 41–44.

26. Dean Kelley, *Why Conservative Churches Are Growing* (New York: Harper and Row, 1972), 53; Roger Finke and Rodney Stark, *The Churching of America, 1776–1990* (New Brunswick, N.J.: Rutgers University Press, 1992). The economist Laurence Iannccone is credited with the rational choice application.

27. Donald A. McGavran, *The Bridges of God* (London: World Dominion Press, 1955), 8; Donald A. McGavran, *Understanding Church Growth* (Grand Rapids, Mich.: Eerdmans Publishing Company, 1970), 85.

28. Gibson Winter, *The Suburban Captivity of the Churches* (Garden City, N.Y.: Doubleday, 1961), 81; Ralph H. Elliot, "Dangers of the Church Growth Movement," *CT*, August 12–19, 1981, 801.

29. C. Peter Wagner, *Our Kind of People* (Atlanta, Ga.: John Knox Press, 1979), 1, 32, 33.

30. Schuller's *Your Church Has Real Possibilities* is updated as, Robert H. Schuller, *Your Church Has a Fantastic Future* (Ventura, Calif.: Regal Books, 1986); David S. Leucke, "Is Willow Creek the Way of the Future?" *CC*, May 1, 1997, 482.

31. Schuller, *Your Church Has a Fantastic Future*, 99, 148 (emphasis in original).

32. Quoted in Tim Stafford, "The Third Coming of George Barna," *CT*, August 5, 2002, 27, 34. See also Barna, *Marketing the Church* (Colorado Springs, Colo.: NavPress, 1988; and Barna, *The Power of Vision* (Ventura, Calif.: Regal Books, 1992).

33. Schaller, *What Have We Learned?*, 125; Schuller, *Your Church Has a Fantastic Future*, 141.

34. Ammerman, *Congregation and Community*, 319. She and her research team studied twenty-three congregations. See also Nancy Ammerman, "Organized Religion in a Voluntary Society," *Sociology of Religion* 58 (Fall 1997): 203–15.

35. Ammerman, *Congregation and Community*, 5, 327.

36. Robert D. Putnam, *Bowling Alone* (New York: Simon and Schuster, 2000), 22, 65–79. Synonyms for "bonding" and "bridging" are inward and outward, private and public, exclusive and inclusive.

37. See Harvy Lipman, "Giving in 2002 Didn't Outpace Inflation," *Chronicle of Philanthropy*, June 26, 2003, 7. The "Giving USA" report for 2002 estimated that 35 percent of all giving was to religious causes, totaling $84.3 billion. See also Elizabeth Schwinn, "Donors to Religious Groups Give More Than Others," *Chronicle of Philanthropy*, June 27, 2002, 34; John L. Ronsvalle and Sylvia Ronsvalle, *The State of Church Giving Through 2000* (Champaign, Ill.: Empty

Tomb, Inc., 2002), 38–39; Ronsvalle quoted in Julia Duin, "Tithing Falls by Wayside," *WT*, January 18, 2002, A2.

38. Hoge, *Money Matters*, 13, 162, 169.

39. Ibid., 172, 169, 168.

40. Ibid., 165, 166, 163 (emphasis in original).

41. Schaller, *What Have We Learned?*, 25.

42. Hoge, *Money Matters*, 15; budget estimates are from *FGC*, 19, and Barna Research Group cited in Duin, "Tithing Falls," A2; Loren B. Mead, *Five Challenges for the Once and Future Church* (Bethesda, Md.: The Alban Institute, Inc., 1996), 5; historian James Hudnut-Beumler quoted in HM, 28.

43. Barna poll cited in Duin, "Tithing Falls," A2; Bible cited in Berkley, *The Dynamics of Church Finance*, 18, 17.

44. Quoted in Stafford, "A Regular Purpose-Driven Guy," 42.

45. Judge quoted in Larry Witham, "Clergy Exemption for Homes Backed," *WT*, April 2, 2002, A7.

46. Quoted in Adolfo Pesquera, "New Law Aims to Protect Clergy Tax Break," *San Antonio Express-News*, May 23, 2002, 1E; Curt Anderson, "House Bill Would Protect Tax Exemption for Clergy Housing," *AP*, April 16, 2002.

47. Warrens quoted in Stafford, "A Regular Purpose-Driven Guy," 45; interview with Vickie Sickles, February 8, 2001, Gettysburg, Pa.

48. Hoge, *Money Matters*, 7; see Proverbs 30:8, Luke 10:7, and I Corinthians 9:14.

49. HM, 2; John G. Stackhouse, Jr., "Money and Theology in American Evangelicalism," in *More Money, More Ministry*, ed. Larry Eskridge and Mark A. Noll (Grand Rapids, Mich.: Eerdmans Publishing Company, 2000), 415.

50. Bureau of Labor Statistic cited in HM, 13; telephone interview with Dan Busby, December 23, 2002.

51. HM, 8.

52. Ibid., 2, 10, 6.

53. Ibid., 6.

54. Ibid., 16; Matthew Price, "Fear of Falling," *CC*, August 15–22, 2001, 20.

55. Already 31 percent of congregational pastors and 21 percent of connectional pastors work part time. HM, 8, 19, 29.

56. Mead, *The Once and Future Church*, 12, 15.

57. Becky R. McMillan and Matthew Price, "At Cross Purposes? Clergy Salaries," Pulpit and Pew working paper, 2001, 26, at http://www.pulpitandpew.duke.edu/atcrosspurposes.pdf.

58. Jackson W. Carroll and Robert L. Wilson, *Too Many Pastors?* (New York: Pilgrim Press, 1980), 123–24.

59. McMillan, "Cross Purposes," 25; HM, 3; see Don Terry, "For 2 Denominations, One Cleric Fills a Need," *New York Times*, October 20, 1996, A1.

60. Price, "Fear of Falling," 21.

61. Interview with Michael L. Cooper-White, February 8, 2001, Gettysburg, Pa.

Chapter 9

1. The phrase "decently and in order" is in the Westminster Confession (1647) and was first used by Paul in I Corinthian 14:40.

2. See "justice-love" in Larry Witham, "Presbyterian Panel Backs Liberal Ethic on

Adultery," *WT*, February 13, 1991, A1; Witham, "Presbyterians Reject Report on Sex," *WT*, June 11, 1991, A1.

3. Laura R. Olson and Wendy Cadge, "Talking About Homosexuality," *JSSR* 41 (March 2002): 161; Anson Shupe, ed., *Wolves Within the Fold* (New Brunswick, N.J.: Rutgers University Press, 1998), 5.

4. Carey quoted in Peter T. Chattaway, "Canadian Anglican Diocese Endorses Same-Sex Unions," *CT*, August 5, 2002, 18; Editorials, "Mortified in Vancouver," *CT*, August 5, 2002, 29.

5. This account of Presbyterian Church (USA) events is based on a variety of news reports.

6. See section G-6.0106b in *The Book of Order* of the Presbyterian Church (USA) at http://www.pcusa.org/oga/publications/boo-04-05.pdf.

7. Commission member Kathy Runyeon quoted in Jerry Van Marter, "News Summary," *Presbyterian News Service*, June 23, 1999.

8. See for example John Dart, "Gay Presbyterian Minister Quits After Being 'Outed,'" *Los Angeles Times*, February 27, 1998, 3; quoted in John Dart, "Presbyterian Turnabout," *CC*, July 4–11, 2001, 6–7; Stokes quoted in John Filiatreau, "Morrison Ordination Upheld," *Presbyterian News Service* (release 03127), March 5, 2003.

9. The 1993 ecclesiastical court case was *LeTourneau vs. Twin Cities Presbytery*.

10. See Larry Witham, "Episcopal Bishops Dismiss 'Heresy,'" *WT*, May 16, 1996, A6; Witham, "Heresy Trial Examines Morality," *WT*, February 28, 1996, A3; Witham, "Episcopal Bishop Going on Trial on Heresy Charge," *WT*, February 25, 1996, A3.

11. Quoted in Megan Tench, "Gay Man is Elected Bishop in N.H.," *Boston Globe*, June 8, 2003, B1.

12. Quoted in Larry Witham, "Churches Debate Role in Gay Unions," *WT*, June 18, 2000, C6.

13. Ibid.

14. Bill Lindelof, "Lesbian 'Blessing' Rekindles Tensions," *CT*, March 1, 1999, 17; for the ban on gay ceremonies see *The Book of Discipline of the United Methodist Church, 1996* (Nashville: United Methodist Publishing House, 1996), 87. The 2004 General Conference extended the ban beyond churches to include "chapels of institutions related to the United Methodist Church."

15. Talbert quoted in *Religion News Service*, "UMC Bishop Begins Probe," *CC*, April 7, 1999, 383; quoted in Rene Sanchez, "At Gay Wedding, Methodists Take a Vow Against Church Ban," *Washington Post*, January 17, 1999, A3.

16. See Lulia McCord, "Creech Again Fuels Church Gay Debate," *Omaha World-Herald*, November 15, 1999, A1; McCord, "Creech Loses Credentials," *Omaha World-Herald*, November 18, 1999, A1.

17. Dell quoted in *AP*, "Minister Tried for Marrying Gay Couple," in *Washington Post*, March 26, 1999, A5; Steve Kloehn, "Church Faces Trial with Its Pastor," *Chicago Tribune*, March 25, 1999, A1.

18. *AP*, "Pastor Punished Over Gay Nuptials," *Los Angeles Times*, March 27, 1999, A10; Dell quoted in Witham, "Church Debates Role," C6.

19. Joe Mandak, "Methodists Order Review of Lesbian Case," *AP*, May 1, 2004; Rachel Zoll, "Methodist Court Won't Review Lesbian Case," *AP*, May 4, 2004.

20. Robert Wuthnow, *The Restructuring of American Religion* (Princeton: Princeton University Press, 1988), 112–16, 16, 147.

21. Jackson W. Carroll, et. al., *Being There* (New York: Oxford University Press, 1997), 205, 230, 208; quoted in Witham, "Churches Debate Role," C6.

22. *CFP*, 107.

23. Enrique Rueda, *The Homosexual Network* (Old Greenwich, Conn.: Devin Adair, 1982); see Louisiana story in Jason Berry, *Lead Us Not Into Temptation* (New York: Doubleday, 1992).

24. Congregation for the Doctrine of the Faith, "Letter to the Bishops of the Catholic Church on the Pastoral Care of Homosexual Persons," October 1, 1986; Richard P. McBrien, "Homosexuality and the Priesthood," *Commonweal*, June 19, 1987, 380–83; Andrew Greeley, "Bishops Paralyzed Over Heavily Gay Priesthood," *National Catholic Reporter*, November 10, 1989, 13–14.

25. *CFP*, 103, 135; McBrien, "Homosexuality," 380.

26. Twenty thousand estimate in A. W. Richard Sipe, *Sex, Priests, and Power* (New York: Brunner Mazel, 1995), 90; *CFP*, 100.

27. Dean R. Hoge, *The First Five Years of the Priesthood* (Collegeville, Minn.: Liturgical Press, 2002), 3, 31; Richard Ostling, "Many U.S. Priests See a Gay 'Subculture' Among Clergy," *AP*, August 16, 2002. See also Larry B. Stammer, "15% Identify as Gay or 'on Homosexual Side,'" *Los Angeles Times*, October 20, 2002, A32. In this major survey, 9 percent identified themselves as homosexual and 6 percent as "somewhere in between, but more on the homosexual side." For younger priests (ordained 20 years or less) the total was 23 percent.

28. Quoted in Stammer, "15% Identify," A32; David Briggs, "Study: Gay Culture Growing Among Catholic Priests," *Plain Dealer*, August 16, 2002, A18; Rachel Zoll, "Catholic Official Argues Against Gay Priests," *AP*, September 20, 2002. Catholic writer George Weigel argues that ordination could be open to celibate men of a same-sex "orientation" who accept church teaching on human sexuality and reject a "gay" self-identity. See Weigel, *The Courage to Be Catholic* (New York: Basic Books, 2002), 162–63.

29. Peter Steinfels, "The Church's Sex-Abuse Crisis," *Commonweal*, April 19, 2002, 18.

30. Richard A. Blackmon and Archibald D. Hart, "Personal Growth for Clergy," in *CACD*, 36; Shupe, *Wolves Within the Fold*, 1; see survey in Nils C. Friberg and Mark R. Laaser, *Before the Fall* (Collegeville, Minn.: Liturgical Press, 1998), vii.

31. Blackmon, "Personal Growth," 39; quoted in "Defeating the Demons," *Christian Ethics Today* 6 (October 2000), at http://www.christianethicstoday.com/Index_Christian_Ethics_Today/Index_Full.htm.

32. *Didache* quoted in *CFP*, 124; quoted in *RAL*, 123; interview with Russell P. Spittler, February 26, 2001, Pasadena, Calif.

33. Quoted in "Defeating the Demons."

34. Interview with Robert Wicks, December 3, 2002, Columbia, Md.; Blackmon, "Personal Growth," 40–41.

35. Karen Lebacqz and Ronald Barton, *Sex in the Parish* (Louisville, Ky.: Westminster John Knox, 1991), 34.

36. Blackmon, "Personal Growth," 40; interview with Wicks.

37. Interview with John O. Lundin, November 22, 2002, Alexandria, Va.

38. Anson Shupe, William A. Stacey, and Susan E. Darnell, eds., *Bad Pastors* (New York: New York University Press, 2000), 201, 199.

39. Interview with Lundin and Wicks; Shupe, *Bad Pastors*, 201, 207.
40. Ibid., 207; quoted from "Lehrer News Hour," Public Broadcasting Service, December 13, 2002; John Jay College of Criminal Justice, *The Nature and Scope of Sexual Abuse of Minors by Catholic Priests and Deacons in the United States, 1950–2002* (Washington, D.C.: USCCB, 2004), 26–27.
41. Bobby Ross Jr., "Victims of Lutheran Abuse Win $37M Award," *AP*, April 22, 2004.
42. Gayle White, "Promise Keepers Hosts 42,000 Clergy at Dome," *Atlanta Journal Constitution*, February 14, 1996, 4B.
43. Michael Clancy, "Promise Keepers See Decline in Attendance," *The Arizona Republic*, February 22, 2003, A8; quoted in Patrick Morley, "The Next Christian Men's Movement," *CT*, September 4, 2000, 84.
44. For attendance by sex see *FGC*, 12; Barna and his survey are cited in Julia Duin, "Does 'Death by Estrogen' Threaten the Churches?" *WT*, September 27, 1999, A13.
45. See Larry Witham, "Promise Keepers Seeks Revival With Mass-Mailed Video," *WT*, November 11, 1999, A7; Laurie Goodstein, "A Marriage Gone Bad Struggles for Redemption," *NYT*, October 29, 1997, A24; Bill McCartney with Dave Diles, *From Ashes to Glory* (Nashville: Thomas Nelson, 1995), xv.
46. Leon J. Podles, *The Church Impotent* (Dallas: Spence Publishing, 1999), 208.
47. For a conservative disagreement with Podles, see Daniel P. Moloney, "Separation Anxiety," book review, *First Things*, 9 (October 1999): 57–59; Chavis quoted in Duin, "Does 'Death by Estrogen' Threaten the Churches?" A13.
48. Paula D. Nesbitt, *Feminization of the Clergy in America* (New York: Oxford University Press, 1997), 107, 109.
49. *BCA*, 306; Marcia Louise Dyson comments at SBU.
50. *BCA*, 304–6; *FGC*, 12.
51. For the Catholic concern see Mitch Finley, *For Men Only* (Liguori, Mo.: Liguori Publications, 1998); quoted in Morley, "The Next Christian Men's Movement," 85.

Chapter 10

1. Telephone interview with Robert K. Johnston, January 29, 2003; see Robert K. Johnston, *Reel Spirituality* (Grand Rapids, Mich.: Baker Academic, 2000), 29–30.
2. Frank Lambert, *"Pedlar in Divinity"* (Princeton: Princeton University Press, 1994), 5, 6.
3. Quentin J. Schultze, *Televangelism and American Culture* (Grand Rapids. Mich.: Baker, 1991), 12.
4. Raymond Chapman, ed., *Godly and Righteous, Peevish and Perverse* (Grand Rapids, Mich.: Eerdmans Publishing Company, 2002), 1; *Religion News Service*, "Clergy Ratings at Lowest Point Ever," *CT*, February 2003, 21.
5. William Martin quoted in Bill Smith and Carolyn Tuft, "TV Evangelists Call Signals From Same Playbook," *St. Louis Post Dispatch*, November 19, 2003, A13.
6. Donald E. Messer, *Contemporary Images of Christian Ministry* (Nashville: Abingdon Press, 1989), 24.
7. Ibid., 21.

8. Ibid., 21, 25–28.

9. Les Keyser and Barbara Keyser, *Hollywood and the Catholic Church* (Chicago: Loyola University Press, 1984), xii; these film themes are from the author's research.

10. Stewart M. Hoover, "Visual Religion in Media Culture," in *The Visual Culture of American Religions*, ed. David Morgan and Sally M. Promey (Berkeley: University of California Press, 2001), 152.

11. A. W. Richard Sipe, *Sex, Priests and Power* (New York: Brunner Mazel, 1995), 76.

12. Ronald B. Bond and David L. Jeffrey, "Preaching," in *A Dictionary of Biblical Tradition in English Literature*, ed. David L. Jeffrey (Grand Rapids, Mich.: Eerdmans Publishing Company, 1992), 631–35; James P. Wind, "Clergy Ethics in Modern Fiction," in *Clergy Ethics in a Changing Society*, ed. James P. Wind et al. (Louisville, Ky.: Westminster John Knox, 1991), 111. The novels are: Andrew Greeley, *The Passover Trilogy*; Walker Percy, *The Thanatos Syndrome*; J. F. Powers, *Wheat That Springeth Green*; and John Updike, *Roger's Version*.

13. David Paul Nord, "The Evangelical Origins of Mass Media in America, 1815–1835," *Journalism Monographs* no. 88 (May 1984): 2; Debra L. Mason, "God in the News Ghetto," Ph.D. Dissertation, Ohio University, November 1995), 203.

14. Author's count. See *Time* archive at http://www.time.com/time/magazine/coversearch/; and Donald J. Lehunus, *Who's on Time?* (New York: Oceana Publications, 1980).

15. John Dart and Jimmy Allen, *Bridging the Gap: Religion and the News Media* (Nashville: First Amendment Center, 1993), 5, 6, 35, 36.

16. Laurence I. Barrett, "The 'Religious Right' and the Pagan Press," *Columbia Journalism Review* (July–August 1993): 33.

17. Gregory quoted in an interview on NBC's *Meet the Press*, June 16, 2002.

18. Kenneth L. Woodward, "The Last Respectable Prejudice," *First Things* 126 (October 2002): 23–35; Philip Jenkins, *The New Anti-Catholicism* (New York: Oxford University Press, 2003), 113.

19. Stephen Powers, David J. Rothman, and Stanley Rothman, *Hollywood's America* (Boulder, Colo.: Westview, 1996), 127, 124.

20. Keyser, *Hollywood and the Catholic Church*, xi; Wade Clark Roof, "Blurred Boundaries," in *Religion and Prime Time Television*, ed. Michael Suman (Westport, Conn.: Praeger, 1997), 61.

21. Richard Maltby, "The Production Code and the Hays Office," in *Grand Designs: Hollywood Cinema in the 1930s*, ed. Tino Balio (New York: Charles Scribner's, 1998), 37–72; and Ted Baehr, *The Media-Wise Family* (Colorado Springs, Colo.: Chariot Victor Publishing, 1998), 228–39.

22. *CFP*, 111.

23. Telephone interview with James Wall, January 3, 2003.

24. The 1968 code is quoted in Powers, *Hollywood's America*, 23.

25. Ibid., 126.

26. Baehr, *The Media-Wise Family*, 229; Mark Hulsether, "Sorting Out the Relationships Among Christian Values, U.S. Popular Religion, and Hollywood Films," *Religious Studies Review* 25 (January 1999): 3.

27. Quoted in Baehr, *The Media-Wise Family*, 238.

28. Powers, *Hollywood's America*, 128–29, 120, 131.

29. Hoover, "Visual Religion," 151; Billy Graham, "TV Evangelism," *TV Guide,* March 5, 1983, 5; Joan Brown Campbell, "Tuning In to Common Concerns," in *Religion and Prime Time,* 9.

30. Robert Lichter et al., *Prime Time* (Washington, D.C.: Regnery Publishing, 1994), 390, 392, 391, 400.

31. Ibid., 400, 389; Lionel Chetwynd, "Religion, Revenue, and Ratings," in *Religion and Prime Time,* 133.

32. Hoover, "Visual Religion," 158.

33. E-mail interview with Stewart M. Hoover, August 9, 2004.

34. Baehr, *The Media-Wise Family,* 43; number of films based on author's survey; Joyce Smith, "The Ministry and the Message: What Americans See and Read About Their Leaders," Pulpit and Pew report, Duke Divinity School, 2003, 5, at http://www.pulpitandpew.duke.edu/Smith.pdf. Looking at feature films across the twentieth century, Smith found that 1996 had the largest ever segment of movies (6.66 percent of the total) with a credited actor playing some kind of religious figure (from clergy to nuns and Catholic brothers), though usually in the background. Also high were 1994 (5.38 percent) and 1996 (5.35 percent).

35. "God and Television," *TV Guide,* March 29, 1997, 24–45; Andrew Greeley, "Do Priests Fall in Love?" *TV Guide,* March 28, 1983, 5–6.

36. M. S. Mason, "Religious Themes Get Wider Play, More Nuanced Portrayal in Fall Shows," *Christian Science Monitor,* October 14, 1997, 13; Victoria A. Rebeck, "Soul Men," *CC,* November 12, 1996, 1047; Gerald Zelizer, "TV to Focus on Atypical Clergy's Lives," *Los Angeles Times,* August 4, 1997, F3.

37. The annual reports monitored the content of CBS, NBC, ABC, Fox, UPN, and WB. See Thomas Johnson, "Faith in a Box: Entertainment Television on Religion, 1993–1996, at http://secure.mediaresearch.org/specialreports/ent/relcov.html; Johnson, "Faith in a Box," 1997, at http://secure.mediaresearch.org/specialreports/ent/sr041998.html.

38. Hoover, "Visual Religion," 147.

39. Avery Dulles, *Models of the Church,* expanded edition (New York: Doubleday, 1987), 161.

40. Messer, *Contemporary Images,* 186–88.

41. Bob Gale, "Ramblings on Why Things Are the Way They Are," in *Religion and Prime Time,* 140.

42. Campbell, "Tuning In," 10; Smith, "The Ministry and the Message," 25.

Chapter 11

1. Isaiah 42:9; Revelation 21:5.

2. Interview with Eddie Gibbs, February 26, 2001, Pasadena, Calif. See Gibbs, *Church Next* (Downers Grove, Ill.: InterVarsity, 2000).

3. On marriages see Bryan T. Froehle and Mary L. Gautier, "National Parish Inventory Project Report," Center for Applied Research in the Apostolate (CARA), Georgetown University, Washington, D.C, October 1999, 19; on "switching" see Robert Wuthnow, *The Restructuring of American Religion* (Princeton: Princeton University Press, 1988), 88; on attendance see Michael Hout and Andrew Greeley, "What Church Officials' Reports Don't Show,"

American Sociological Review 63 (February 1998): 113–19; and C. Kirk Hadaway, Penny L. Marler, and Mark Chaves, "Overreporting Church Attendance in America," *American Sociological Review* 63 (February 1998): 122–30.

4. Interview with Nathan Hieb, February 26, 2001, Pasadena, Calif.

5. David J. Wood, "The Conditions of Call," *Congregations*, March–April, 2001, 18.

6. "Selected Findings From the National Clergy Survey," Pulpit and Pew Report, February 2002, 3, at http://www.pulpitandpew.duke.edu/clergy_letter_1 .pdf.

7. Ibid., 3, 1, 4. Male clergy are 79 percent overweight or obese; Bryan Froehle, "Priests in the United States: Satisfaction, Work Load, and Support Structures," *CARA Working Paper No. 5*, September 2002, 23.

8. Interview with Robert Wicks, December 3, 2002, Columbia, Md.

9. Susanne C. Monahan, "Role Ambiguity Among Protestant Clergy," *RRS* 41 (Fall 1999): 80, 92–93.

10. Becky R. McMillan, "What Do Clergy Do All Week?," Pulpit and Pew report, Duke Divinity School, 2002, at http://www.pulpitandpew.duke.edu/clergy week.html.

11. Bill Hybels, *Courageous Leadership* (Grand Rapids, Mich.: Zondervan, 2002), 243.

12. WDL, 29.

13. David Aleshire quoted in Q&A in John Dart, "Is It Worth It? The Value of a Theological Education," *CC*, February 22, 2003, 34.

14. See Elizabeth Eisenstadt-Evens, "Farm Boy Makes Good," *CT*, August 5, 2002, 59.

15. Kenneth L. Carder, "Market and Mission," a lecture presented at Duke Divinity School, Durham, N.C., October 16, 2001, at http://www.pulpitandpew. duke.edu.kencarderlecture.pdf; see two kinds of spirituality in Robert Wuthnow, *After Heaven* (Berkeley: University of California Press, 1998).

16. Interview with Chad Rimmer, February 8, 2001, Gettyburg, Pa.; Jack Wertheimer, "The Rabbi Crisis," *Commentary* 115 (May 2003): 36.

17. Jackson W. Carroll, "Leadership in a Time of Change," *The Circuit Rider*, July/August, 2002, 27, 28.

18. WDL, 6.

19. Quoted in Stephen Fried, *The New Rabbi* (New York: Bantam Books, 2002), 33.

20. Francine Parnes, "An Appreciation Day Passes Quietly," *NYT*, October 5, 2002, A15.

21. Interview with Lloyd John Ogilvie, February 12, 2003, Washington, D.C.

22. Quoted in Matthew J. Price, "After the Revolution," *Theology Today* 59 (October 2002): 439.

23. "64% of Online Americans Have Used the Internet for Religious or Spiritual Purposes," press release, Pew Internet and American Life Project, Washington, D.C., April 7, 2004. While this study, "Faith Online," reports 82 million religion surfers, an earlier one, "Cyberfaith," gave a 20 million figure for 2000. See both studies at http://www.pewinternet.org; see the virtual church at http://www.shipoffools.com/church.

24. See Lutheran data in James P. Wind, "The Leadership Situation Facing American Congregation," Alban Institute Special Report, Bethesda, Md., September

2001, 12; Mark A. Shibley, *Resurgent Evangelicalism in the United States* (Columbia: University of South Carolina Press, 1996), 113.

25. Roger Finke, "Innovative Returns to Tradition," paper presented at the Society for the Scientific Study of Religion, Columbus, Ohio, 2001.

26. Aleshire quoted in Dart, "Is It Worth It?" 35.

27. The honors track is recommended in Barbara Wheeler, "Fit for Ministry?" *CC*, April 11, 2001, 23; Melissa Wiginton, "Who Should Be Our Pastors?" Talk given to the Fund for Theological Education, Inc., Indianapolis, January 8, 2003, at http://www.pulpitandpew.duke.edu/wiginton.html.

28. Ibid.

29. *Diagnostic and Statistical Manual of Psychological Disorders: DSM-IV-TR*, 4th ed., text revision (Washington, D.C.: American Psychiatric Association, 2000).

30. John Esau, "Ten Things I Didn't Learn in Seminary," *CC*, February 22, 2003, 12; quoted in Amanda Mantone, "Review Board Probes 'Causes and Contexts' of Abuse," *Religion News Service*, February 27, 2004.

31. James Dittes, "Tracking God's Call," in *CACD*, 22.

32. Donald B. Cozzens, "The Seven Skills of Highly Effective Pastors," *U.S. Catholic*, February 2002, 33.

33. For MAS functions and skills, see Allen Nauss, "Ministerial Effectiveness in Ten Functions," *RRS* 36 (September 1994): 58, 62, 63. (Functions include: evangelist; preacher/priest; equipper of laity; minister to youth/children; personal enabler; visitor/counselor; personal/spiritual model; administrator; overall effective; community minded-minister; teacher. Skills include being: tolerant of uncertainty or freedom; persuasive; task-oriented; assertive in leading; relations-oriented; goal-oriented; accurate in predicting, cool under pressure; integrative; able to represent a congregation); quote from H. Malony and Richard Hunt, *The Psychology of Clergy* (Harrisburg, Pa.: Morehouse, 1991), 136.

34. Nauss, "Ministerial Effectiveness," 65.

35. Tim Stafford, "The Business of the Kingdom," *CT*, November 15, 1999, 50; Peter F. Drucker, "Foreword," *The Leaders of the Future*, ed. Frances Hesselbein, Marshall Goldsmith, and Richard Beckhard (San Francisco: Jossey-Bass, 1996), xii (emphasis in original).

36. Hybels, *Courageous Leadership*, 12; Cozzens, "The Seven Skill," 33 (emphasis in original); Anthony B. Robinson, "Leadership That Matters," *CC*, December 15, 1999, 1228; Robinson, "Lessons in Leadership," *CC*, December 15, 1999, 1230.

37. Jackson W. Carroll, "How Do Pastors Practice Leadership?" Pulpit and Pew report, Duke Divinity School, 2000, at http://www.pulpitandpew.duke.edu/pastorlead.html.

38. For Benke story, see *AP*, "Lutheran Panel Reinstates Pastor After Post–9/11 Interfaith Service," in *NYT*, May 13, 2003, B4; Todd Hertz, "Lutheran Leader Suspended Over September 11 Service," *CT*, September 9, 2002, 17–18.

39. See Peter Steinfels, "A Vatican Office Attacks Relativism," *NYT*, October 7, 2000, B8; "Evangelical Views of Islam," April 7, 2003, survey by the Ethics and Public Policy Center and *Beliefnet*, at http://www.beliefnet.com/story/124/story_12447_1.html.

40. "In Jesus' Name?" *CC*, September 25–October 8, 2002, 5; for survey see *FGC*, 30; Edward Wimberly, "Spiritual Formation in Theological Education and Psychological Assessment," in *CACD*, 27, 28.

41. Robert D. Putnam, *Bowling Alone* (New York: Simon and Schuster, 2000), 22.

42. James MacGregor Burns, *Leadership* (New York: Harper and Row, 1978), 4.

43. Interview with Greg Ogden, February 26, 2001, Pasadena, Calif.

44. Shelley quoted in Stafford, "The Third Coming of George Barna," 38.

45. E. Brooks Holifield, *A History of Pastoral Care in America* (Nashville: Abingdon Press, 1983).

46. Cozzens, "The Seven Skills," 33; interview with John O. Lundin, November 22, 2002, Alexandria, Va.; Barbara Brown Zikmund, Adair T. Lummis, and Patricia M.Y. Chang, "Women, Men and Styles of Clergy Leadership," *CC*, May 6, 1998, 478.

47. Esau, "Ten Things," 12; 2 Corinthians 4:1.

Index